# THE UNITED STATES
# AND ARGENTINA

OTHER TITLES IN THE
CONTEMPORARY INTER-AMERICAN RELATIONS SERIES,
EDITED BY JORGE DOMÍNGUEZ
AND RAFAEL FERNÁNDEZ DE CASTRO


THE UNITED STATES AND MEXICO:
BETWEEN PARTNERSHIP AND CONFLICT

*Jorge Domínguez and Rafael Fernández de Castro*


THE UNITED STATES AND CHILE:
COMING IN FROM THE COLD

*David R. Mares and Francisco Rojas Aravena*


THE UNITED STATES AND VENEZUELA:
RETHINKING A RELATIONSHIP

*Janet Kelly and Carlos A. Romero*


THE UNITED STATES AND ARGENTINA:
CHANGING RELATIONS IN A CHANGING WORLD

*Deborah L. Norden and Roberto Russell*

# THE UNITED STATES AND ARGENTINA

## CHANGING RELATIONS IN A CHANGING WORLD

Deborah L. Norden
and
Roberto Russell

ROUTLEDGE
New York  London

Published in 2002 by
Routledge
29 West 35th Street
New York, NY 10001

Published in Great Britain by
Routledge
11 New Fetter Lane
London EC4P 4EE

Routledge is an imprint of the Taylor & Francis Group.

Printed in the United States of America on acid-free paper.

10  9  8  7  6  5  4 3  2  1

Cataloging-in-Publication Data is available from the Library of Congress.
Norden, Deborah L. and Roberto Russell
The United States and Argentina: changing relations in a changing world
ISBN: 0-415-93279-3 (hardback)
ISBN: 0-415-93280-7 (paperback)
Includes references and index.

# CONTENTS

ACKNOWLEDGMENTS

This book was initiated at the invitation of Jorge Domínguez and Rafael Fernández de Castro, for their series on U.S.-Latin American relations. It was an unusual inception, since the two authors had never even met, and it led to a somewhat rough beginning. However, we have spent the past few years getting to know each other's work and working habits, learning to respect and trust each other, and finally, learning to actually collaborate as partners on this project. It has been a productive partnership for the authors; we hope that our readers will also find it valuable. With a few thousand miles between Buenos Aires and California, most of this process has occurred through e-mail.

We owe much of the success of this project to Jorge and Rafael. Not only did they originate it, but they also organized the Mexico City conferences that allowed us to begin exchanging views and to gain crucial feedback and ideas from our other colleagues involved in this project. (Relaxation, however, was certainly not a large part of those meetings!) In addition, Jorge and Rafael provided us with their substantial insights along the way, as well as with an inspiring example of two extremely dedicated and hard-working professionals. We thank them for this opportunity. We also wish to acknowledge the very thoughtful and helpful comments of an anonymous reviewer.

*Deborah L. Norden*: I would like to express my appreciation to my colleagues at the University of California-Riverside and Whittier College for their support during the creation of this book. In particular, my thanks to my research assistant, Barry Peterson, for his invaluable help at the last stages of this project. Most of all, however, I wish to thank my family. The first meeting for this project began only a couple of months after my first daughter, Meghann, was born. The book goes to press just a few months after the birth of my second daughter, Rebecca. It would never have been completed without the help of my husband, Frank Bright, who cheerfully shouldered far more than his share of child-care responsibilities during this time, and still managed to discuss the substance of the book with me.

*Roberto Russell:* I wish to thank Veronica De Majo for her invaluable help typing numerous revisions and for helping enormously with the frequent e-mails between the authors; Analía Trouvé for her constant assistance in searching for data and bibliographic information from the library of the Institute of Foreign Service, Argentina; my colleagues from the Universidad Torcuato Di Tella for their astute comments. Finally, I wish to thank my wife, Marcela Gianzone, for accompanying me in this effort, for her intelligent critiques of the first drafts, and especially, for entertaining and taking care of our small son, Guillermo, during the many weekends I spent writing this.

*The transition from authoritarian rule to constitutional government.*

*The continent-wide economic depression of the 1980s and the subsequent shift toward more open-market–conforming economies.*

*The end of the Cold War in Europe.*

*The transformation of relations with the United States.*

Each of these major events and processes was an epochal change in the history of Latin America and the Caribbean. What is more striking is that all four changes took place within the same relatively short time, though not all four affected each and every country in the same way. They became interconnected, with change on each dimension fostering convergent changes on other dimensions. Thus at the beginning of the new millennium we witnessed an important transformation and intensification in U.S.–Latin American relations.

This book is part of a series of ten books on U.S. relations with Latin American and Caribbean countries. Each of these books is focused on the fourth of these four transformations, namely, the change in U.S. relations with Latin America and the Caribbean. Our premise is that the first three transformations provide pieces of the explanation for the change in the United States' relations with its neighbors in the Americas and for the changes in the foreign policies of Latin American and Caribbean states. Each of the books in the series assesses the impact of the epoch-making changes upon each other.

The process of widest impact was the economic transformation. By the end of 1982, much of North America, Western Europe, and East Asia launched into an economic boom at the very instant when Latin America plunged into an economic depression of great severity that lasted approximately to the end of the decade. As a consequence of such economic collapse, nearly all Latin American governments readjusted their economic strategies. They departed from principal reliance on import-substitution industrialization, opened their economies to international trade and investment, and adopted policies to create more open-market-conforming economies. (Even Cuba had changed its economic strategy by the 1990s, making its economy more open to direct foreign investment and trade.)

The regionwide economic changes had direct and immediate impact upon U.S.–Latin American relations. The share of U.S. trade accounted for by Latin America and the Caribbean had declined fairly steadily from the end of World War II to the end of the 1980s. In the 1990s, in contrast, U.S. trade with Latin America grew at a rate significantly higher than the growth of U.S. trade world-wide; Latin America had become the fastest-growing market for U.S. exports. The United States, at long last, did take notice of Latin America. Trade between some Latin American countries also boomed, especially within subregions such as the Southern Cone of South America, Venezuela and Colombia, the Central American countries, and, to a lesser extent, the Anglophone Caribbean countries. The establishment of formal freer-trade areas facilitated the growth of trade and other economic relations. These included the North American Free Trade Agreement (NAFTA), which grouped Mexico, the United States, and Canada; Mercosur, the southern common market, with Argentina, Brazil, Paraguay, and Uruguay; the Andean Community, whose members were Bolivia, Colombia, Ecuador, Peru, and Venezuela; the Central American Common Market; and the Caribbean Community. U.S. foreign direct and portfolio investment flowed into Latin America and the Caribbean, financing the expansion of tradable economic activities; the speed of portfolio investment transactions, however, also exposed these and other countries to marked financial volatility and recurrent financial panics. The transformation in hemispheric international economic relations—and specifically in U.S. economic relations with the rest of the hemisphere—was already far-reaching as the twenty-first century began.

These structural economic changes had specific and common impacts on the conduct of international economic diplomacy. All governments in the Americas, large and small, had to develop a cadre of experts who could negotiate concrete technical trade, investment, and other economic issues with the United States and with other countries in the region. All had to create teams of international trade lawyers and experts capable of defending national interests, and the interests of particular business firms, in international, inter-American, or subregional dispute-resolution panels or "court-like" proceedings. The discourse and practice of inter-American relations, broadly understood, became much more professional—less the province of eloquent poets and more the domain of number-crunching litigators and mediators.

The changes in Latin America's domestic political regimes began in the late 1970s. These, too, would contribute to change the texture of inter-American relations. By the end of 1990, democratization based on fair elections, competitive parties, constitutionalism, and respect for the rule of law and the liberties of citizens had advanced and was still advancing throughout the region, albeit unevenly and with persisting serious problems, Cuba being the principal exception.

Democratization also affected the international relations of Latin American and Caribbean countries, albeit in more subtle ways. The Anglophone Caribbean is a largely archipelagic region long marked by the widespread practice of constitutional government. Since the 1970s, Anglophone Caribbean democratic governments rallied repeatedly to defend constitutional government on any of the islands where it came under threat and, in the specific cases of Grenada and Guyana, to assist the process of democratization in the 1980s and 1990s, respectively. In the 1990s, Latin-American governments also began to act collectively as well to defend and promote democratic rule; with varying degrees of success, they did so—with U.S. support—in Guatemala, Haiti, Paraguay, and Peru. Democratization had a more complex relationship to the content of specific foreign policies. In the 1990s, democratization in Argentina, Brazil, Uruguay, and Chile, on balance, contributed to improved international political, security, and economic relations among these Southern Cone countries. Yet democratic politics at times made it more difficult to manage international relations over boundary or territorial issues between given pairs of countries, including Chile and Peru, Colombia and Venezuela, and Costa Rica and Nicaragua. In general, democratization facilitated better relations between Latin American and Caribbean countries, on the one hand, and between Latin America or Caribbean countries and the United States on the other. Across the Americas, democratic governments, including those of the United States and Canada, acted to defend and promote constitutional government. Much cooperation over security, including the attempt to foster cooperative security and civilian supremacy over the military, would have been unthinkable except in the new, deeper, democratic context in the hemisphere.

At its best, in the 1990s democratic politics made it possible to transform the foreign policies of particular presidential administrations into the foreign policies of states. For example, Argentina's principal political parties endorsed the broad outlines of their nation's foreign policy, including the framework to approach much friendlier relations with the United States. All Chilean political parties were strongly committed to their country's transformation into an international trading state. The principal political parties of the Anglophone Caribbean sustained consistent long-lasting foreign policies across different partisan administrations. Mexico's three leading political parties agreed that NAFTA should be implemented, even if they differed on specifics, binding Mexico to the United States and Canada. And the George H. W. Bush and Clinton administrations in the United

States followed remarkably compatible policies toward Latin America and the Caribbean with regard to the promotion of free trade, pacification in Central America, support for international financial institutions, and the defense of constitutional government in Latin America and the Caribbean. Both administrations acted in concert with other states in the region and often through the Organization of American States. Democratic procedures, in these and other cases, served to establish the credibility of a state's foreign policy because all actors would have reason to expect that the framework of today's foreign policy would endure tomorrow.

The end of the Cold War in Europe began following the accession of Mikhail Gorbachev to the post of general secretary of the Communist Party of the Soviet Union in 1985. It accelerated during the second half of the 1980s, culminating with the collapse of communist regimes in Europe between 1989 and 1991 and the breakup of the Soviet Union itself in late 1991. The impact of the end of the U.S.-Soviet conflict on the Western Hemisphere was subtle but important: the United States was no longer obsessed with the threat of communism. Freed to focus on other international interests, the United States discovered that it shared many practical interests with Latin American and Caribbean countries; the latter, in turn, found it easier to cooperate with the United States. There was one exception to this "benign" international process: the United States was also freed to forget its long-lasting fear of communist guerrillas in Colombia (they remained powerful and continued to operate nonetheless) in order to concentrate on a "war" against drug trafficking, even if it undermined Colombia's constitutional regime.

This process of the end of the Cold War also had a specific component in the Western Hemisphere—namely, the termination of the civil and international wars that had swirled in Central America since the late 1970s. The causes of those wars had been internal and international. In the early 1990s, the collapse of the Soviet Union and the marked weakening of Cuban influence enabled the U.S. government to support negotiations with governments or insurgent movements it had long opposed. All of these international changes made it easier to arrange for domestic political, military, and social settlements of the wars in and around Nicaragua, El Salvador, and Guatemala. The end of the Cold War in Europe had an extraordinary impact on Cuba as well; while it did not end the sharp conflict between the U.S. and Cuban governments, the latter was deprived of Soviet support, forcing it thereby to recall its troops overseas, open its economy to the world, and lower its foreign policy profile. The United States felt freer to conduct a "colder war" against Cuba, seeking to overthrow its government.

Two other large-scale processes, connected to the previous three, had a significant impact on international relations in the Western Hemisphere: these are the booms in international migration and in cocaine-related international organized crime. To be sure, emigration and organized crime on an international scale in the

Americas are as old as the European settlement that began in the late fifteenth century and the growth of state-sponsored piracy in the sixteenth century. Yet the volume and acceleration of these two processes in the 1980s and 1990s were truly extraordinary.

One effect of widespread violence in Central America and in Colombia, and of the economic depression everywhere, was to accelerate the rate of emigration to the United States. Once begun, the process of migration to the United States was sustained through networks of relatives and friends, the family-unification provisions of U.S. legislation, and the lower relative costs of more frequent international transportation and communication. By the mid-1990s, over twelve million people born in Latin America resided in the United States; two-thirds of them had arrived since 1980. The number of people of Latin-American ancestry in the United States was much larger, of course. In the 1980s, migrants came to the United States not just from countries of traditional emigration, such as Mexico, but also from countries that in the past had generated few emigrants, such as Brazil. As the twentieth century ended, more people born in Latin America lived in the United States than lived in the majority of the Latin American states. The United States had also come to play a major role in the production and consumption of the culture of the Spanish-speaking peoples, including music, books, and television. These trends are likely to intensify in the twenty-first century.

Had this series of books been published in the mid-1970s, coca and cocaine would have merited brief mention in one or two books, and no mention in most. The boom in U.S. cocaine consumption in the late 1970s and 1980s changed this. The region-wide economic collapse in the 1980s made it easier to bribe public officials, judges, police, and military officers. U.S. cocaine-supply interdiction policies in the 1980s raised the price of cocaine, making the coca and cocaine businesses the most lucrative in depression-ravaged economies. The generally unregulated sale of weapons in the United States equipped gangsters throughout the Americas. Bolivia and Peru produced the coca. Colombians grew it, refined it, and financed it. Criminal gangs in the Caribbean, Central America, and Mexico transported and distributed it. Everywhere, drug traffic–related violence and corruption escalated.

The impact of economic policy change, democratization, and the end of the Cold War in Europe on U.S.–Latin American relations, therefore, provides important explanations common to the countries of the Americas in their relations with the United States. The acceleration of emigration and the construction and development of international organized crime around the cocaine business are also key common themes in the continent's international relations during the last fifth of the twentieth century. To the extent pertinent, these topics appear in each of the books in this series. Nonetheless, each country's own history, geographic location, set of neighbors, resource endowment, institutional features, and leadership characteristics bear as well on the construction, design, and implementation of its foreign policy. These more particular factors enrich and guide the books in this series in their interplay with the more general arguments.

As the 1990s ended, dark clouds reappeared in the firmament of inter-American relations, raising doubts about the "optimistic" trajectory that seemed set at the beginning of that decade. The role of the military in the running of state agencies and activities that normally belong to civilians rose significantly in Colombia, Venezuela, and Peru, and in January 2000 a military coup overthrew the constitutionally elected president of Ecuador; serious concerns resurfaced concerning the depth and durability of democratic institutions and practices in these countries. Venezuela seemed ready to try once again much heavier government involvement in economic affairs. And the United States had held back from implementing the commitment to hemispheric free trade that Presidents George H. W. Bush and Bill Clinton both had pledged. Only the last of these trends had instant international repercussions, but all of them could affect adversely the future of a Western Hemisphere based on free politics, free markets, and peace.

## THIS PROJECT

Each of the books in this series has two authors, typically one from a Latin American or Caribbean country and another from the United States (and, in one case, the United Kingdom). We chose this approach to facilitate the writing of the books and also to ensure that the books would represent the international perspectives from both parts of the U.S.–Latin American relationship. In addition, we sought to embed each book within international networks of scholarly work in more than one country.

We have attempted to write short books that ask common questions to enable various readers—scholars, students, public officials, international entrepreneurs, and the educated public—to make their own comparisons and judgments as they read two or more volumes in the series. This project sought to foster comparability across the books through two conferences held at the Instituto Tecnológico Autónomo de México (ITAM) in Mexico City. The first, held in June 1998, compared ideas and questions; the second, held in August 1999, discussed preliminary drafts of the books. Both of us read and commented on all the manuscripts; the manuscripts also received commentary from other authors in the project. We also hope that the network of scholars created for this project will continue to function, even if informally, and that the web page created for this project (www.itam.mx/organizacion/divisiones/estgrales/estinter/americalatina.html) will provide access to the ideas, research, and writing associated with it for a wider audience.

We are grateful to the Ford Foundation for its principal support of this project, and to Cristina Eguizábal for her advice and assistance throughout this endeavor.

We are also grateful to John D. and Catherine T. MacArthur Foundation for the support that made it possible to hold a second successful project conference in Mexico City. The Rockefeller Foundation provided the two of us with an opportunity to spend four splendid weeks in Bellagio, Italy, working on our various general responsibilities in this project. The Academic Department of International Studies at ITAM hosted the project throughout its duration and the two international conferences. We appreciate the support of the Asociación Mexicana de Cultura, ITAM's principal supporter in this work. Harvard University's Weatherhead Center for International Affairs also supported aspects of this project, as did Harvard University's David Rockefeller Center for Latin American Studies. We are particularly grateful to Hazel Blackmore and Juana Gómez at ITAM and Amanda Pearson and Kathleen Hoover at the Weatherhead Center for their work on many aspects of the project. At Routledge, Melissa Rosati encouraged us from the start; Eric Nelson supported the project through its conclusion.

*Rafael Fernández de Castro*
ITAM

*Jorge I. Domínguez*
Harvard University

# INTRODUCTION

FOR MOST OF ARGENTINE AND U.S. HISTORY, ARGENTINA HAS defined its relationship with the United States in terms of autonomy. This did not necessarily mean confrontation or hostility, but it did mean independence. Argentine leaders retained the right to choose—based on their own perceptions of national interest—when cooperation with the United States might be desirable, and when more distance might be preferable. Such an option has never been available to the smaller and closer countries of Central America and the Caribbean, which have been compelled historically and geographically to make very definitive decisions about their relationship to the United States. Countries such as Nicaragua and Cuba have had the choice between allegiance and confrontation (when another protector was available); autonomy in these countries has been virtually inconceivable. In contrast, Argentina has always had size, distance, and in Latin-American terms, a relatively high level of development and productivity in its favor.

Thus, Argentina's post–Cold War transformation to among the most devoted of U.S. allies stands as a major break with historical patterns of U.S.-Argentine relations. Under President Carlos Menem (1989–1999), Argentina developed a bond with the United States unlike it had ever had before. Once Latin America's strongest voice against United States intervention in the Americas, now Argentina loyally accompanied the United States on numerous international military missions. Once inclined to shun the United States in favor of European trade partners, now Argentina closely followed U.S. recommended economic policies and pursued improved trade relations within the Americas, albeit while retaining important ties to Europe.

This period of close relations endured even as Menem passed the reins of government to Fernando De la Rúa, and, in the United States, as the presidency passed first from George Bush to William J. Clinton in 1993, and then to George

W. Bush in 2001. Only an extreme political and economic crisis—catastrophic even by Argentine standards—sufficed to challenge this friendship. In December 2001, soaring unemployment and frustration with unrelenting recession finally propelled Argentines into the streets in uncontrolled protests, complete with rioting and looting, De la Rúa abruptly resigned. As a series of interim presidents rapidly passed the hot potato of Argentine government from one to another (five different people occupied the presidency over the course of two weeks), Argentina's leadership was forced to reconsider its resolute economic liberalism, and, in conjunction with this, its strong allegiance to the United States. In the end, the United States' friendship had not been enough to salvage Argentina's economy, nor to compel the northern state to offer a life raft to its rapidly sinking Argentine partner. Yet, in many respects, economic necessity prevented a true rupture in the relationship. Argentina could not afford to entirely turn its back on potential support from the United States, or the U.S.-dominated International Monetary Fund; likewise, the United States could ill afford Argentina's default on its debt.

This study seeks to understand why this friendship occurred, and what some of its limits were. Why did one of the strongest and historically most independent countries of Latin America develop a foreign policy during the post-Cold War period characterized, above all, by strong allegiance to the United States? We look at a variety of possible causes to explain this. What impact did changes in the international system, and in Argentine and U.S. domestic politics, have on this relationship? Should the transformation of U.S.-Argentine relations be seen as an indicator of declining Argentine power in the international system; a shifting Argentine culture and identity; or as a more deliberate Argentine policy choice, based on either changing needs or a new assessment of the potential benefits of friendship?

After briefly assessing the nature of post–Cold War relations between Argentina and the United States, the project first turns toward the past, looking at the long history of conflict between the two countries. We then look at some of the possible sources of the current transformation in U.S.-Argentine relations, considering such factors as the "new world order" and domestic politics and policymaking in both the United States and Argentina. Finally, we explore more extensively the nature of U.S.-Argentine relations, looking at the issues that have shaped and stood out in the dialogue between the two countries, and how the shifting U.S.-Argentine relationship has been played out in international institutions.

We argue that Argentina's dramatic policy shift emanated, above all, from the country's overwhelming need to address its profound economic crisis, and the government's pragmatic assessment of the strategic options available to help it do so. In the early 1990s, Argentina desperately needed to reestablish its international credibility, largely destroyed by economic and political instability, as well as past military aggression, in order to attract foreign loans and investment. The end of the Cold War left a world strongly dominated by the principles of economic and political liberalism, with the United States occupying the most powerful position in the key liberal international institutions, such as the International Monetary Fund, the World Bank, and the United Nations. Thus, despite Argentina's greater trade compatibility with Europe, the United States now became Argentina's most important ally. To prove its credibility, the government sought to reverse prior practices in both economic and security policies, emphasizing on both fronts Argentina's interest in being a "good citizen" of the new liberal order. However, as will be demonstrated, U.S. recognition of Argentina's efforts came primarily in the security arena. In contrast, Argentina's economic reforms failed to entirely convince the United States and, in the end, also failed to ensure Argentina's prosperity.

## U.S.-Argentine Relations during the Post-Cold War Period

The close relationship that developed between Argentina and the United States since the end of the Cold War would have been nearly unimaginable in decades past. On all fronts, political affairs, security arrangements, and economic relations, Argentine foreign policy fell neatly in line with U.S. priorities. Under the leadership of President Carlos Menem, the administration apparently opted to relinquish Argentina's highly valued independence, trading it in for U.S. friendship. Yet the program that resulted was also remarkable with regard to its high level of integration—with political, economic, and security policies tightly interwoven and neatly interdependent—and in many respects with regard to its success, albeit temporarily.

The dramatic change in U.S.-Argentine relations actually began somewhat before the end of the Cold War, when Argentina's military regime handed power to a freely elected civilian government in 1983, after more than seven years of harshly repressive authoritarian rule. Argentina thus entered the wave of political democratization that would gradually engulf the hemisphere and allow a new political convergence throughout the region.

Raúl Alfonsín, Argentina's president from 1983 to 1989, faced the difficult challenges of helping to establish an enduring democracy, an achievement that had long eluded the politically tumultuous nation. The economy was in shambles, with bouts of hyperinflation that plagued Alfonsín until his somewhat precipitous resignation. Equally tricky, the government found it necessary to balance between the competing demands of the many victims of the military's repression, who sought some kind of justice, and the military itself—divided, defensive, and unwilling to easily accept the harsh treatment of the Radical Party administration. The government nonetheless proceeded with a strongly pro–human rights agenda, trying and sentencing numerous military officers. The result was a series of military rebellions that may not have directly threatened the government, but did limit its ability to independently form foreign policy.[1]

Despite these challenges, democracy survived, and in 1989 Argentina carried out a momentous transfer of power from a freely elected president of one political party, the Radicals, to a freely elected president of a second political party, the Peronists. Such a moment had not occurred in Argentine politics since the very beginning of the century, before the Peronist, or "Justicialist," Party had even come into existence. The Radical Party represented moderate democratic reform, while the Peronist Party originated from a nationalist, syndicalist base, bridging elements of the political left and right. Thus, neither party represented the potential extremes of the political spectrum; both, however, had at different times participated in democracy's demise. The smooth electoral transition meant that newly elected president Carlos Menem could continue the process of democratization initiated by Alfonsín, benefiting from his predecessor's earlier efforts to deal with the rocky moments of the initial transition. Menem did not, in many respects, actually deepen democracy— his tendency to bypass the Argentine Congress and rely heavily on decree powers led Guillermo O'Donnell to describe the government as "delegative democracy."[2] Yet the administration did continue to hold free elections and respect civil rights, and managed to design a more positive and proactive agenda that would place Argentina on the path toward a more stable political future.

Veering dramatically away from traditional Peronism, Menem adopted a highly internationalist approach, particularly in the areas of economic and defense policy. This internationalism was especially geared toward cooperation with the United States. For example, in 1991, Argentina modified forty positions in the United Nations, explaining that this was an "expression of an intended greater approximation to the United States."[3] Argentina thus deliberately and explicitly followed the U.S. lead in the international arena, beginning by lending strong support in the United Nations, especially in areas such as international security and support for democracy. However, as will be discussed in chapter 5, Argentina did nonetheless hold firm on issues where the U.S. position conflicted with Argentine interests.

The United Nations also served as the guidepost for Argentina's developing defense policy. The Alfonsín administration had dealt with security issues largely by shrinking the military budget and proscribing military participation in matters of domestic security, but had neglected to provide the armed forces with an alternative role. Menem proceeded to fill that gap—without dipping back into government coffers—by offering troops for international peacekeeping, well in keeping with the principle of cooperation with the United States and U.S.-dominated liberal international institutions. Beginning in 1992, Argentina contributed an army battalion to UN peacekeeping efforts in Croatia; smaller forces were sent to UN missions in Cyprus and Kuwait. However, Argentina also cooperated with U.S.-led military missions with more limited international support, including sending ships to the Persian Gulf in 1990, and peacekeepers to Haiti following the

U.S. invasion in 1994. This approach certainly converged nicely with U.S. priorities and concerns. During the post–Cold War period, the United States was blessed with the burden of having the world's strongest military, but lacked both the economic power and political will for extensive unilateral policing. The United States therefore increasingly encouraged other nations to contribute to peacekeeping, placing this mission near the top of military training programs and sponsoring innumerable related exercises and simulations.

At the same time, Argentina also cooperated with the United States on other key international security issues, such as nuclear weapons and missile nonproliferation. Argentina took such symbolically important measures as relinquishing its missile project (the Condor II), and signing the Treaty on Nuclear Non-Proliferation.

Given the centrality of economic concerns for Argentina, the government naturally also sought more harmonious relations in this sphere, as well. Prioritizing economic recovery was only encouraged further by the undeniable link between economic instability and political instability. In other words, furthering democratization and military subordination also required addressing economic issues; focusing exclusively on security measures would not suffice.

Over the decades, economic relations between the countries underwent many twists and turns. At the beginning of the twentieth century, Argentina appeared to be a true disciple of Adam Smith, while the United States relied more on protectionism. Yet, like many Latin American countries, Argentina adopted import-substituting industrialization plans toward the 1940s and 1950s, building an unwieldy state and substantial debt in the process. Meanwhile, the United States gradually became the world's most determined advocate of free trade. By the late 1980s, however, protectionist models of development (such as import-substituting industrialization) had fallen into disrepute, and neoliberal models began gaining in Latin America.[4] Mexico was probably the first to adopt major economic reforms during this period (other than Chile, whose military regime had embraced economic liberalism long before it became the mode), but Argentina was not far behind.

After the 1989 inflation crisis immediately preceding Menem's presidency, economic stabilization moved to the front of the Argentine agenda. Inflation soared to more than 3000 percent for 1989, fostering considerable consensus about the necessity of economic reform.[5] Menem opted to fully embrace neo-liberalism. Domestically, he followed up on Alfonsín's preliminary steps toward privatization, nearly liquidating state holdings. The telephone company, national airline company, railroads, and oil fields passed into the hands of private capital. Internationally, Argentina sought to encourage trade by taking an active role in the World Trade Organization (WTO), initiating a would-be common market with Brazil, Uruguay, and Paraguay (Mercosur, or the Southern Market), while pursuing—thus far unsuccessfully—acceptance in NAFTA (the North American Free

Trade Agreement). Argentina then bound its economic future more closely to that of the United States by legally pegging the national currency to that of the United States.[6] By the end of the Menem administration, Argentina had even begun to explore the possibility of relinquishing a national currency altogether and replacing it with the U.S. dollar. Discussions of this issue faded considerably once Fernando De la Rúa took office in 1999, although after December 2001, some questioned whether dollarization might have been a good move, after all.

## Explaining U.S.-Argentine Cooperation

As mentioned above, while Argentina's economic concerns were central, a number of factors contributed to this striking transformation in U.S.- Argentine relations. Certainly the changing international climate is part of the picture; political changes in both countries also played a role. These factors and their effect on U.S.-Argentine relations will be explored in further depth through the remainder of this volume.

The changing international climate has certainly been important for U.S.-Argentine relations, and for the region as a whole. On a broad scale, the gradual process of globalization has, over time, increased international interdependence. This has occurred most obviously in terms of economics, with relations becoming far more complex than a simple exchange of raw materials for manufactured goods. However, globalization has also meant more interaction between populations, in part due to the simple fact that communication and transport have become infinitely more efficient over time, as well as more accessible. With this increasing interaction, the barriers between cultures have begun breaking down. Overall, the process helped to create the possibility for more consensus on, for example, preferred political systems (democracy) or economic models (neoliberalism).

While globalization has been a very gradual process, the end of the Cold War transformed the international environment practically overnight. Perhaps this has not meant the "end of history" in Francis Fukuyama's terms, but it did mean that ideology became relatively less important in defining the lines of international conflict.[7] The end of the Cold War left military power more concentrated (with the United States as the predominant power), and economic power more dispersed. With the end of the bipolar order, Latin America ceased functioning as a playing field for "low intensity" Cold War conflicts, leaving the countries of the region somewhat more independence than they might have had previously. However, this also meant that the countries of the region had to compete more for positive attention and aid from the United States.

This has contributed to the process of regional integration in the Americas. Regionalism had, of course, begun before the end of the Cold War, evidenced especially by the formation of the European Union. It has since become stronger, with growing ties both within subregions of the Americas (Central America, the Andean region, and the Southern Cone), and within the Western Hemisphere as a whole. Most of this integration has been on the economic front, but other forms of cooperation also appear to be increasing. For example, the OAS (Organization of American States) seems to have taken on new life during the post–Cold War period.

Western Hemisphere unity has been deliberately encouraged by the United States, seeking to strengthen economic ties and distribute more of the security costs in the region. Notably, around 1997, the U.S. State Department renamed the "Americas Region" section of its organization to "Western Hemisphere"; the new approach of the U.S. government has been to consider Latin America, the Caribbean, and Canada as all part of a single hemispheric bloc with the United States. In some respects, this emphasis continues the Pan-Americanism that the United States began advocating in the late 1800s. However, present day Pan-Americanism seems more weighted toward economics rather than security issues, and in some respects, the United States does seem to be willing to accept somewhat lower-profile leadership.

The shift in the U.S. posture toward the region is only one facet of changing foreign policy. Since the end of the Cold War, and the end of Ronald Reagan's presidency (1988), the greatest shift was naturally the diminishing relevance of anticommunism. What has replaced this is somewhat less clear; U.S. foreign policy concerns became more diverse, and—until terrorism raised its head in September 2001—less defined around a single, overriding priority. Despite their political differences, the foreign policy approaches of George H. W. Bush and Bill Clinton were quite similar. Both emphasized economic cooperation and collective security; for both administrations, immigration and narcotics trafficking were also issues, although the two presidents took somewhat different tactics with respect to the drug issue.

Because of the timing of Argentina's reforms and the end of the Cold War, U.S.-Argentine relations probably became closest during the Clinton administration, building on important advances already initiated during the Bush administration. This is more a consequence of the inevitable imbalance between the two countries than of a dramatic shift in U.S. policies. The United States develops foreign policy toward Latin America, or the Western Hemisphere, as a region; Argentina develops foreign policy toward the United States. Thus, it was not until the end of Bush's government and the beginning of the Clinton administration that the cumulative effects of Argentina's 1983 democratization, the 1987–1990 military rebellions, the end of the Cold War, and, above all, the economic crisis originating in 1989 collectively pushed the Argentine government to initiate the momentous change in relations between the two countries.

In other words, in many respects, Argentina policymakers have been much more responsible for the changes in U.S.-Argentine relations than their U.S. peers. Why have Argentine leaders, especially the Menem administration, sought such a change? Again, the answers are multiple. To begin with, the 1976–1983 military regime left Argentina with a very poor international image—Argentina became known not for its relatively high level of development, education, and sophistication, but for harsh repression and impulsive international aggression. The military regime also left behind a faltering economy. Following the 1989 round of hyperinflation, reform began to seem increasingly pressing. Argentina's assertive internationalism thus stands out as a well-designed tactic for increasing international confidence in Argentina, and attracting the kind of foreign aid and investment that would be needed to salvage the economy, albeit temporarily. At the same time, cooperation on the security front offered Argentina the opportunity to use the armed forces for a productive and respected purpose, thereby also helping to strengthen democratization.

Hence, various factors contributed to the immensely improved relations between the United States and Argentina. Political convergence found its roots in Argentina's democratic transition, as well as the international gains of the democratic paradigm following the end of the Cold War. Economic cooperation and integration stemmed from the pressures of economic crisis in Argentina, the growing trend toward regional economic blocs, as well as broader processes of globalization and Argentina's need for economic stability to obtain political stability. Finally, security cooperation can be explained both by global trends toward cooperative security and Argentina's more particular need to find a productive role for its armed forces.

What is most clear is that U.S.-Argentine relations improved enormously during the last decade of the 1900s. While the interests of the two countries unavoidably still conflicted at times, the ways of dealing with these conflicts differed dramatically from the selective and intermittent cooperation characterizing past U.S.-Argentine relations. Previously, disagreements tended to define the relationship, rather than being subsumed within it. Points of dissent colored the entire picture of U.S.-Argentine relations and became its central elements, overshadowing areas of convergence and cooperation. In contrast, during the immediate post–Cold War period, U.S.-Argentine friendship became the overriding characteristic of the relationship, with Argentina deliberately defining the United States as its closest ally.

When the reality of Argentina's profound economic troubles erupted at the end of 2001, Argentina's new leaders began reevaluating policies of this period, particularly questioning the convertibility program that had bound the peso so tightly to the U.S. dollar. As it sought to drag itself from the quagmire of its latest economic and political crisis, some softening of the Menem era focus on the United States appeared in order. Looking toward a broader array of friendships now seemed a more promising approach to finding help through newly challenging times. Yet, the legacies of the honeymoon period remained. Argentina's post–Cold War policies of devout loyalty towards the United States had, in many respects, broken the long pattern of pervasive conflict and mistrust.

# AUTONOMOUS ARGENTINA: A HISTORY OF U.S.-ARGENTINE RELATIONS

THE CLOSE FRIENDSHIP BETWEEN ARGENTINA AND THE UNITED States in the 1990s is intriguing for a number of reasons. As a case study, it demonstrates changing patterns in international relations, with growing emphasis on regional blocs and a surprisingly high level of consensus about such practices as free trade and democracy. Argentina's outreach also exemplifies renewed U.S. hegemony in the region, combined with somewhat diminished U.S. interest in the Americas. However, the transformation of U.S.-Argentine relations is also fascinating from a historical perspective. Perhaps the most notable aspect of the friendship after the end of the Cold War was its sheer novelty. It was a friendship built on the rocky foundation of a century during which cooperation, albeit frequent, still seemed unable to overcome the predominant pattern of mutual distrust. Nonetheless, the government of Carlos Menem made a strong commitment to this relationship, taking important steps to eradicate past distrust and to prevent any future government from erasing its achievements.

This chapter will look at the development of U.S.-Argentine relations from the early years (1800s) through the Cold War in order to compare earlier patterns with that of the Menem period. Particular attention will be given to critical moments in U.S.-Argentine relations before World War I, during and immediately after World War II, and during the Argentine military regime of 1976–1983. Over the course of history, U.S.-Argentine relations took a number of different forms, including (1) divergent interests during the prewar period; (2) conflict during and shortly after World War II; and (3) pragmatic, but intermittent, cooperation during the Cold War period. Only with the Menem administration did Argentina begin to define its foreign policy interests as virtually one with the United States, allowing this friendship to directly shape both foreign and domestic policy choices, despite the continued existence of unavoidable areas of disagreement.

Relations between the United States and Argentina have traditionally been far from smooth. Since quite early in its history, the United States has pursued a strategy of aggrandizement in the Americas, well in keeping with the practices of its colonial parent, Great Britain. Encouraged by its own early promises of grandeur, Argentina has typically rejected such ambitious U.S. designs in the region, adopting a posture of resistance and even confrontation. This position developed first during the late 1800s, when trade interests began to conquer distance and Argentina and the United States first really began to take notice of one another. Confrontation peaked during World War II, with Argentina's prolonged refusal to join the U.S. condemnation of the Axis Powers, and the United States' continuing accusations of Argentine collusion with the Nazis. Finally, during the Cold War, adamant anticommunism facilitated some convergence between U.S. foreign policymakers and the Argentine military regimes—only to have cooperation again dissolve in distrust following the 1982 Falklands/Malvinas war between Argentina and Great Britain.

## EARLY RELATIONS: COMPETING FOR INFLUENCE IN SOUTH AMERICA

Friendship has often eluded the United States and Argentina for a variety of reasons. Distance and competing exports certainly worked against the development of early bonds between the two countries, which simply did not need each other. Somewhat similar early economic successes also encouraged similarly ambitious aspirations, with both countries seeking grand "destinies" within the region. For the United States, this meant, first, trying to keep the then more powerful Europeans out of the region; secondly, seeking to expand territory within the North American continent and hegemony throughout the Americas; and, third, seeking Western Hemispheric unity to strengthen the U.S. position internationally. In contrast, Argentina sought to retain strong relations with Europe, to protect Argentine autonomy, and, intermittently, to unite Latin America against U.S. pretenses at dominance.

Both U.S. and Argentine foreign policies have received innumerable criticisms. The United States has been portrayed more often than not (and for good reason) as a heavy-handed imperialist in Latin America, with a history of stealing territory from its closest neighbor and coercing political loyalty from those only slightly farther down the road. Argentina's international postures have also been criticized, however. According to Carlos Escudé, Argentina's determined nationalism has verged on "pathology"; he claims that a "lack of contact with reality has transformed our nationalism into a destructive force for the very nation."[1] However, while Argentina's determined nationalism may at times have created unnecessary international conflicts or even obstacles to development, it also helped preserve a level of foreign policy freedom available to few others in the

Americas. Argentine obstructionism created one of the few protections against U.S. ambitions in the region during the nineteenth and early twentieth centuries.

### Ends of the Earth: Distance and Trade

During much of the nineteenth century, Argentina and the United States were shielded from too much conflict simply through limited interaction. In an age prior to telephones and commercial airplanes, the considerable distance from the midsection of North America to the southern tip of South America prevented extensive contact between Argentina and the United States. Furthermore, Argentina and the United States had little need to seek out such contact. According to Joseph Tulchin, during the early 1800s "trade consisted mainly of flour, lumber, and furniture from the United States in return for hides, tallow, and wool. . . ."[2] Such trade was limited, however. With similar climates and large expanses of fertile land, cattle and wheat were major products of both countries, which tended to mean more competition than exchange.

Argentina thus looked toward Europe instead of the United States. Throughout the 1800s, Europe still stood out as the heart of Western civilization and imperial power; U.S. ambitions for international status were only beginning to move beyond wishful thinking. The Argentine population blossomed with waves of European immigrants, their numbers vastly exceeding those of the very limited native population. Architecture copied from France found its way into Buenos Aires streets, and Spanish and Italian influences permeated virtually all aspects of Argentine culture. Yet with respect to trade, Great Britain was by far the most important player. Not only were the British far more interested in Argentine products than was the United States, but British ships could provide the transportation necessary to facilitate these exchanges.

While Europe continued to attract the most trade with Argentina, toward the mid-1880s trade between the United States and Argentina did begin to expand. Up to the early 1880s, the balance of trade between the two countries distinctly favored Argentina. According to Thomas McGann, "As late as 1881 the value of the goods which Argentina sent to the United States was more than two and one-half times the value of United States products imported by Argentina."[3] By this time, however, the United States had begun to industrialize, developing increasing numbers of manufactured goods. Thus, while Argentina continued to export around the same quantity of goods—still primarily agricultural—it began importing more of the United States' new exports, until, by 1885, imports had exceeded exports (see table 1.1). The United States' advances in manufacturing meant that long before it would be noticed, Argentina had already begun to lose the competition for hemispheric leadership.

While increasing trade did encourage more contact between the two countries, U.S. trade barriers ensured that some of that contact would involve discord. At

**TABLE 1.1**

**Argentine Trade with the United States and Europe, 1880–1910 (as percentage of total exports and imports)**

|  | Imports | | | Exports | | |
|---|---|---|---|---|---|---|
|  | 1880 | 1900 | 1910 | 1880 | 1900 | 1910 |
| Great Britain | 30.4% | 33.5% | 31.5% | 9.9% | 20.7% | 21.7% |
| Other Europe | 45.3% | 47.5% | 49.3% | 67.4% | 61.4% | 36.3% |
| United States | 7.8% | 13.4% | 13.9% | 9.5% | 5.9% | 6.8% |

Source: José Paradiso, *Debates y Trayectoria de la Política Exterior Argentina* (Buenos Aires: Grupo Exterior Latinoamericano, 1993), 27.

different points, the United States sought to block two major Argentine exports, wool and beef. Legislation passed in 1867 raised duties on wool, then Argentina's primary export to the United States.[4] More important, in later years were restrictions placed on Argentine beef. In 1927, during a period in which the United States had greatly expanded its economic ties to South America, it opted to prevent imports of meat from Argentina, as well as from fifteen other countries where foot-and-mouth disease had been suspected.[5] Widely perceived as a protectionist measure, the United States kept the policy in place until 1997, when limited quantities of chilled Argentine beef were finally allowed into the U.S. market.

America for . . . whom?

While expanding its economic presence, the United States also sought to expand its political presence in Latin America. In 1823, with the United States still a new nation and with very limited capacity to exert an international influence, President James Monroe formulated what would come to be known as the Monroe Doctrine. In brief, the Monroe Doctrine warned the European powers that "'we should consider any attempt on their part to extend their political system to any portion of this hemisphere as dangerous to our peace and safety. . . . We could not view any interposition . . . in any other light than as the manifestation of an unfriendly disposition toward the United States.'"[6] The Monroe Doctrine thus promised the Americas that they would be safe from European intervention, but not from that of the United States. Given that the European powers were, at the time, the most meddlesome external actors, the potentially threatening statement from the United States looked to some like a promise of support.

Ironically, even Argentina—one of the countries subsequently most suspicious of U.S. designs in the region—found encouragement in the Monroe Doctrine. In 1824, embroiled in a conflict with Brazil, Argentina again sought support from the United States, suggesting that this might "prevent European intervention in the dispute."[7] U.S. leaders criticized the Brazilian monarchy harshly, but stopped short at becoming directly involved in a battle between American states.[8] Argentina sought U.S. aid against a more demonstrable European incursion after Great Britain laid claim to the Falklands/Malvinas Islands in 1833, retaking possession after a nearly sixty-year absence.[9] Again, the United States refused. Argentine hopes for U.S. sympathy with their claim would be similarly disappointed 150 years later, when Argentina's military government sought to reclaim the islands they called the Malvinas.

If in the early years Argentines perceived the Monroe Doctrine as a promise the United States refused to fulfill, with the 1904 Roosevelt Corollary the doctrine became more of a threat. In the late 1800s and early 1900s, creditor countries such as the United States began facing difficulties with debtors unable to make payments. When Venezuela reached such a crisis, British, German and Italian ships sailed south, seeking to force compliance. Argentina and the United States both reacted. In 1902, Argentine foreign minister Luís María Drago sent a statement to Washington strongly opposing the use of force to pursue debt payments, once more appealing to the Monroe Doctrine as an argument against external intervention.[10] The Roosevelt Corollary incorporated the Drago Doctrine's opposition to the Europeans' use of force to collect debt, but now promised that the U.S. would assume the responsibility for enforcing good behavior in the Americas. By this time, however, the Argentine government sought only the promise of non-interference, and opposed the principle of unity of the Americas implied by Drago's invocation of the Monroe Doctrine. Thus, as the United States gradually became more inclined and able to intervene in South American affairs, Argentina grew increasingly suspicious of the Monroe Doctrine. Most Argentine leaders seemed inclined to turn to European allies rather than supporting a unified and U.S.-led American region.

### Manifest Destinies and Pan-Americanism

Different approaches by the United States and Argentina with respect to Pan-Americanism perhaps demonstrate more than any other early issue or event the nature of U.S.-Argentine relations. U.S. interest in Pan-Americanism emanated from the idea of Manifest Destiny, a term coined in the 1840s to refer to the supposed "destiny" of the United States to eventually occupy the entire continent, sharing its political system with all inhabitants. Gradually, the concept became even more ambitious, expanding to include the dissemination of U.S. political values and free trade principles even beyond the continent. The United States thus followed a trajectory characterized by increasingly broad aspirations toward leadership in the Americas.

When convenient, Argentina sought—generally unsuccessfully—to utilize U.S. ambitions to garner U.S. support in international conflicts. As a rule, however,

Argentina maintained far deeper relations with Europe than with the United States, and sought to protect both that relationship and its own promise of regional greatness from the United States. Thus, from the Argentine perspective, the country's "destiny" was more appropriately parallel to the United States than subordinate. Domingo Sarmiento, one of Argentina's most noted thinkers, and its president in the late 1800s, predicted that "'We shall reach the level of the United States. . . . We shall be the United States.'"[11] For many Argentines, their country's superiority in the region stemmed from its highly European character. Toward the late 1800s, Argentina appeared both wealthier than its neighbors and more democratic than most, achievements often attributed to the European heritage. According to Peter Smith, these advantages were interpreted as giving Argentina a responsibility "to spread the gospels of development through South America."[12]

Argentines thus highly valued their ties with Europe, for cultural as well as trade reasons, and resisted U.S. efforts to unify the Americas independent of Europe. Throughout the 1800s, Argentines consistently rejected proposals for regional collective security agreements, claiming that they preferred bilateral agreements, and saw no need for defense against Europe's "protective and civilizing" influence.[13] Later in the 1800s, Argentina continued to pose an obstacle to the U.S. quest for solidarity in the region.

In 1889, the United States hosted the first Pan-American conference, hoping to encourage trade in the region, as well as to set up a mechanism for resolving disputes. More specifically, it sought to use "macroregionalism," defined by Andrew Hurrell as "bloc regionalism, often built around a hegemonic or potentially hegemonic power," as a means of furthering its own economic prowess.[14] An Argentine delegation attended the conference, but primarily to obstruct U.S. proposals. In particular, Argentina opposed North American plans for a customs union (potentially impeding Argentine trade with Europe), and to establish a permanent court—in Washington, D.C.—with the authority to mediate regional disputes.[15] Argentina continued to demonstrate disinterest in subsequent Pan-American conferences, hindering and delaying the development of inter-American unity.

Yet it was not Pan-Americanism that Argentina truly opposed as much as it was regionalism with U.S. leadership.[16] In 1888, around the same time that plans for the first Pan-American conference were developing, Argentina and Uruguay hosted a South American conference, designed to foster cooperation—especially on trade issues—within the region.[17] During World War I, Argentina again sought to lead Latin-American solidarity, this time pursing a collective approach to the war.[18]

In sum, conflicts between the United States and Argentina up through World War II had to do not only with competing agendas but also with competing ambitions. Argentina was willing to seek U.S. aid, but would not easily accept U.S.

leadership of a unified Latin-American bloc. Argentina sought to protect its own autonomy, opportunities for trade, and potential for subregional leadership. In sum, both countries defended their own interests, but those interests did not place them on the path to easy cooperation.

## WORLD WAR II: FROM COMPETITION TO CONFLICT

Following World War I, the relationship between Argentina and the United States began to deteriorate further. Even without Pan-American unity, the United States achieved the hegemony in Latin America that Argentina had fought. Increasingly, the paths of the two countries diverged—the United States becoming a world power, and Argentina gradually losing its position of regional privilege. Trade between the countries had increased, with Europe gradually losing ground to the United States in South America, but now noncommercial interests began moving into the U.S. agenda. New ideological issues began to permeate U.S. foreign policy—specifically, a concern with the spread of fascism—and in light of this, there was increased determination to ensure hemispheric unity. For Argentina, this period encompassed dramatic political changes, spanning from the elimination of recent voting rights to the emergence of the country's historically most important and inclusive political movement, Peronism. However, trade and national autonomy continued to be Argentine priorities, and, at this point, acquiescing to U.S. pressures seemed unlikely to support these objectives. Argentine and U.S. hostility peaked around issues such as Argentine neutrality during World War II, and U.S. suspicions of Argentine motivations for this neutrality.

### Competing Neutrality: World War II

Although three very different regimes governed Argentina during the period between World War I and World War II, none of these naturally sympathized with the United States. From 1916 to 1930 the major force in Argentine politics was the middle-class Radical Party, led by Hipólito Yrigoyen, the first president to be elected through relatively inclusive elections.[19] Antagonistic toward the United States and suspicious of U.S.-led inter-American collaboration, Yrigoyen sought to bring together the countries of Latin America under Argentine leadership. After a pivotal coup toppled Yrigoyen's government in 1930, a conservative regime monopolized power until another coup in 1943.

The 1930 coup brought to power a less nationalist leadership than that of Yrigoyen, but one that, for other reasons, tended to be disinclined to cooperate with the United States. The conservatives who replaced Yrigoyen used a combination of electoral fraud, military support, and exclusion of the more popular Radical Party to return Argentina to the more restrictive politics that had previously characterized the country.[20] Given Yrigoyen's opposition to the United States, the new leadership was not unwelcome for Washington, D.C. However, the restored oligarchs represented, above all, the agricultural elites, a sector strongly interested in trade and inclined toward an export economy.[21] Argentina's new government did not dismiss the possibility of cooperation with the United States, but the latter's protectionist policies, including restrictions on imports of Argentine beef and wool, discouraged a strong shift toward a U.S.-oriented foreign policy. Argentina thus again sought markets in Europe, and in 1933, negotiated the Roca-Runciman pact with Great Britain to ensure that Argentine beef would be sold. The pact committed Great Britain to purchase a minimum of 390,000 tons of chilled Argentine beef annually, in exchange for a number of concessions by Argentina, including a commitment to reduce tariffs and give preferential treatment to British companies.[22] Widely criticized in Argentina as excessively favorable to Great Britain, the pact nonetheless underscored the historic ties between the two countries.

The United States, on the other hand, remained primarily a competitor for Argentina, with respect to regional influence as well as trade. Thus, for these two countries, the Chaco War between Bolivia and Paraguay implied another opportunity to demonstrate who—Argentina or the United States—would wield the most influence in South America. Following the 1865–1870 war between Paraguay and the Triple Alliance of Argentina, Brazil, and Uruguay, in which Paraguay lost vast amounts of its territory, borders remained unclear. By the early 1900s disagreements over rights in the Chaco region had led to a number of military clashes between Paraguay, to whom the territory had been ceded in the late 1880s, and Bolivia, whose interests had largely been ignored up to this point. The conflict intensified toward the late 1920s, and by 1932, Bolivia and Paraguay had become engaged in outright war. Both Argentina and the United States proclaimed neutrality (although according to historical accounts, Argentina actually favored and aided Paraguay), but both sought to set rules for resolving the dispute.[23] Echoing the debates of the 1889 Pan-American conference, the United States sought to oversee mediation in a Washington-based court of arbitration, which, in 1928, created a commission (Comision de Neutrales) of five neutral countries to deal with the conflict—the United States, Colombia, Cuba, Mexico, and Uruguay. The Commission of Neutral Powers not only sought to convince Bolivia and Paraguay to accept their authority to arbitrate the dispute, but also suggested that should either party break a resulting agreement, the other American countries "should treat the violator as an aggressor and should immediately withdraw all diplomatic and consular representatives from that country."[24] Argentina, which had already organized a competing group of border countries as mediators, objected both to the interventionist nature of the commission's approach, and to the idea of a regional response without a broader legal basis. Argentine Foreign Minister Carlos Saavedra Lamas thus suggested that the

League of Nations might be the appropriate forum for mediating the conflict. With Bolivia and Paraguay's acceptance, the League of Nations took over as mediator, effectively obstructing U.S. pretensions at leadership. In the end, however, the league's failure to terminate the war led to Argentina's resuming its efforts, which ultimately were successful.[25]

Once World War II erupted in Europe, U.S.-Argentine relations appeared to gain an increasingly ideological tint. Underneath the surface, however, the two countries' competing quest for influence in Latin America, and the Argentine concern with trade, remained at the heart of the countries' differences. Both countries initially opted for neutrality, and, in 1939, both governments even shared an underlying sympathy for the Allies. Despite this, the war in Europe soon deepened the rift between Argentina and the United States.

Two moments proved especially critical to increasing tensions: first, President Franklin Delano Roosevelt's 1940 declaration that the United States would help provide supplies to the Allies, and second, the U.S. entrance into the war in 1941 and ensuing demand that all other American states relinquish their neutrality. Rather than encouraging Argentine cooperation, the manner in which U.S. decisions were announced and implemented achieved the opposite result. U.S. actions appear to have actually weakened the more pro-U.S. elements in the Argentine government, and strengthened anti-U.S. and pro-Axis sentiment.

In early 1940, the Argentine government proposed to the United States that the countries of the Americas relinquish neutrality and adopt a position of "non-belligerents" in the war, thereby favoring the Allies without directly entering the war.[26] The initiative was an attempt by President Roberto M. Ortiz, one of the Argentine leaders most sympathetic to the United States, to strengthen his position within the divisive ruling coalition and attract more democratic supporters.[27] The United States flatly refused the proposal, claiming that it would be problematic both domestically and within the Americas.[28] However, later in the year, President Roosevelt proceeded to adopt, in essence, the very strategy that the Argentines had suggested—with no acknowledgement of Argentine authorship. Whereas Argentina had early on suggested abandoning neutrality, the United States now virtually demanded that the countries in the region follow its lead. The demand became more insistent following the United States' entrance into the war in 1941. In January 1942, the foreign ministers of the region met in Rio de Janeiro to discuss the posture of the Americas toward the war. The United States was adamant that all the countries of the Americas should break relations with the Axis. By the time the conference concluded, only Argentina and Chile had failed to do.[29] The United States responded to Argentina's refusal to follow suit by punishing what the secretary of state perceived as the "bad neighbor."[30] The United States blocked arms sales to

Argentina, froze Argentine funds in the United States, and sought to impose an economic blockade.

The United States could not, however, promise Argentina the trade and investment that would make abandoning neutrality at this point a lucrative choice. Germany had been an important market for Argentina since World War I, and, despite some interruption in trade during the Second World War, this was not a trading partner that Argentina would easily abandon.[31] Furthermore, the United States showed little inclination to compensate Argentina for the losses such a decision would entail; nor could it compensate Argentina for its wounded pride, a not inconsequential issue following the 1940 rebuff. According to Carlos Escudé, this act made "an Argentine rupture with the Axis due to U.S. pressures after the U.S. entry into the war close to politically impossible, considering the importance that an independent foreign policy had in Argentina's political culture."[32] By 1943, the government—now under the leadership of President Ramón Castillo—had become more firmly anti–United States and according to some observers, unabashedly pro-Axis.[33]

### The 1943 Military Regime, Perón, and the United States

Thus, like the 1930 coup, the 1943 military coup brought the possibility of improved relations with the United States. Nevertheless, as before, no transformation was immediately forthcoming. While the coup leaders "gave early indications that they would be more cooperative with the Allies than their predecessors," the coalition included strongly nationalist sectors with little sympathy for the United States.[34] Ironically, it would be one of the more adamantly nationalist leaders and the victim of an aggressive U.S. propaganda campaign who would oversee improving relations between the two countries.

At the time of the 1943 coup, Colonel Juan Domingo Perón still appeared to be a background member of the coup coalition, less senior than the generals who would initially assume the most prominent positions in the government. The first leader of the junta, General Pedro Pablo Rámirez represented one of the more moderate sectors, and demonstrated a willingness to cooperate with the Allies—if this meant that Argentina would again be able to acquire needed arms. When the United States refused, Argentina sought to instead purchase weapons from the Axis powers. The United States responded angrily, threatening that if Argentina did not break off relations with the Axis, it would "cut off all trade with Argentina" and reveal Argentina's purported role in the recent Bolivian coup.[35] Rámirez's decision to concede opened the path to the rise of the more nationalist faction, led by General Edelmiro Farrell and Colonel Perón.

By late 1945, Perón's deft mobilization of Argentina's urban working class had helped him to consolidate his position as the most powerful figure in the country, setting the stage for his 1946 election to the presidency. Given his roots in an army strongly influenced by German trainers, his own experience studying in Italy, and his known nationalism, his relatively pragmatic course with respect to the United States was somewhat surprising. Perón sought secure trade relations (preferably with Great Britain), an international leadership role for Argentina, and, like Rámirez, the weapons with which to ensure that position. In early 1945, with plans to form a major new international organization—the United Nations—in the works, Perón also sought to ensure that Argentina would be active in that potentially powerful forum. To reach these ends, Perón thus found it expedient to negotiate with the United States.

### Reconciliation?

The United States, however, set the terms. In early 1945, the United States initiated a meeting of American foreign ministers in Mexico City. At the Chapultapec Conference, the United States set forth a number of conditions which, if accepted by Argentina, would allow the normalization of Argentina's relations with the inter-American system, and, especially important, would permit Argentina to be a founding member in the planned United Nations. With Perón's urging, Argentina complied, and after years of defending neutrality, finally took the ultimate step of declaring war on the Axis.[36] The Argentine government thus finally won diplomatic recognition from the United States, a founding position in the United Nations, and ultimately, access to arms.

Perón's reconciliation with the United States can perhaps best be understood in light of his coalition and economic interests. Perón's support base was primarily in the military, and in the modern sectors of the economy—the urban working class, above all, but also some industrialists. In this respect, Peronism made a strong break with Argentina's historically powerful rural elite, the high society of Sociedad Rural and the polo fields. Both the military and industry had a direct interest in what the United States could provide. For the armed forces, the issue was clearly weapons. For the industrializing sectors of Argentina, it was access to capital and equipment, which the United States was now much better positioned to supply than Great Britain. Thus, circumstances favored a certain degree of Argentine cooperation, albeit still within a climate dominated by distrust.

### Perón versus Braden

For probably similar reasons, Perón dealt cautiously with virulent attacks by U.S. official Spruille Braden on the eve of the 1946 elections, which Perón was strongly favored to win. Braden, who first became Ambassador to Argentina in May of 1945 and then replaced Nelson Rockefeller as assistant secretary of state that August, was a determined enemy of Perón. Convinced that Perón would preserve Nazi and anti-American influence in Argentina, Braden directed an intensive investigation of the pro-Nazi activities and connections of Argentina's leadership. The resulting document, known as the "Blue Book," accused Argentina's military government of "collaborat[ing] with enemy agents in important espionage activities" and "conspir[ing] with the enemy to undermine the governments of neighboring countries in order to destroy their collaboration with the allies. . . . "[37] However, most of the information apparently dealt with President Castillo; despite Braden's best efforts, the investigation was unable to establish strong links between Perón and the Nazis.[38]

Braden released the Blue Book shortly before Argentina's presidential elections, hoping to sway Argentine voters to turn against Perón at the polls. Instead, the master politician turned Braden's attack into his own advantage. The campaign switched course from a competition between Argentine political parties to "Braden or Perón," practically eliminating Perón's opponents from the headlines and guaranteeing his success. Furthermore, Perón issued his own response to Braden, calling it the "Blue *and White* Book," in reference to Argentina's national colors. In the document, Perón carefully focuses his wrath on Braden, instead of the United States, writing that "the malicious interpretations [the Blue Book] contains are his work. We will conclusively demonstrate here that this official has failed in his duty as faithful informant, deceiving the government that placed its trust in him."[39] After responding to the different points in the Blue Book, primarily by pointing to Castillo and the preceding oligarchic regime as the culprits, Perón concludes by inviting the United States to engage in a more friendly relationship, writing, "May we recognize the United States with brotherly love, and may they know that here in the extreme south of the continent there is a people of free men, jealous of their liberties and rights, qualified as few others to cooperate in the tasks of the American civilization. And may we both know that there are no true reasons that can distance us from the attainment of our parallel destinies."[40] Perón's carefully designed response to Braden's onslaught thus not only boosted his popularity in the elections but opened up possibilities for a smoother relationship with the United States during the Cold War.

Nevertheless, the scars of World War II and Braden's attack remained. The United States continued to distrust and oppose Perón, and complaints about American imperialism remained common in Perón's discourse, even while the two sides took practical steps toward cooperation. During the Cold War, and especially from 1953 on, perceived national interests encouraged both governments to set aside some of their antagonism. For Argentina, key concerns were economic, particularly the need to attract foreign investment to help finance industrialization.[41] The United States also developed renewed economic interests in Latin America. However, with the Cold War enveloping U.S. perspectives in a new icy prism, strategic concerns in the region provided the strongest motivation for a more diplomatic posture toward Perón.

## U.S.-ARGENTINE COOPERATION AND CONFLICT DURING THE COLD WAR

Following World War II, the United States became less concerned with fascism and more wary of communism. Now allies were sought for a different war—the Cold War against the Soviet Union. Throughout most of this period, relations between Argentina and the United States tended to be occasionally rocky, but generally more peaceful than previously. Perón's efforts to establish a "third position" between the East and the West caused some consternation for the United States, as did increasing trade between Argentina and the Soviet Union from the 1950s onward. However, trade with the United States increased as well, and by the time the United States became more seriously concerned with the potential for communism in Latin America, the Peronists had been ousted from power. Despite occasional conflicts over issues such as Argentine grain sales to the Soviet Union, relations with Cuba, Argentina's nuclear policies, and varying Argentine policies toward U.S. oil companies, from 1955—when Perón was ousted—until the end of 1976, overall the two countries maintained more stable and cooperative relations than had been the case historically.

This relative stability occurred despite Argentina's profound political instability during this period. From 1955 to 1976, Argentina experienced two military regimes (1955–1958 and 1966–1973), each of which involved multiple additional changes in the leadership, and three civilian governments (1958–1962, 1963–1966, and 1973–1976), each of which was displaced by a military coup. Nevertheless, U.S. preoccupation with matters in Europe and in Asia to some extent muted U.S. interest in Argentine events during this period. At the same time, Argentine leaders tended to be more concerned with potential and actual insurrection within, and relatively less inclined than some of their predecessors to directly confront the United States.

### Chaotic Cooperation

The military regimes, in particular, preferred to seek an accommodation with the United States. The military leaders of 1955–1958 felt even more discomfort with Peronist mobilization than the United States did, and sought "a more positive relationship with the acknowledged leader of the Western world," with whom they clearly identified.[42] Following the December 1958 Cuban Revolution, and Fidel Castro's gradual shift from "pink" to "red," the militaries of Latin America also came to see communism as a much more immediate threat in the region. This was the era of the national security doctrines in Latin America, an approach that linked development, politics, and security, and which gave the military responsibility for "ensuring that security is achieved."[43] Unambiguously anticommunist, the "national security doctrine" helped justify the military regime of 1966–1973 as a necessity to save Argentina from insurrection and impose sufficient order for economic progress. General Juan Carlos Ongania, in particular, pursued an alliance with the United States, as well as with other anticommunist regimes in the region.

Yet civilian regimes during this period also found important points of convergence with the United States. Arturo Frondizi's elected government, 1958–1962, coincided with a period in which the U.S. had regained an interest in democracy and development as bulwarks against possible leftist insurrection.[44] Frondizi's "developmentalism" also encouraged foreign investment—always an interest of the United States—though he balanced this with nationalist controls and friendliness toward Cuba. Overall, however, the Frondizi government maintained good relations with the United States. Surprisingly, the Peronist governments of 1973–1976 for the most part also sustained relatively peaceful relations with the United States. While Hector Cámpora, the first to be elected, represented the more left-wing and nationalist sentiments in the party, he governed only briefly before Perón was able to return to power. At this point, Perón appeared much more moderate than during the 1940s, when tensions with the United States peaked. He now not only pursued friendly relations with the United States, but also sought to shut down the guerrilla groups that had emerged in his party. After Perón's death in 1974, his wife and successor, Isabel, deepened Argentina's alignment with the United States. Thus, among the civilian presidents of the period, only Cámpora and Arturo Illia (1963–1966)—who reversed Frondizi's oil contracts with U.S. companies—directly confronted the United States.

Diminished friction with the United States could not, however, mask the fact that internally Argentina was falling apart. Small guerrilla groups—some Peronist, others leftist—and their equally violent paramilitary enemies had created an atmosphere of frightening ungovernability. Terrorism reigned, and neither military nor civilian governments seemed capable of containing it. The military governments, in fact, exacerbated the problem, as much guerrilla violence initially stemmed from frustration with political exclusion. The only civilian president with the potential to pacify the country was Juan Perón, as his 1973 election represented a return to open political competition. However, Isabel unfortunately did not inherit his political skills along with his office, and the situation continued to deteriorate.

### The Era of the Generals: Initiation of the *Proceso*

In 1976 a new military *junta* took power, with the intent of restoring order to Argentina and permanently eliminating any potential "subversion" in Argentina. Known as the Proceso de Reorganización Nacional (Process of National Reorganization), the regime posed a number of dilemmas for the United States. On the one hand, the new military government was strongly anticommunist, and a dependable ally in the Cold War struggle. In an initial document, it explicitly declared its intention to ally Argentina with the "Western and Christian world."[45] The military leaders also soon made clear their rejection of a "third world" identity during this era of increasing north/south tensions. For them, the United States offered the best hope of defeating the forces of international communism, and Argentina should thus join with the north in that endeavor. Military presidents General Jorge Videla, General Leopoldo Galtieri and, for the most part, General Roberto Viola all adhered to this position, despite other conflicts among them.[46]

The military rulers also had the capacity to finally establish some level of control in the increasingly anarchic situation, given their determination to use whatever means necessary. Yet the violence used by the government to ensure order converted Argentina into one of the region's worst human rights offenders. The military regime tested relations with the United States even further when Argentina turned to international aggression in 1982, occupying the Falkland/Malvinas Islands. Shared anticommunism proved an insufficient bond to overcome these actions by the Argentine leaders.

### Carter and Argentine Human Rights

The military junta that took control of Argentina in March 1976 made no secret of its intention to combat the guerrillas. The military's primary aim in taking power was to ensure "national security" in Argentina, a concept that now seemed to focus primarily on eliminating leftist ideologies. Consequently, the military went far beyond fighting Argentina's relatively small, armed guerrilla groups. Seeking to ensure a more permanent transformation and stabilization of Argentine politics, the military targeted a much wider range of suspected "subversives," kidnapping, torturing, and killing suspected leftists or leftist sympathizers. According to official reports, close to nine thousand people disappeared during this period;[47] unofficial estimates place the number closer to thirty thousand or even more.

Political trends in the United States were quite different. Within a year of the 1976 coup, President Jimmy Carter was inaugurated in the United States. Carter deliberately sought to distance himself from his Cold War predecessors, designing a foreign policy in which ethics, and especially respect for human rights, would head the agenda; this was clearly not an area where Argentina excelled in the 1970s. The United States thus launched a campaign against the Argentine military regime, publicly critiquing its human rights record, blocking loans and international financing,[48] and establishing an embargo against "the sale of arms and spare parts to Argentina . . . or the training of its military personnel."[49] The Argentine government responded by ignoring and bypassing U.S. sanctions, since the repression (fighting "subversion," in the military's terms) was an intrinsic part of the military government's mission.

This mutually hostile relationship made cooperation in other areas very difficult, as demonstrated by Argentina's reaction to the U.S. grain embargo against
the Soviet Union. The United States formulated this policy in the wake of the
Soviet invasion of Afghanistan in 1979, requesting that all major producers—
Argentina, Australia, Canada, and the European Community—also participate.[50]
However, not only had the United States planned this approach entirely independent of its would-be partners in the venture, but it failed to in any way establish a
prior foundation for cooperation with Argentina. Offended by the United States'
lack of consultation in deciding on the embargo, and mistrustful of economic
sanctions in general, the Argentine government refused to comply. Instead,
Argentina increased grain sales to the Soviet Union significantly, thereby greatly
diminishing the impact of the sanctions.

Following this, however, the tide began to turn in U.S.-Argentine relations.
Human rights violations gradually diminished, largely because by 1979 the military leaders believed that they had already succeeded in defeating the
"subversives." Around the same time, many in the United States were reaching
the conclusion that sanctions had not been effective, and perhaps a new position
toward Argentina was in order.[51] The 1980 election of Ronald Reagan dramatically sped the reform of U.S. policy toward Argentina.

### Reagan and Central America

If Carter was known for his single-minded advocacy of human rights, Reagan
was known for his equally single-minded anticommunism. With respect to
Argentina, he demonstrated the change by welcoming military leader Roberto
Viola (soon to be president) as his first official visitor from Latin America.[52]
Almost immediately, Reagan sought to lift sanctions against Argentina, attempting to reinstate not only support for loans, but military aid and training.
Congress, however, continued to resist. According to Mark Falcoff, "The Reagan
administration finally compromised on military aid by allowing the Humphrey-
Kennedy Amendment to be replaced by another law . . . which permitted the sale
of arms and the resumption of military training for both Argentina and Chile
when and if the United States certified that a significant (though unverified)
improvement in human rights had occurred." [53] The new administration thus successfully renewed a cooperative relationship with Argentina, well in keeping with
Reagan's policy of supporting friendly, anticommunist, authoritarian regimes.[54]
The U.S. began supporting loans and financing for Argentina, and invited
Argentina to engage in joint naval exercises.[55]

Yet nowhere would Reagan demonstrate his foreign policy priorities as clearly
as in Central America, openly supporting the repressive Salvadoran regime and
pursuing the overthrow of Nicaragua's leftist Sandinistas by any conceivable
means. And here the interests of U.S. and Argentine leaders converged. The small

nations of the isthmus, plagued by revolutionary movements and repressive regimes, epitomized Reagan's fear of an advancing communist threat and a growing Soviet and Cuban foothold in the Americas. For Argentina, the Central America crises were much further away, but still quite significant. Like the United States, Argentina sought political influence within the region, as both had historically, now in the fight against communism.[56] The issue also reflected the continuation of the military regime's domestic policies. The military suspected that many of the Argentine guerrillas who escaped fled to Central America, and may have become integrated into the more successful revolutionary movements in that area.[57] According to Falcoff, "these exiles were seen by the Argentine military as part of a world wide conspiracy to bring down Latin American military institutions and Western civilization with it."[58]

Thus, as the countersubversive war wound down within Argentina, the Argentine military became increasingly active abroad. Argentina began by offering weapons and military assistance to Nicaraguan dictator Anastasio Somoza Debayle during the late 1970s.[59] Similar support would be provided to regimes in El Salvador and Guatemala, which were engaged in their own battles with revolutionary guerrillas. After the 1979 Sandinista revolution, the Argentine military began aiding Nicaraguan counterrevolutionaries, helping to "organize and train the dispersed and ill-equipped bands of Nicaraguan guardsmen exiled in Guatemala."[60]

Argentina thus actively fought in the Central American wars, even during periods when the United States appeared to stay more on the sidelines. During the 1970s, while the Carter government withdrew support from human rights offenders, the Argentine military sought to substitute for the United States in the Central-American battle against communism. Once Reagan came to power, fighting the Central-American Left became a more cooperative venture. Argentine trainers helped to hide U.S. involvement, which primarily consisted of financial support, thereby protecting the Reagan administration from the disapproval of the American public and the wrath of the U.S. Congress. The Argentine military thus aided the Reagan administration in its agenda, but in a way that preserved Argentina's cherished foreign policy autonomy and still avoided making friendship with the United States into a priority.

### Conflict in the Falklands/Malvinas War

Relations between the U.S. and Argentine governments soon deteriorated again, however. In April 1982, 150 years after Great Britain had reasserted its sovereignty in the Falkland Islands, Argentina sought to reclaim them. Just as in the 1800s, the quarrel between Argentina and Great Britain also soured relations between Argentina and the United States. Again, the United States refused to support Argentina's claims.

The military's decision to occupy the islands stemmed from a number of important misplaced expectations. First, the military gambled that Great Britain would not bother to defend the islands, given the cost of such an endeavor, and the matter could therefore be settled at the bargaining table. Second, Argentine leaders expected that the United States would, at the very least, remain neutral, given the latter's perceived debt to Argentina in the Central America matter, and that they would be able to garner further support from other developing countries. Third, military leaders expected that the war would be popular enough to allow them to shore up their severely dwindling legitimacy, and avoid transferring power to an elected civilian. None of these expectations proved well-founded.[61]

Consequently, the Argentine military found itself fighting a war with Great Britain for which it had neither planned nor prepared. The international reaction, furthermore, proved a considerable disappointment to Argentina. While many Latin-American countries did sympathize with Argentina (Venezuela and Peru offered supplies, and the Nicaraguan Sandinistas even offered troops),[62] the Organization of American States was unwilling to openly back Argentina's actions.[63] The United States turned out to be an even less reliable ally. After first assuming an active diplomatic role, with U.S. Secretary of State Alexander Haig shuttling between London and Buenos Aires in the hopes of preventing the war, the United States came down firmly on the side of Great Britain. The United States permitted Great Britain to use American satellites, gave them access to Ascensión Island, provided some two hundred Sidewinder missiles, and reportedly offered to supply aircraft fuel and aircraft carriers, if necessary.[64] Furthermore, the United States renewed essentially the same set of sanctions that had previously been used to punish Argentina for human rights offenses during the Carter government. Hence, on April 30, "the United States announced that it would withhold certification of Argentine eligibility for military sales, Eximbank credits and guarantees, and loans from the Commodity Credit Corporation."[65] Argentina was soundly defeated in the war, and U.S.-Argentine relations had reverted to the historic pattern of distrust and mutual hostility.

## RESOLVING A HISTORY OF CONFLICT?

In sum, for approximately a century, from the time the United States and Argentina first began to interact more consistently in the 1880s through the early 1980s, U.S.-Argentine relations tended to be defined more by the issues that divided the countries than those that brought them together. Cooperation did penetrate the haze of distrust between the two countries, especially during the Cold War, but Argentina never entirely relinquished its proud independence enough to allow these convergences to blossom into friendship. Despite radical regime changes, Argentine leaders preserved considerable consistency with respect to their foreign policy priorities. The Argentine government sought to protect Argentine markets, establish relations with the most promising trade partners (whether or not their politics were compatible with those of Argentina), preserve national autonomy, and advance Argentine leadership within the region. These priorities often clashed with U.S. foreign policy aims and practices, especially U.S. protectionism, its hegemonic aims in the Americas, and its more ideological approach to foreign policy.

In the 1980s, and especially the 1990s, the pattern of U.S.-Argentine relations finally began to change. In the wake of the Falklands/Malvinas debacle, the Argentine military fled from power, allowing free elections to take place at the end of 1983. The rebirth of democracy in Argentina began the shift toward more peaceful relations between the United States and Argentina, eased by the surprise election of human rights activist Raúl Alfonsín of the Unión Cívica Radical. It was the first time that the Radicals had defeated the Peronists in open presidential elections since Perón's first rise to power.

The new democratic administration sought to improve the Argentine-U.S. relationship, severely scarred by human rights issues and devastated after the Falklands/Malvinas War. As stated by Minister of Foreign Affairs Dante Caputo, Argentina sought to establish a "mature relationship" based on shared values of "democracy, pluralism, the dignity of mankind, human rights, liberty and social justice."[66] Domestically, the Alfonsín administration actively pursued these values, most visibly in their efforts to bring members of the military to justice for the human rights violations of the military regime. Such measures incurred unavoidable costs. Feeling directly under attack by the new government, in 1987 a group of army officers organized the first of a series of rebellions, challenging both the government's policies and their military superiors' compliance.[67] Gradually the government was forced to retreat.

Despite Argentina's dire need for outside support under these conditions, autonomy continued to be valued more than the benefits that could be attained from a more conciliatory approach to the United States. The Alfonsín administration held fast to its positions on issues such as the Central-American conflicts—where Argentina now took an active role in pursuing a peaceful settlement—and Cuba, and refused to bow to U.S. pressures regarding nuclear nonproliferation. U.S.-Argentine relations also suffered during this period due to U.S. doubts about the Alfonsín administration's initial approach to dealing with its economic crisis. The 1985 Plan Austral, with its emphasis on fighting inflation and reducing the deficit, did win U.S. approval. However, in part due to the intense political backlash against the government's austerity plans, neither the Plan Austral nor the later Plan Primavera could prevent the continued deterioration of the Argentine economy. Alfonsín's administration ended in 1989 in the midst of a bout of hyperinflation, as the value of the new austral currency plummeted to only a small fraction of its 1988 value. Only at this point did U.S. friendship and confidence begin to appear critical to rebuilding Argentina's international image, and to Argentina's gaining support from international economic institutions.

Hence, it was not until the Cold War had ended and the second freely elected president of the period, Carlos Menem, had taken office that U.S.-Argentine relations truly appeared to be en route to a new pattern of committed cooperation and friendship. Menem, who had campaigned as a traditional Peronist, radically shifted his policies once in office. It was Menem who truly implemented the economic reforms for which the Alfonsín administration had merely planted the seeds. Furthermore, the Menem government deliberately set aside Argentina's traditionally obdurate independence, seeking instead a more profound friendship with the United States than these countries had enjoyed before.

# THE NEW INTERNATIONAL ORDER AND THE TRANSFORMATION OF U.S.-ARGENTINE RELATIONS

THE END OF THE COLD WAR CREATED BOTH NEW OPPORTUNITIES and new challenges for U.S.-Argentine relations. For more than forty years, relations between the United States and Latin America had been shaped by the ideological struggle led by the United States and the Soviet Union. Argentine leaders had alternately sought—unsuccessfully—to forge an independent path, and had wholeheartedly embraced the U.S-led anticommunist struggle, though still without sacrificing political independence. Throughout, as before, the relationship between the United States and Argentina tended to be characterized by a certain distrust, which several bouts of cooperation still failed to dispel. This pattern would change dramatically with the end of the Cold War.

As both the prowess and promise of communism disintegrated, the ideological struggle lost meaning and ceased serving as the guidepost for international affairs. Patterns of global change previously obscured by the overpowering influence of the Cold War now became far more important in defining foreign relations. At the same time other, newer patterns began to emerge, alternately spurred on by the sudden lack of obvious constraints, or inspired by the need to create some semblance of order in an apparently disordered world. It was a transformation that brought elation, hope, and above all, confusion. But for U.S.-Argentine relations, the new global order brought important new prospects. As U.S. leaders wrestled with what the "new world order" should mean for U.S. foreign policy, Argentine leaders seized the change as an opportunity. If the end of the Cold War left the United States somewhat without direction, it helped create a direction for Argentina. The emerging tendencies in the post–Cold War system and in the developing U.S. foreign policy offered Argentine policymakers a possible solution to their major problems, including hyperinflation, a disruptive military, and an international reputation damaged by recent political instability and foreign aggression.

The end of the Cold War created new opportunities for U.S.-Argentine relations largely because of a convergence between (1) a changing international environment, in which political democracy and economic liberalism predominated, with the United States as the dominant liberal power; (2) changing U.S. priorities, as the United States sought to limit the costs of its newfound power and counter relative economic gains of competitors by strengthening regional alliances; and (3) a critical moment in Argentina, with an infant democracy threatened by economic crisis and a historically problematic military with an as yet undefined role. Argentina's chaotic domestic situation—especially the faltering economy—provided the incentive to shift its foreign policy focus toward alignment with the strongest international power, now the United States. This chapter focuses on the nature of the international changes that invited this foreign policy shift.

### Defining the "New World Order": Continuity and Change

With the dramatic changes in Eastern Europe during the late 1980s and 1990s, observers rushed to define the emerging international system. One thing was clear: the superpower struggle between the United States and the Soviet Union would no longer set the parameters for interstate relations. The Cold War began to end with Mikhail Gorbachev's reforms of the 1980s, *glasnost* and *perestroika*, which gradually expanded political freedoms and economic competition in the Soviet Union. The 1989 collapse of the Berlin Wall and the subsequent 1991 dissolution of the Soviet Union finalized the process which Gorbachev had unwittingly begun: the conclusion not only of the Cold War, but of a bipolar system organized around the ideological tension between two competing superpowers able to engage political players worldwide in their battle.

What, then, would succeed the Cold War world order? Speculation began even before the fate of the Soviet Union had been sealed. Some welcomed the end of the Cold War enthusiastically. From the White House, George H. W. Bush greeted events in Eastern Europe with the triumphant claim that the United States had "won" the Cold War, and a "new world order" would emerge. Similarly, Francis Fukuyama gleefully announced that we had reached the "end of history," with the "unabashed victory of economic and political liberalism"and the conclusion, if not of all conflict, at least of ideological conflict.[1] Others, however, predicted a new era of chaos emerging from a period which could actually be characterized as the "long peace."[2] While the utter destruction of the world through nuclear weapons may have diminished as a threat, without superpower enforcement of "order" in and between their client states other conflicts could proliferate, either between civilizations (per Samuel Huntington) or along socioeconomic lines (per Zbigniew Brzezinski).[3] Yet a third group of observers regarded the developments with relative calm, claiming that in reality, little had changed.[4]

Despite the vast differences, it is possible to reconcile these perspectives. As will be discussed, at the end of the Cold War, both continuity and change can be found in the world system. Among the changes, many may be discomforting, but others offer promise and opportunity, as Argentine policymakers quickly observed. In many respects, the end of the Cold War resembled blowing away a large, dark cloud, so that preexisting trends and patterns could finally come to light. In particular, trends in domestic politics (i.e. democratization), transnational issues (economic globalization), and international institutions became both more evident and more important once the Cold War ceased to cast its shadow. Yet the Cold War was not so superficial or ephemeral that its passing would leave no further mark. In particular, the relations between and among states and blocs of states could not avoid change with the collapse of Cold War bipolarity. This bundle of factors created the environment of the post–Cold War period and, more specifically, encouraged Argentine leaders to adopt the pro-United States liberal internationalism that would so definitively characterize foreign policy at this time.

## Emerging Trends

Without U.S.-Soviet tensions as a referent, a number of characteristics of the world system came to the fore. Some of these originated nearly simultaneously to the Cold War, while others developed over time or emerged only toward the end of this period. According to G. John Ikenberry, one of the earliest trends was toward setting up institutions for interstate competition. This trend, known as liberal internationalism, or "the liberal democratic order . . . culminated in a wide range of new institutions and relations among Western industrial democracies, built around economic openness, political reciprocity, and multilateral management of an American-led liberal political system."[5] Institutions representing liberal internationalism include the United Nations, the World Bank, the International Monetary Fund (IMF) and the General Agreement on Tariffs and Trade (GATT), which were formed in the aftermath of World War II, and the recent successor to GATT, the World Trade Organization. The premise of these organizations was that peace and prosperity for all could best be achieved through cooperation within the framework of these international institutions, under the guidance of the liberal West and, particularly, the United States.[6] During the Cold War, however, the power and range of influence of these institutions was circumscribed by the existence of a competing international model. The United Nations, for example, remained somewhat limited in its ability to act, given the presence of both superpowers in its Security Council and the diversity of the organization's membership.[7] Particularly since the 1960s, growing numbers of new, small countries in some respects shifted the General Assembly to a forum dominated by the world's poorer nations, which contributed further to the United States' lukewarm support for the organization.

During the post–Cold War period, however, the United Nations' overall activity, and especially its involvement in peacekeeping, expanded exponentially, not in small part due to the reform and subsequent disintegration of the Soviet Union. As the Gulf War dramatically demonstrated, the United States and Russia could, in the post–Cold War world, cooperate on international missions. Without such a strong likelihood of a veto by one of the five permanent members of the Security Council (the United States, the Soviet Union, China, Great Britain and France), the UN would be much freer to act. When the UN did not have the capability, the practice developed of UN authorization of U.S.-led actions or, alternatively, NATO-led cooperative missions. Not coincidentally, cooperative security was one of the linchpins of Argentina's foreign policy approach in the 1990s, and a pivotal point for U.S.-Argentine friendship, with Argentine involvement in both UN-directed and U.S.-led military missions.

Liberal economic institutions also gained influence in the post–Cold War world, particularly the new creation of this period, the World Trade Organization. Not only did the WTO create a more formal organizational structure to replace the looser agreements of its predecessor, but it also significantly expanded its scope. The GATT had focused primarily on the pursuit of unfettered trade in goods, seeking to reduce, and ultimately eliminate, tariffs and nontariff trade barriers. To this, the WTO added the pursuit of free trade in services, as well as seeking to address growing issues such as technology and intellectual property, along with sensitive agricultural products.

The IMF and the World Bank also saw their potential influence expand following the end of the Cold War. The IMF, originally designed to provide short-term loans to help stabilize the fixed exchange rate system of the postwar period, had already witnessed considerable growth of its function. Following the debt crises of the early 1980s, the IMF was called upon to assume a broader role in economic stabilization than originally anticipated, now providing a wider range of loans, with quite a few conditions attached. With the end of the Cold War, both the IMF and the World Bank—responsible for longer-term development loans—came to serve a much larger constituency, as numerous new developing countries, former members of the communist bloc, joined the liberal international economy. Since the United States has historically exercised disproportionate influence in these organizations, as with the United Nations, U.S. international influence grew concomitantly with this expansion of liberalism and with the growing authority of the associated institutions.

The growing role of international institutions has also been encouraged by the more gradual trend toward globalization. Globalization refers, in essence, to the ever-expanding linkages and interdependence throughout the international community. Beginning with profound technological advances in transportation and communication, states, communities and peoples have, in practice, been brought into increasing contact with one another. Perhaps even more important, the economies of the world have become profoundly intertwined and interdependent, with goods, finances, and even labor largely leaving borders behind.[8] For some, this economic integration and the concomitant blurring of lines between nation-states is a sign of promise, an indication that we are on the path toward a peaceful, undivided world community. Others, however, have pointed to some of the more troublesome aspects of globalization. Stanley Hoffmann, for example, notes that globalization to some extent diminishes the ability of governments to effectively govern. He writes, "The new transnational economy has not merely, and beneficially, constrained the power of states. . . . It has, alas, also deprived them of their ability to perform necessary tasks, to carry out basic functions liberalism never intended to remove from them. The free flow of drugs and the free circulation of crime have accompanied the formation of a global world economy. . . . Moreover, the ability of governments to define their own monetary policies and to orient investments, employment, and growth has been seriously curtailed by the very size and weight of the transnational economy."[9] Globalization may also actually *increase* socioeconomic inequality, or at the very least, awareness of such inequalities.[10]

Globalization thus appears to be something of a mixed blessing, but an unavoidable reality. Economic interdependence means that isolation may be an increasingly difficult option for all countries. During the Cold War, states that sought, like Juan Domingo Perón's Argentina, to achieve a "third way," avoiding absorption into either the U.S. or Soviet camps, often found themselves under considerable pressure from the superpowers to relinquish their idealistic neutrality. At the end of the Cold War, ideological forces and international political allegiances became somewhat less important, while economic participation and integration into the world economy became more so. Even without direct pressure from world powers, the need to buy and sell goods and attract investment discouraged countries from shoring up national boundaries and stepping outside the system.

A more recent trend is democratization. While globalization may bend the boundaries between domestic and foreign policies,[11] democratization is a phenomenon of domestic politics, but one both influenced by globalization and carrying global implications. Particularly in the 1980s, many countries throughout the world began leaving behind authoritarian regimes and establishing democratic institutions, or at a minimum, liberalizing the existing political order.[12] Internal dynamics, such as the difficulty of legitimizing and institutionalizing military regimes, stand out as the most obvious causes of these democratic transitions.[13] However, globalization also had an influence, with enhanced communication facilitating "demonstration effects" in later democratizers.[14] The democratization of Eastern Europe and the collapse of the Soviet Union can, in some respects, be seen as the culmination of this process, with incipient democracies emerging in those polities previously most hostile to liberalism.

Because of this wave of democratization, democracy became a central characteristic of the post–Cold War order. It also helped to define Argentina's position within this order. Argentina's transition to democracy began with the 1983 elections, which placed Argentina as one of Latin America's earlier democratizers of this period. This allowed Argentina to play a leadership role with respect to democratization in the region, standing out as a model for subsequent democratizers. The new government's efforts to punish human rights offenders and the subsequent backlash from the military became an important example of both democratic ambition and the constraints on new democratizers. In sum, as democratization became a trend both within the region and the world, Argentina became an important point of reference, in a much more positive sense than during the prior, authoritarian years.

### Power and Influence after the Cold War

The end of the Cold War thus meant that many preexisting trends came to the surface, intensifying in the process and helping to define the emerging world order. Nevertheless, other defining characteristics of the new era emanated specifically from the end of the Cold War and the bipolar order. Notably, the interstate system and the role of ideology within that system would be profoundly altered during the post–Cold War period.

In many regards, the Cold War can be seen as a competition between two ideologies, liberalism and communism. While communism did not entirely disappear from the world after the Soviet Union's demise, it had undeniably suffered a considerable defeat: no country remained that could truly advance the communist cause. Without Soviet financial support, Cuba was quite weak; the most powerful remaining communist country, the People's Republic of China, had, in practice, been moving away from a communist economic system since the late 1970s. Communism may have collapsed of its own weight, rather than due to the power of liberalism to convince, but the effect was the same. Liberalism emerged triumphant, with the "total exhaustion of viable systemic alternatives,"[15] and would remain as the dominant ideological model for the post–Cold War system.

This outcome had a variety of practical consequences. To begin with, it meant increased legitimacy for new and struggling democratic regimes, and diminished international legitimacy and support for insurgent movements from either the left or the right. Little international backing remained for revolutionary guerrilla movements, encouraging several Latin American groups to accept peace settlements. Likewise, military rule lost acceptance as a political alternative; Venezuela's 1992 coup attempts drew harsh criticism from the region, particularly from the Organization of American States (OAS). Economic liberalism—especially free trade—also surged, replacing not only state communism, but common Latin-American approaches such as import-substituting industrialization. Thus, governments like Argentina's, which had already been struggling to counter the oversized states and debts inherited from ISI and subsequent models, as well as raging inflation and fiscal crisis, were encouraged to take further steps toward liberal economic reforms.

The other major developments in the post–Cold War order had to do with the changes in the overall balance and configuration of states within the international system. The loss of the Soviet Union meant ending bipolarity, but left a situation that was neither entirely unipolar or multipolar. With respect to military power, the United States could no longer be challenged. As Brzezinski writes, "America possesses not only overwhelming strategic power—constantly enhanced by technological innovation—but also an unmatched capability to project its conventional forces to distant areas."[16] Nuclear weapons could, of course, still threaten the United States, but the dismantling of the Soviet Union dispersed its holdings, and no other nuclear weapons state had the capability to compete.

Yet in economic affairs, U.S. superiority was less certain. Since World War II, economic development has led to increasing competition with U.S. prowess, and overall, a multipolar world in the economic sphere.[17] As Raimo Vayrynen writes, "Economic resources have dispersed to such an extent that the United States has no chance of claiming hegemony over them."[18] In part, this is due to globalization, which diminishes the government's control of the country's resources. However, it is also due to the growing importance of other economic players—both individual countries and blocs—in economic production and world trade. While the United States may have been left with the strongest single economy and enjoyed a prolonged boom in the 1990s, both the European Community and Japan came to present much more of a challenge to the United States during the second half of the twentieth century. By 1990, the Japanese gross domestic product (GDP) had grown to 53.5 percent of the U.S. GDP ($2970.1 billion and $5554.1 billion, respectively); the countries of the European Union, on the other hand, boasted a combined GDP of $6742.4 billion, surpassing that of the United States.[19] The United States also lost some ground in world trade through the latter 1900s, with Germany surpassing the U.S. share of exports, and Japan coming in close behind (see table 2.1); the European Union seemed likely to compete even more effectively with the United States. For Argentina, trade with Europe and Mercosur (the Southern Market) consistently outpaced trade with the United States in the 1990s, even as Argentina's imports from all these countries expanded exponentially (see table 2.2). Nevertheless, during the immediate post–Cold War period, the United States for the most part retained and even strengthened its hegemonic position in Latin America with respect to both politics and economics. This was the result of various factors, including U.S. predominance within the increasingly

**Table 2.1**

**Exports As a Share of Total World Exports, 1950–1996
(in millions of U.S. dollars)**

|  | 1950 | 1960 | 1970 | 1980 | 1990 | 1992 | 1994 | 1996 |
|---|---|---|---|---|---|---|---|---|
| United | 9993 | 19626 | 42659 | 225566 | 393592 | 448163 | 512627 | 625073 |
| States | 16% | 15% | 14% | 11% | 11% | 12% | 12% | 12% |
| Japan | 825 | 4055 | 19317 | 130441 | 287581 | 339885 | 397005 | 410901 |
|  | 1% | 3% | 6% | 6% | 8% | 9% | 9% | 7% |
| Germany | 1993 | 11415 | 34228 | 192860 | 410104 | 422271 | 429722 | 521111 |
|  | 3% | 9% | 11% | 10% | 12% | 11% | 10% | 10% |
| EU (15)* | 19022 | 48162 | 128438 | 753825 | 1496061 | 1575811 | 1669539 | 2103812 |
|  | 31% | 48% | 13% | 37% | 43% | 42% | 39% | 40% |
| Total | 61893 | 129886 | 314614 | 2022400 | 3490909 | 3755842 | 4279208 | 5329657 |

*Source*: United Nations Conference on Trade and Development, *Handbook of International Trade and Development Statistics 1996/1997* (New York: United Nations, 1999), 2

*\*Note*: The combined data for the European Union for these years is estimated for illustration purposes, as all fifteen countries did not join the EU until the late 1990s.

important liberal international institutions mentioned previously; U.S. ability to offer security in an insecure world; and the growing tendency toward regionalism, with more countries turning to their geographic neighbors both for reasons of security and to improve economic performance.

The end of bipolarity implied the loss of a certain amount of security. Given the horrific possibilities of conflict in the Cold War, the two superpowers deftly avoided directly confronting one another, allowing ideological battles to be fought only on others' terrain. The risks also meant that it was in the interest of both powers to keep such wars relatively limited. The Cold War period was not without bloodshed, but the scale of war remained somewhat confined.

In contrast, during the post–Cold War period, no such powerful deterrent exists, especially since the relevant players are not always obvious. Consequently, there is the risk that this new era of "peace" could instead be an era of less controlled and potentially more devastating conflict; September 11, 2001 underscored that risk.

Two post–Cold War patterns have been particularly important in helping to counter this insecurity, both of them building on preexisting trends. First of all, cooperative security has gained support, in large part to help impose peace in areas of post–Cold War crisis (e.g., the former Yugoslavia). Organizations such as the United Nations and the OAS, along with various ongoing practices of engagement, have thus in some respects filled in for the superpowers, replacing deterrence with international cooperation as a means of preventing and limiting war. Second, countries have now turned to their neighbors for support in this new,

**Table 2.2**

**Argentine Trade with Major Trading Partners, 1991–1999**

**Exports (as percentage of total Argentine exports; total in millions of U.S. dollars)**

|          | 1991   | 1992   | 1993   | 1994   | 1995   | 1996   | 1997   | 1998   | 1999   |
|----------|--------|--------|--------|--------|--------|--------|--------|--------|--------|
| Mercosur | 16.5%  | 19.0%  | 28.1%  | 30.7%  | 31.1%  | 33.3%  | 35.3%  | 36.7%  | 29.9%  |
| Brazil   | 12.4%  | 13.7%  | 21.4%  | 23.3%  | 25.5%  | 27.8%  | 30.4%  | 31.4%  | 24.1%  |
| E.U.     | 33.6%  | 31.1%  | 28.1%  | 26.0%  | 20.7%  | 19.2%  | 15.6%  | 18.2%  | 20.3%  |
| U.S.     | 10.4%  | 11.%   | 9.8%   | 11.1%  | 7.1%   | 8.3%   | 7.8%   | 8.2%   | 11.2%  |
| Total    | 11978  | 12235  | 13118  | 15659  | 20967  | 23811  | 25516  | 25227  | 23333  |

**Imports (as percentage of total Argentine exports; total in millions of U.S. dollars)**

|          | 1991   | 1992   | 1993   | 1994   | 1995   | 1996   | 1997   | 1998   | 1999   |
|----------|--------|--------|--------|--------|--------|--------|--------|--------|--------|
| Mercosur | 21.0%  | 25.3%  | 25.1%  | 23.9%  | 21.8%  | 24.5%  | 24.7%  | 25.4%  | 24.6%  |
| Brazil   | 18.5%  | 22.5%  | 21.3%  | 19.9%  | 20.1%  | 22.4%  | 22.5%  | 22.6%  | 21.9%  |
| E.U.     | 24.2%  | 25.6%  | 25.8%  | 30.0%  | 27.9%  | 29.0%  | 27.3%  | 27.7%  | 29.2%  |
| U.S.     | 18.1%  | 21.7%  | 23.0%  | 22.9%  | 18.3%  | 20.0%  | 20.0%  | 19.4%  | 19.5%  |
| Total    | 8275   | 14872  | 16784  | 21527  | 20122  | 23762  | 30349  | 31402  | 25538  |

*Sources*: International Money Fund, *Direction of Trade Statistics Yearbook* (Washington, D.C.: IMF, 1998–2000), 102–4; *Direction of Trade Statistics* (Washington, D.C.: IMF, December 1999), 41; *Direction of Trade Statistics* (Washington, D.C.: IMF, March 2001), 43.

disorderly world. In part, this is due to increased freedom from cross-regional, ideological ties during the post–Cold War period.[20] However, such regional bonding also replaces these ideological ties, generating a new frame of reference, stronger economic blocs, and relatively more protection from security threats. As will be discussed, these responses were embraced by both the United States and Argentina, and helped Argentina find ways of pursuing their newly valued friendship with the United States.

## THE UNITED STATES IN THE NEW WORLD ORDER

The United States' pivotal position following the Cold War meant that whichever posture the country assumed would play an important role in determining how the threat of chaos would be dealt with. One possibility would be for the United States to assume an active leadership position, assuming a guardian role in the new world order. Alternatively, the United States could either retreat from an active international role or seek allies to help share the costs of policing; the nation would also, however, need to deal with the economic uncertainty emanating from increasingly strong competition. The end of the Cold War also meant that many Americans initially expected a "peace dividend"—an increase in spending (or reduction in taxes) from funds no longer necessary for defense. These economic factors influenced both U.S. policymakers' inclination and their ability to assume an active international role.

Despite the United States' relative power following the Cold War, it was not left with either a monopoly or sufficient economic resources to easily absorb the costs of extensive unilateral policing. Beyond this, there is the question of will. Until September 11, the memory of Vietnam still caused many Americans to shy away from anything but the smallest and shortest commitment of U.S. troops abroad. Furthermore, without the Cold War, the U.S. government lost much of its ability to justify extensive interventionism, which meant even more resistance from a doubtful public. During the Cold War, the United States could be the torchbearer for liberal democracy, saving the world from communism; during the post–Cold War period that position was essentially drowned out by the swelling chorus of liberal democratic states, with no communist enemy to fight. For many Americans, it is simply unclear why wars abroad should be U.S. wars. These public sentiments were transformed following the September 11, 2001 terrorist attack. Immediately, Americans went on the defense, patriotism soared, and war came to be seen as inevitable—and for some, even desirable. Everywhere, Americans raised the flag. The American flag waved on homes, on cars, on businesses; red, white, and blue even became the fashion for clothing and jewelry. The American public was unquestionably ready for a new international role.

Nevertheless, in Latin America, the United States had taken on a policing role long before U.S. policing expanded internationally for the war against terrorism. In 1989, as the Cold War was just coming to an end, the United States invaded Panama to oust and arrest General Manuel Noriega, subsequently convicted in the U.S. of narcotics-related charges. The lack of an ideological incentive for the invasion made this the United States' first clearly post–Cold War military action. According to Jorge Castañeda, the United States' failure to avoid "blatantly violating diplomatic protocol, immunity, or asylum in Latin America" also indicated the clear dominance of the United States, without the Soviet Union as a counterbalance.[21] In 1994, now clearly into the post–Cold War period, the United States launched another invasion in the region, this time occupying Haiti. Ostensibly, the action was motivated by the desire to restore (or establish) democracy in that state; by most accounts, countering immigration was a stronger influence. By early 2000, the enormous levels of U.S. military aid flowing to Colombia had inspired widespread concerns about U.S. intentions toward that country.[22]

Argentina, at least during Carlos Menem's presidency, was among the Latin American states most willing to cooperate with the United States in these adventures. Argentina did not support U.S. actions in Panama, but President Raúl Alfonsín did offer to act as mediator during the period of crisis and negotiations prior to the U.S. invasion.[23] President Menem offered considerably more support in the Haiti operation, although not without some definite domestic dissent. Early plans to participate in the invasion were eventually swapped for a more moderate commitment to join the subsequent peacekeeping force.

From the other side of the spectrum, isolationists argued that the United States should refrain from foreign involvement altogether and focus instead on domestic affairs. Yet while isolationist influences may have temporarily limited U.S. involvement abroad, in the post–Cold War world it was difficult to maintain this posture. With military and economic power, the United States also gained a broader range of international interests than it may have had prior to World War I. Thus, while unilateral policing is too costly to serve as the standard practice for the United States, isolationism also seemed an unlikely choice during the post–Cold War period, and an impossible one once terrorism became an immediate threat to the United States.

Two alternatives have thus emerged as strong trends in post–Cold War U.S. foreign policy: cooperative security and regionalism. The former approach seeks to reduce U.S. costs in controlling post–Cold War chaos, while the latter seeks to increase U.S. economic security and thereby strengthen the United States' international position.

As discussed above, cooperative security in many respects continues the tradition of liberal internationalism (or, perhaps, liberal institutionalism) that originated in the aftermath of World War II. However, the United States demonstrated further interest in cooperative security and peacekeeping following the end of the Cold War, particularly once President Bill Clinton took office.[24] This change had much to do with the more diffuse and uncertain nature of the United States' potential threats during this period. Ashton Carter, William Perry (Clinton's first secretary of defense), and John Steinbrunner write, "The new security problems require more constructive and more sophisticated forms of influence that concentrate more on the initial preparation of military forces than on the final decisions to use them."[25] They explain that "cooperative engagement" involves military cooperation on such issues as size, composition, and standards *prior* to the emergence of conflict. These positive interactions, exemplified with the conferences of Western Hemisphere defense ministers begun in 1995, would theoretically make interstate war less likely through a much more positive mechanism than deterrence. This approach reduces risks for all by using confidence-building measures and transparency to reduce the possibility of conflict. Many of these measures in fact do occur with clear U.S. leadership, indicating continued U.S. interest in controlling the agenda, even while inviting others to

**Table 2.3**

## U.S. Economic Assistance and Military Aid, 1985-1997

|                                | 1985  | 1990  | 1991  | 1995  | 1996  | 1997  |
| ------------------------------ | ----- | ----- | ----- | ----- | ----- | ----- |
| **U.S. Economic Aid (in millions)** |       |       |       |       |       |       |
| Latin America                  | 1506  | 1486  | 1075  | 717   | 681   | 741   |
| % Total                        | 18.5% | 21.3% | 14.0% | 6.3%  | 7.1%  | 8.1%  |
| NIS                            | —     | —     | —     | 843   | 629   | 559   |
| % Total                        | —     | —     | —     | 7.5%  | 6.6%  | 6.1%  |
| Total                          | 8132  | 6964  | 7668  | 11295 | 9589  | 9170  |
| **U.S. Military Aid (in millions)** |       |       |       |       |       |       |
| Latin America                  | 269   | 234   | 237   | 22    | 11    | 11    |
| % Total                        | 4.64% | 4.78% | 4.96% | 0.58% | 0.28% | 0.28% |
| NIS                            | —     | —     | —     | 1.7   | 4.5   | 3.9   |
| % Total                        | —     | —     | —     | 0.04% | 0.11% | 0.10% |
| Total                          | 5801  | 4893  | 4783  | 3813  | 3970  | 3864  |

Source: U.S. Census Bureau, *Statistical Abstract of the United States 1999* (Washington, D.C., 1999); U.S. Census Bureau, *Statistical Abstract of the United States 1994* (Washington, D.C., 1994)

participate. In theory, such multilateral approaches would also benefit the United States by allowing it to share some of the costs;[26] in practice, the United States has tended to absorb much of the costs and responsibility for UN missions.

Safety in Numbers: Regionalism

The end of the Cold War also increased U.S. interest in strengthening its ties to its neighbors. Latin-American democratization allowed less controversial cooperation in matters of security and defense. The United States was able to take advantage of a reinvigorated Organization of American States for this purpose, while also pursuing new initiatives, such as the meetings of the Western Hemisphere defense ministers. These developments both helped diminish the risks of regional conflict and improved the possibility for reducing potential U.S. military expenditures in the area.

One thing was clear, however: growing security cooperation with Latin America did not indicate a substantial U.S. preoccupation with military "threats" from, or within, the region. On the contrary, the end of the Cold War immediately diminished U.S. concerns with conflict in the Americas, given that domestic and regional strife had lost its global implications. U.S. attentions instead initially turned to the newly dangerous—and newly promising—former communist states of Eastern Europe. Shattered from within, the area became ridden with conflicts rooted in long-standing ethnic and religious divisions, and inspired by the battle to establish new state boundaries. With nuclear weapons now unpredictably dispersed, chaos in the region carried even more ominous implications. Shortly after the beginning of the new millennium, the U.S. focus shifted toward the Islamic states of central Asia and the mid-East, as Islamic militants came to pose the greatest threat. Thus, U.S. funds that previously might have been spent fighting or seeking to prevent communism in Latin America now went to help pacify, rebuild, and co-opt the remnants of the former communist states (see table 2.3), and subsequently, to build up defenses against terrorism.

In sum, while the United States lost much of its foreign policy focus after the Cold War, certain tendencies did emerge. Despite the hopes of some Americans that the United States would retreat from international involvement, U.S. policy-makers showed an inclination to remain involved and even to preserve some leadership while relying more on their allies. Cooperative security and regionalism thus emerged as strong tendencies in U.S. foreign policy, as useful means of reducing U.S. security costs and improving the United States' economic position.

The uncertainties of the post–Cold War period were not, however, all military. Economic issues also contribute to uncertainty, not in the least mitigated by globalization. Thus, the United States began pursuing improved trade relations with its Western Hemisphere neighbors, especially those in closest proximity. This quest was undoubtedly aided by the apparent triumph of liberalism, which gave the United States new possibilities to pursue an old agenda—the expansion of free trade and elimination of trade barriers (at least those established by other countries)—while also allowing it the freedom to pursue new agenda items, such as labor standards and trade. And in post–Cold War Latin America, the United States found new interest in this approach. Mexico, in particular, radically reversed its traditional nationalism and showed surprising interest in a broad free trade agreement with the United States and, subsequently, Canada (especially notable given the considerable concessions Mexico would need to make). The North American Free Trade Agreement (NAFTA) formed the cornerstone of the U.S. Western Hemisphere approach, and anticipated both bilateral free trade agreements with a number of countries in the region as well as plans for an ambitious, hemispheric Free Trade Area of the Americas (FTAA).[27]

This stronger regionalism helped provide the United States with the basis to improve its own position in the international market, and to compete with growing regional blocs in Europe and Asia. Partly as a consequence of this policy, along with the economic reforms in the region, U.S. exports to Latin America expanded from 12.5 percent of total U.S. exports in 1990 to 19.9 percent in 1998 (see chapter 4, table 4.2). U.S. imports from Latin America also increased during this period, although somewhat more moderately; in 1990, 12.1 percent of the United States' total imports came from Latin America, compared to 15.3 percent in 1998.

## CREATING CONVERGENCE: ARGENTINE FOREIGN POLICY

The changes in the international order, the position of the United States, and U.S. policies following the end of the Cold War unavoidably also changed conditions for Argentina. On the positive side, the end of the Cold War meant that there were no longer dueling superpowers to exacerbate internal conflicts in Latin America, as had occurred in Nicaragua and elsewhere. This also meant a diminished threat from either armed revolutionaries or coup-prone militaries. But as a consequence, Latin American politics and conflicts ceased to have much international impact, and the United States lost much of its motivation for providing aid to the region. The United States did, as mentioned, look to its neighbors for trading partners. However, at least initially, this economic interest was really only manifested in NAFTA, linking only the United States, Mexico, and Canada. Without a clear path toward the FTAA, NAFTA implied as much risk as it did promise for the rest of Latin America—the risk that Latin American countries outside of NAFTA could end up excluded from the lucrative U.S. market.

Latin American countries thus needed to find other ways to attract U.S. attention, especially since they no longer had the option of shifting their alignment to a competing superpower. The only regional "threat" that could now consistently attract U.S. support was narcotics trafficking; thus many militaries and police forces in the region acquiesced to U.S. pressures and began to emphasize counternarcotics missions. In countries still suffering from guerrilla warfare, especially Colombia, purported ties between the guerrillas and the narcotics industry suddenly gained increasing attention. Argentina had neither guerrillas nor substantial narcotics to easily draw U.S. concern and funds. On the other hand, Latin-American countries also sought to ensure that they would be perceived as having favorable conditions for U.S. investors. Thus, neoliberal reforms, including most notably privatization and measures to reduce trade barriers, began gaining popularity. Latin American countries also began uniting on a subregional basis, partly to create more interesting potential partners for the United States, and partly to achieve some measure of counterbalance to NAFTA. Along these lines, four of the region's southernmost countries—Argentina, Brazil, Uruguay, and Paraguay—agreed in 1991 to form the Southern Common Market, Mercosur, both to expand this subregion's own economic potential and to create stronger bonds among these newly democratic regimes.

## Argentina and the New World Order

Given Argentina's long history of carefully guarded national autonomy and conflictive relations with the United States, the former's post–Cold War foreign policy approach seems quite remarkable. Yet, Argentina's foreign policy choices at this time were in fact a very pragmatic response to a number of domestic challenges carefully tailored to the new international environment. Following Menem's 1989 election, the new administration developed a tightly knit package of foreign and domestic policy that very clearly presumed U.S. hegemony in the region and bowed to U.S. influence in international institutions. The Menem administration was also in the forefront of the post–Cold War movements toward both cooperative security and regionalism. This package of policies helped resolve some of the sources of instability plaguing Argentina's still relatively new and fragile democracy.

As the Cold War ended, Argentina had reached a critical juncture of its own. In 1983, the country had undergone a successful transition from democracy after more than seven years of military rule. The military regime forced the new elected government to deal with a number of legacies, including the extensive human rights offenses, a much-weakened economy, and an international reputation further soured by Argentina's invasion of the British-held Falkland (Malvinas) Islands in 1982. President Alfonsín began the difficult task of securing Argentina's democracy, attempting to reverse the country's economic decline, and improving its international reputation and relations. While he made some important progress in resolving some of the country's problems, these were rocky years for Argentina. Perhaps Alfonsín's most important accomplishment was his success in maintaining Argentina's democracy until the next round of civilian elections in 1989—no small feat in this coup-prone country. Nonetheless, Carlos Menem's 1989 government still inherited a broad array of domestic policy problems.

One of the most pressing was the country's ongoing economic crisis. Despite the Alfonsín administration's best efforts to deal with the country's problems with overwhelming debt, high unemployment, and soaring inflation, the government's stabilization programs (Plan Austral and Plan Primavera) achieved only very temporary results. By the time of the 1989 elections, chaos had taken firm control of the economy. Inflation skyrocketed to above 70 percent per month in May, when the elections were held, and to 114.5 percent in the following month.[28] The consequences were, naturally, devastating: savings became unthinkable, living standards declined, and only the exchange houses found business booming.

While the economy became the Menem administration's central concern, it was not the only challenging area of domestic politics. The Alfonsín government had also failed to fully resolve the issue of military insubordination. Long accustomed to overseeing the civilians rather than the reverse, many sectors in the military did not easily accept Alfonsín's efforts to reassert control. Particularly irritating for the armed forces were the government's attempts at "justice," which involved trying and sentencing military officers for human rights offenses. In 1987, a group of lieutenant colonels led the first of a series of four rebellions, demanding a change in the government's policies and the military's leadership.[29] The third of these rebellions occurred in December 1988, only a few months before the elections, under new leadership and with apparently new momentum; a fourth took place two years later, with Menem already in the presidency. Thus, another important challenge for the Menem administration would be dealing with the armed forces, redefining their role in such a way that they could begin to serve as a productive element of the state and establishing more secure, long-term civilian control.

The most urgent issues facing the Menem administration thus involved domestic crises, but these were linked to foreign policy issues. Argentina's political and economic instability inevitably had injured its credibility with international investors. In addition, Argentina's international reputation had suffered considerably during the military regime. Not only did the country come to symbolize repression, but the 1982 Falklands/Malvinas war with Great Britain labeled Argentina a dangerous aggressor. Alfonsín did make some notable progress in this area. In particular, he began improving Argentina's international reputation by negotiating agreements to resolve border disputes. The government also sought to "normalize" relations with the United States[30] which immediately improved simply due to democratization. However, Argentina's instability still precluded establishing a new and trustworthy image in the eyes of international lenders and investors.

## Argentina's Foreign Policy Response

How could Argentina simultaneously resolve these issues? Clearly, some kind of dramatic action was necessary to prevent the further deterioration of the country's new democracy. The response selected by the Menem administration seemed to draw its inspiration from the changes occurring in the international environment at that time. Menem thus seized on four apparent aspects of the emerging world order in defining his government's policies: (1) U.S. leadership, especially in the Americas; (2) economic liberalism; (3) cooperative security; and (4) increasing regionalism. A fifth factor, democratization, further facilitated Argentina's insertion into an increasingly democratic international environment, but since Argentina's democratization had actually occurred earlier, this was largely a case of convenient convergence rather than design. In fact, while Menem formally respected the rules of democracy, he nonetheless frustrated the deepening of democracy through his extensive use of decree laws, concentration of decision making, and efforts to change the rules to allow his own reelection.

At the heart of Menem's foreign policy program was the government's wholehearted embrace of the United States. This approach followed logically from the United States' new international prominence and regional hegemony following the disintegration of the Soviet Union. Thus, the Menem administration "prize[d] its relations with the United States, emphasizing the elimination of each and every possible area of conflict on their joint policy agenda, as well as increasing cooperation with the US government on various global issues, such as the narcotraffic or problems of the environment."[31] In essence, Argentina opted to throw in its lot with the apparent "winner," now finding cooperation more profitable than resolute expressions of its autonomy. As the centerpiece of the administration's foreign policy, alignment with the United States also implied embracing the major post–Cold War postures of the United States. In particular, economic liberalism now became essentially a nonnegotiable option for a country hoping for a close relationship with the United States. The extensive neoliberal program adopted by Menem thus greatly facilitated improving the relationship.

In many respects, Argentina's program of privatization and free trade policies became the hallmark of the Menem government, reflecting the centrality of economic concerns to Argentina's foreign policy agenda. Reforms included the relatively radical decision to officially peg the Argentine peso to the U.S. dollar in 1991, reducing tariffs and privatizing such important nationally owned companies as ENTEL, the telephone company, and Aerolíneas Argentinas, a major airline.[32] Yet, while free trade certainly did help solidify the newly entwined relationship between the United States and Argentina, and trade between the two countries clearly expanded during this period, economic liberalization itself did not suffice to earn Argentina the U.S. approbation and international credibility it sought. Economic stability and aid may have been the primary goals, but reestablishing credibility required investing in other foreign policy areas beyond those of economic relations.

The area of reform that proved most fruitful for U.S.-Argentine relations was cooperative security. Argentina's participation in international military missions—especially through the United Nations—not only coincided with the broader post–Cold War trend in this direction, but particularly aided the United States. Argentina's troop contributions both helped lower the manpower costs for the United States and gave U.S.-led missions the added legitimacy of a multilateral appearance. Furthermore, participation in international military missions also helped resolve one of Argentina's stickiest domestic issues: what to do with the armed forces. Peacekeeping not only improved the international reputation of the Argentine military, but it offered participants an opportunity to carry out a truly professional mission in conjunction with some of the finest militaries in the world; members of the armed forces were thus quite satisfied with this policy.[33]

Finally, another new element in Argentine foreign policy was regionalism, especially in economic affairs, but also in terms of security. This orientation also emulated both a shift in some U.S. policies and a broader international trend. Argentina thus was a founding member of Mercosur, the Southern Cone's common market, along with Brazil, Paraguay, and Uruguay. Based initially on a 1986 agreement between Argentina and Brazil, and officially initiated by the 1991 Treaty of Asunción, Mercosur quickly led to the massive expansion of trade within the region.[34] Despite its primarily economic focus, Mercosur also contained an important political component, as future agreement explicitly required that Mercosur members remain democratic. Thus, Mercosur sought to strengthen not only the economies of its member countries, but also their new democratic regimes.

This regionalism—probably especially with the added "democratic" content—did help to attract U.S. attention, in that the formation of an economic bloc made all of the Mercosur countries appear as more interesting and attractive trading partners, and U.S. trade with Argentina and Latin America as a whole (even when Mexico is excluded from the numbers) rose significantly during the 1990s (see table 2.3). Notably, however, Mercosur did seem to develop an even stronger economic relationship with Europe than with the United States. According to Thomas O'Keefe, by 1996, European direct investment in the countries of Mercosur had once again surpassed that of the United States, restoring the pattern normal to the region until the late 1980s.[35] Mercosur's considerable successes of most of the 1990s were also unable to protect its members or its union from economic crisis, though. Thus, Brazil's currency devaluation in early 1999, as well as the recession in both Brazil and Argentina, appeared to place some serious obstacles in the way of continued Mercosur success.[36]

Along with pursuing economic regionalism, albeit with some obstacles, Argentina also sought to increase regional cooperation in security affairs. As Monica Hirst writes, "Argentina has been the country in the area most concerned with the need to link economic integration with regional security. Since the early nineties the idea of creating a security system for the Southern Cone has been defended in Argentine academic, military, and diplomatic circles. According to certain proposals this system would include the formation of a center responsible for avoiding subregional conflicts, a strategic data center, military technical exchange, armaments industry cooperation, and cooperation for civil protection."[37] However, like the movement toward economic regionalism, Argentina's interest in regional security was undoubtedly partly defensive. The Southern Cone's economic bloc was formed at least in part to compensate for a potential turn inward on the part of NAFTA. Regional security thus appears to be an appropriate reaction to another post–Cold War shift, the United States' possibly reduced concern with regional conflicts when these conflicts do not appear to directly infringe on U.S. interests. While U.S. interference has often been unwelcome in Latin America, and arguably quite damaging to the countries the United States sought to "aid," U.S. oversight nonetheless did impose certain external limits on regional conflicts. Increasing regionalism promised to both reduce the likelihood of interstate regional conflict and provide some external bounds in the event that conflict should occur. Nevertheless, probably one of the most important implications of Argentina's involvement in regional security had to do with domestic issues: regional security cooperation also helped Argentina keep its military budget small, and further diminished possible military justifications for interfering with the government. In other words, regional security was also one more way to keep the military out of politics.

## CONCLUSION

The end of the Cold War thus helped create the appropriate context for a new era in U.S.-Argentine relations. The United States' new position in the world encouraged its leaders to support efforts, such as cooperative security and regionalism, that would reduce the costs of increased military hegemony and responsibility. At the same time, the collapse of the Soviet Union also allowed the United States to expect policies from its allies that it had previously only desired—namely, economic and political liberalism.

This approach served as an invitation to Argentina's new leaders: to use the guidelines emerging from the developing post–Cold War environment and indicators of new U.S. foreign-policy interests to design Argentina's own policy approach, an approach that could help answer such pressing domestic problems as the continuing economic crisis. Was this a necessary or automatic reaction on the part of Argentina? This is unlikely. Such a radical shift in Argentine foreign policy required deliberate design and direction, and probably still could not have been implemented without particularly strong leadership and public desperation following the crises of 1988 and 1989. Yet, the approach initially succeeded. Aided by a fixed exchange rate, Argentina's economy became far more stable during the Menem years than it had been for decades. Furthermore, from 1991 until 1999, the end of Menem's second term, the armed forces remained peacefully in the barracks. In sum, the government had put together a tightly integrated, creative policy package, which appeared to be well adapted to the emerging post–Cold War order. Nevertheless, the policies of the administration were by no means flawless; some of the government's shortcomings contributed to Menem's decline in popularity prior to the 1999 elections. More importantly, Menem's economic policies—especially the overly rigid fixed exchange rates—were largely responsible for Argentina's prolonged recession and the consequent economic and political crises of 2001–2002.

# THE MAKING OF FOREIGN POLICY: COMPETING MODELS IN THE UNITED STATES AND ARGENTINA

CHAPTER 3

WHILE THE END OF THE COLD WAR FACILITATED A CHANGE IN U.S.-Argentine relations, it was the policymakers in those countries who actually made it happen. Yet U.S. and Argentine policymakers do not hold equal responsibility for the transformation. The United States may be the more powerful player internationally, but it was the Argentines who took the initiative in redefining the relationship. In part, this has to do with interest. Cold as it may sound, the United States simply matters more to Argentina than Argentina matters to the United States. Thus, while the United States develops general foreign policies, or perhaps policies toward the Latin American region, Argentina is more inclined to develop policies explicitly toward the United States. However, another part of the explanation has to do with capacity. The nature of the Argentine political system permits radical changes in foreign policy far more easily than the rather sluggish and bulky U.S. system. During the immediate post–Cold War period, the contrast between decision-making capabilities in the two countries became even stronger, as considerable consensus about foreign policy began developing in Argentina, just as U.S. foreign policy began losing cohesion. The United States did not regain some sense of common purpose with respect to foreign policy until 2001.

This chapter thus compares the U.S. foreign policy process to that of Argentina in order to understand how these processes influence foreign policies in these countries. We then explore the policies of the men who have led these countries during the immediate post–Cold War period: in the United States, George H. W. Bush Sr. and Bill Clinton, and in Argentina, Carlos Menem. As will be demonstrated, President Carlos Menem was probably the most important player in building the new post–Cold War friendship between the United States and Argentina.

## POWER AND POLICY IN ARGENTINA AND THE UNITED STATES

Why was Menem able to play such a determining role in this relationship? In brief, the Argentine political system is characterized by a much higher concentration of power and commensurately higher flexibility than that of the United States. Not only has Argentina historically been characterized by numerous shifts between democratic and authoritarian rule,[1] but even during democratic periods, Argentine presidents have been endowed with a fairly high degree of discretion in making foreign policy, limited primarily by the military's informal "veto" power during much of the twentieth century. With the armed forces finally more firmly under the thumb of civilians,[2] President Menem probably had more freedom to independently form foreign policy than any elected Argentine president since the early 1900s. It is a freedom which Menem used liberally. Menem enacted many times more decree laws than any civilian president in Argentine history, bypassing the Argentine Congress and earning his regime the designation of "delegative democracy."[3] Menem also was inclined to sidestep his own bureaucracies when forming policy, thereby concentrating policymaking even further.[4] Such an approach may be somewhat problematic for the long-term deepening of democracy, but it did permit more policy innovation and potentially more effective crisis resolution.

In contrast, the U.S. policy process is notoriously slow. Ostensibly under the leadership of the president,[5] the U.S. foreign policy process actually involves a number of actors. Not only do the bureaucracies compete among themselves, but Congress plays a critical role in both impeding and even designing foreign policy. Dramatic foreign policy transformations in the U.S. thus tend to be unusual, and foreign policy tends to be characterized by confusing contradictions rather than logical coherence, especially since the Cold War ceased providing a point of concordance. Given the complexity of the process, the United States thus found itself responding relatively passively to its Argentine suitor, rather than developing a more deliberate and proactive Argentina policy.

## The U.S. Foreign Policy Process

From the outside, most observers tend to expect that the policy process is more or less "rational," with policy decisions emanating from certain broad principles, designed by the president and his closest advisors. Such a view of coherence is vaguely comforting—it presumes strong and knowledgeable leadership, and a highly responsive and capable bureaucracy. Any policy decisions that do not entirely "fit" with stated presidential goals can, along these lines, be explained away as part of a conspiracy: the "government" must really have other goals than the lofty ideals that the administration presents.[6] However, in the United States, the policy process tends to be far more complex than this model would suggest, particularly since the end of the Cold War. Among the implications of the end of the Cold War were, first, the elimination of an important source of consensus and cooperation between the office of the president and Congress, and secondly, the need to reorganize foreign policy bureaucracies to better reflect the requirements of the post–Cold War order. At least in the short run, both of these processes have deterred the United States from making rapid and radical policy changes.

### Presidency and Foreign Policy

In contrast to the turn-of-the-millennium period, the Cold War allowed the president and his inner circle comparative autonomy in conducting foreign policy. With the constant threat from the Soviet Union, Cold War presidents had the requisite mandate and support to exercise a "presidential government model of leadership." According to Glenn Hastedt and Anthony J. Eksterowicz, this model is based on the presumption that "successful leadership required that presidents guard and protect their power, especially from congressional encroachment."[7] This autonomy allows presidents to act decisively and rapidly in forming and enacting foreign policy.

While most presidents would likely prefer this strong leadership model, their ability to actually exercise such authority varies. Unlike the Argentine constitution and laws, the United States Constitution does not grant the president generous rights to decree legislation. The foreign policy powers of the U.S. president include heading the administration; acting as the chief of state, and consequently, the symbolic leader of the country; commanding the military; negotiating treaties; appointing personnel; and recognizing foreign governments.[8] However, these are not absolute powers. As head of the administration and military commander, the president must unavoidably rely on career personnel to faithfully elaborate, inform, and enact his policies. Furthermore, most of the powers of the president are constitutionally balanced or "checked" by congressional powers. For example, the Senate must ratify treaties, and Congress decides what funds will be allocated to the administration and the armed forces. Thus, strong presidential leadership relies as much on the cooperation of Congress as on the powers and inclinations of the president.

During much of the Cold War, the relative consensus about the threat from the Soviet Union encouraged Congress to cooperate with the president in foreign affairs issues, at least until the 1960s.[9] Vietnam placed something of a damper on this relationship, due to the widespread public disapproval of a war commonly seen as needlessly wasteful of American lives. Hastedt and Eksterowicz write, "During the war effort in Vietnam, no matter how vocal the opposition of individual legislators, Congress did not act to curtail presidential foreign-policy powers. Only after the war ended and the Watergate scandal unfolded did Congress act to cut off funding for the war, pass such legislation as the War Powers Act and the Case Act, and regularly began to attach 'barnacles' to foreign aid and military assistance legislation."[10]

This was the beginning of a trend toward diminished presidential autonomy in foreign affairs that appears to have deepened after the end of the Cold War, at least until the 2001 World Trade Center attack. The demise of the Soviet Union eliminated the sense of urgency in foreign policy.[11]

At the same time, the foreign policy office closest to the president—the National Security Council—gained strength and influence during these decades. Formed as an advisory body in 1947, the NSC began expanding its influence with a 1949 reform that streamlined the organization and placed it directly in the executive office building. Under John F. Kennedy, the NSC staff became directly responsible to the president.[12] The small size, personal relationship to the president, and White House position allowed the NSC to develop as the president's personal foreign policy organization, partially supplanting the State Department.[13] According to Geoffrey Kemp, the NSC has become increasingly strong in recent years, in part due to the media.[14] With news channels like CNN broadcasting international news as it breaks, presidents are more frequently compelled to respond instantly to the waiting public, without the time to fully consult with the larger bureaucracies. This demand for instantaneous presidential policy would presumably partially counter some of the other recent pressures against presidential power.

Nevertheless, even when the presidency has been strongest, the U.S. president himself has tended to have little involvement with foreign policy toward specific countries in Latin America. There are exceptions, of course—most notably, "problem" countries. Cuba, for example, has been a national obsession at least since the Kennedy administration. President Ronald Reagan and his advisors appeared to be strongly involved with policies toward Nicaragua during the Sandinista years. However, Argentina—distant and relatively unthreatening—has rarely been an issue for the Oval Office, while the United States has been increasingly central for Argentina's presidents. Argentina's initiatives have, however, drawn some attention from the north, as reflected in the increased visits from top U.S. officials. Not only did secretaries of state and defense visit Argentina on several occasions, but both President George H. W. Bush (December 1990) and President Bill Clinton (October 1997) did travel to Buenos Aires themselves. During the same period, though, President Menem made multiple trips to the United States, again underlining the persistent inequality in the relationship.

Congress

Because Congress does not deal with the daily workings of foreign affairs, it is sometimes portrayed as relatively peripheral to the foreign-policy process.[15] Yet Congress in fact has a range of important responsibilities with respect to foreign policy, not the least of which is budgetary power. Particularly since the 1970s, this power has been habitually used in conjunction with foreign assistance and defense appropriations acts to limit the kinds of activities in which the president could engage.[16] The government has thus, on various occasions, been limited from providing aid or training troops for countries that Congress has deemed undesirable. Other legislation has forced the executive to accept certain issues as foreign policy priorities—for example, the 1986 legislation requiring the president to "certify" counternarcotic compliance in source and transit countries.

As suggested above, this congressional activism has tended to increase over time. According to Hastedt and Eksterowicz, Congressional capacity with respect to foreign affairs has increased due to such developments as an expanding number of subcommittees, improved research capabilities, and increasing staff.[17] They argue that presidential control of foreign policy has further faded due to "the emergence of a class of policy issues that do not respect the foreign-domestic boundary line. The environment, drugs, immigration, foreign investment in the United States, the national debt, education, investment policy, and military base closings are among the most prominent of these 'intermestic' issues."[18] These issues thus inevitably fall into the ambit of congressional concerns.

The end of the Cold War thus furthered an already developing tendency in executive-congressional relations. With the end of the Cold War, Congress appeared more inclined to place limits on foreign policy, particularly in the area of foreign-affairs spending. Much of this played out along party lines, and was especially noticeable when the Republicans took control of Congress during Clinton's Democratic administration.[19] However, a general perception that U.S. priorities no longer necessitated extensive foreign spending undoubtedly also contributed to the cuts.

Congress has also sought on several occasions to influence U.S. policy toward Argentina, albeit often through mostly symbolic means. For example, in August 1994, the Senate passed a resolution condemning a recent attack against an Argentine Jewish community center and "recognizing the efforts of the Argentine government in investigating the case."[20] Later efforts from within the House of Representatives to make a more critical statement met with only limited success, despite growing concern with the slowness of the investigation. Several legislators have also sought to establish a productive informal relationship with their Argentine counterparts, potentially deepening congressional influence in the area of U.S.-Argentine relations.

Most Congressional actions, however, have involved either approving executive initiatives or obstructing them. Thus, Congress backed executive initiatives to restore Argentine eligibility for military assistance and surplus defense material, and to proclaim Argentina a "major non-NATO Ally" in 1997.[21] For Argentina, though, probably the most important congressional action of the post–Cold War period was a lack of action. In 1997, Congress refused the president's request for "fast track" authority. With this new power, the president would have the right to negotiate free trade treaties without the persistent threat that Congress would subsequently tack on amendments unacceptable to his counterparts in other countries. The refusal slowed possibilities of expanding the North American Free Trade Agreement (NAFTA) and pursuing an eventual Western Hemisphere free-trade zone.[22] Although it was Chile, rather than Argentina, that had been assumed to be next in line for NAFTA incorporation, congressional resistance to fast track authority disappointed many in the region. By the time "fast track"—now known as Trade Promotion Authority—returned to Congress in December 2001, Argentina's economic crisis greatly overshadowed anticipation of the Free Trade Area of the Americas.

### Foreign Affairs Bureaucracies

Neither the President nor the Congress frequently deal with the daily workings of foreign affairs, however. The sheer volume of issues confronting the U.S. government precludes this for elected officials with a broader mandate. Thus, most foreign policy issues tend to be worked out by regional and issue specialists within the bureaucracy, particularly the State Department and the Department of Defense, although, as will be discussed, other departments and agencies have also been key protagonists. Within the State Department, the Americas Region has historically been the office dealing with Latin-American policy; within the Department of Defense (DOD), Inter-American Affairs, in the Office of the Secretary of Defense, has had this responsibility. Neither the State Department nor the Defense Department has any office specializing in Argentina, other than on-site foreign service personnel; in fact, the DOD's Inter-American Affairs typically has not even had a single desk officer responsible solely for Argentina. The intelligence agencies do, however, have more country specialists.

Certain changes in the organization of the State Department and the Department of Defense both reflect policy changes toward Latin America and are likely to help shape future changes. In the State Department, the major change was to abolish the Americas Region office, replacing it with the more inclusive office of the Western Hemispheric Region. This change corresponds to a general shift toward macroregionalism, including the United States and Canada with their southern neighbors as a single hemispheric bloc. The shift to some extent is a logical extension of NAFTA, which bound Mexico, the United States, and Canada into a tightly intertwined economic bloc. However, it also institutionalized the possibilities for furthering macroregionalism by including all of the Americas within one office.

In the Department of Defense, changes have also been far-reaching, if somewhat more subtle in their implications for Latin America. First, in the mid-1990s, the office of Inter-American Affairs acquired responsibility for the countries of the Caribbean, similarly broadening its regional scope. This occurred following the incorporation of the Caribbean into the army's Southern Command. Subsequently, in 1998, the office of Inter-American Affairs quietly shifted from ISA (International Security Affairs) to SOLIC (Special Operations and Low-Intensity Conflict).[23] Most importantly, this places Inter-American Affairs under the same umbrella as the counternarcotics office, emphasizing one of the new priorities in U.S. defense. The peacekeeping office became another important functional office within the DOD's undersecretariat for policy, suggesting another shift in the direction of U.S. security policy with respect to Latin America.

What implications did these organizational changes have for U.S. relations with Argentina? First of all, the new hemispheric approach demonstrated increasing U.S. interest in regional cooperation, especially in the area of trade. Even if Congress continued to prevent the president from directly expanding regional economic integration in the region, the State Department could act to further the notion of hemispheric solidarity. Thus, one of the means through which Argentina would be most likely to win U.S. favor would be by demonstrating support of regional free trade and cooperation. The State Department also continued to monitor such issues as narcotics trafficking and control (through the Office of International Narcotics and Law Enforcement) and human rights, areas in which Argentina could easily gain U.S. approval. Similarly, organizational developments in the Department of Defense also demonstrated increasing U.S. interest in regional cooperation, with a particular emphasis on nontraditional military roles such as counternarcotics and peacekeeping. William Perry, secretary of defense during Clinton's first term in office, helped push security cooperation on a variety of fronts to the top of the U.S. defense agenda,[24] an approach that coincided very well with Argentine inclinations during this period. The United States could thus be expected to continue to encourage its Latin American allies to also engage in counternarcotics and peacekeeping missions, and to expand peacetime cooperation and collaboration.

However, some of the most important initiatives in U.S. policy toward Argentina have come from departments and agencies other than those traditionally responsible for foreign policy. For Argentina, one of the symbolically most important shifts in U.S. policy of this period involved the 1997 decision to allow Argentine beef to enter the United States for the first time in sixty years. Given the centrality of cattle to both Argentina's economy and its culture, epitomized by the image of the cattle-herding gaucho of the pampas, the decades-long prohibition of Argentine beef has been a prolonged source of friction and resentment. Nevertheless, it was a more technocratic than diplomatic office that carried out the policy change. In 1996, the Animal and Plant Health Inspection Service of the U.S. Department of Agriculture began inviting reactions to their proposal to remove certain restrictions on Argentine beef, given the lack of evidence of any threat from foot-and-mouth disease (purportedly the reason that the beef had been excluded).[25] In August 1997 the rule officially went into effect, and for the first time in most Argentines' or Americans' lives, U.S. consumers began seeing small quantities of the celebrated Argentine steaks appearing in their restaurants.

Other parts of the U.S. federal bureaucracy that have helped elaborate policy toward Argentina include the Justice and Treasury Departments. The Justice Department has been involved with respect to such issues as negotiating a 1996 extradition treaty with Argentina, which was connected to broader efforts by the attorney general's office to facilitate international extradition.[26] In addition, the FBI, in particular, had both pressured Argentina to pursue its investigations of the 1992 bombing of the Israeli embassy and the 1994 bombing of a Buenos Aires Jewish community center (the Asociación Mutual Israelita Argentina), and contributed to the investigations.[27] The Treasury Department moved into the limelight toward the end of Menem's term, after Menem had raised the possibility of completely adopting the U.S. dollar as Argentina's national currency. Without completely dismissing the option, Treasury Department representatives (especially Deputy Secretary Lawrence Summers) apparently sought to discourage such a move by clarifying that adopting the dollar would not be likely to mean acquiring support from U.S. monetary policy or the Federal Reserve.[28] The actions of the Agriculture, Justice, and Treasury Departments thus demonstrate that U.S. policy toward Argentina has been formed in a variety of bureaucratic offices. The State Department may be the bureaucracy predominantly responsible for foreign policy, but it is by no means solely responsible.

## POST–COLD WAR U.S. FOREIGN POLICY

Regardless of bureaucratic continuities and changes, and the evolving role of Congress, individual presidents still have a central part to play in setting foreign policy priorities. During the initial shift into the post–Cold War period, the United States was governed by two presidents: George H. W. Bush, during whose presidency the Berlin Wall crumbled, and Bill Clinton, who came to power as the dust began to clear. The third president of the period, George W. Bush, held office during a new phase of international politics, as the fog of post–Cold War euphoria and uncertainty gradually began to clear.

The Bush presidency can best be seen as a transitional period in terms of foreign policy. As former vice-president to Ronald Reagan, Bush inherited a strong legacy of Cold War anticommunism. However, it was during the Bush administration that the United States "won"—from the administration's perspective—the Cold War. The enemy had disappeared, and the rallying cry for threat-driven unity in national policy ceased to resonate in policy circles. Thus, Bush's foreign policies—both in general, and toward Latin America—tended to be somewhat inconsistent and lacking in vision, despite the fact that Bush was expected to be particularly experienced and skilled in foreign affairs. Nevertheless, it was the Bush administration that first negotiated NAFTA with Mexico and Canada, and Bush who proposed the hemisphere-wide Free Trade Area of the Americas. At the time, however, the disintegration of the Soviet Union was a more pressing issue for U.S. foreign policy.

Clinton began his administration as the first clearly post–Cold War president, after the collapse of the Soviet Union and well after the fall of the Berlin Wall. In theory, this would mean that Clinton would have more opportunity to come into office with an appropriate post–Cold War foreign-policy vision. However, in contrast to Bush, Clinton's skills and interests lay in domestic politics, not foreign affairs. Thus, Clinton's presidency began with little more definition than Bush's had of how post–Cold War foreign policy would be defined.

Yet certain consistencies emerged. A 1993 speech by National Security Advisor Anthony Lake has generally been construed as the major statement of Clinton's position. In this, Lake proclaimed that the United States would pursue the "'enlargement of the world's free community of market democracies.'"[29] Undeniably vague, the statement did indicate, first of all, that Clinton intended the United States to adopt an active role in the international arena, rather than succumbing to post–Cold War isolationism. It also pointed to two administrative priorities: political democracy and free trade. Overall, this position differed little from that taken by Bush. If anything, however, Clinton emphasized economic issues even more than Bush had, energizing the Commerce Department and initiating a new economic council.[30] One difference did appear to be Clinton's approach to the nature of U.S. involvement in foreign affairs. According to James Lindsay, Clinton "favored a multilateral approach that emphasized collective action through international institutions such as the United Nations. In contrast, many Congressional Republicans preferred a unilateral approach to foreign policy.[31]

These priorities coincided nicely with Argentina's developing internationalism. By the time the Cold War ended, Argentina appeared to be smoothly on the path to democratic consolidation, as well as moving toward ever-deepening economic liberalism. With Menem, Argentina adopted other U.S. priorities, especially emphasizing cooperative security and peacekeeping, and giving at least lip service to counternarcotics (narcotics-trafficking is far less of an issue in Argentina than in the more northern areas of Latin America). However, the convergence, and the decision to seek convergence, again largely emanated from the Argentine side. While the United States fumbled toward a new set of post–Cold War foreign policy priorities, Argentina moved decisively to forge a new relationship. It was not until after the 2001 terrorist attacks, with George W. Bush now seated in the oval office, that the United States again assumed a more protagonistic role in foreign policy. Counter-terrorism moved to the top of the U.S. agenda, and while the United States welcomed any support from allies, it proved more than willing to fight this war alone, if need be. With respect to Latin America—which still did not top the U.S. agenda—the George W. Bush administration seemed to prioritize counter-narcotics, free trade (including support for the Free Trade Area of the Americas), economic liberalism, and economic and political stability. For Argentina, however, stability continued to be infuriatingly elusive.

## THE ARGENTINE FOREIGN POLICY PROCESS

From the dawn of the Cold War until the beginning of democratization (1983), Argentina's foreign-policy decision-making process was strongly affected by political and institutional instability. Furthermore, in contrast to the U.S. case, the rivalry of the Cold War—as much in terms of power as ideas—increased Argentina's external options, and, consequently, the amount of disagreement about foreign policy. Argentine political actors had different and often irreconcilable visions about international political and economic matters, in particular about the nature of the East-West conflict, and thus championed different international postures. As was common in Latin America, the military assumed that the global battle between capitalism and communism should be central in defining foreign policies and alliances. This spirit of the Cold War oriented foreign policy when the armed forces took power, and inspired many of the military's challenges to civilian authorities during the latter's brief and turbulent governments.

Nonetheless, the fear of communism did not suffice to unify the military around a common foreign policy project. Like the civilians, military governments could not escape the factionalism and internal power struggles that accelerated their declines. The military leaders who displaced Isabel Perón in March 1976 sought to avoid the failures of their predecessors by designing a distinctive system of power sharing between the different military branches, assigning responsibility for one-third of the state apparatus to each one. According to its authors, this "quota" system was designed to discourage personalism, impede the supremacy of one branch (obviously, the army) over the others, and foster corporate unity in the military. Nonetheless, the cure was worse than the disease. In practice, the divisions of governmental power and responsibilities never followed functional criteria, but instead responded to generally arbitrary motivations, having to do with each force's obsession with protecting its political space from the others. Complicating this further was the right of each force to veto any undesired policies.[32] This made it very difficult to reach even the minimal levels of internal coherence and rationality necessary for government action.[33] On the contrary, the military's system opened the way for personal power battles and allowed each arm to sabotage projects instigated by the others. These intramilitary conflicts provide abundant evidence of the high level of autonomy enjoyed by the armed forces vis-à-vis civil society demonstrating as well that the military cannot be considered merely an armed branch of any social class.

In sum, weak and tutelary governments, and others that appeared to be strong but soon fell, lacked the conditions to execute consistent foreign policy. Beyond this, many foreign policy decisions were made in order to influence relations between internal political forces, seeking to weaken competing actors or affect the frustrated democratization processes initiated in this era. The major decision units were small, temporary circles of political leaders, at times overlapping. This encouraged the formation of parallel diplomacies, with the principal goal of expanding their promoters' domestic political influence by developing various kinds of external ties.

The most notorious case was that of Leopoldo Fortunato Galtieri, who, as commander in chief of the army and a military junta member, systematically attacked the foreign policies promoted by president Roberto Viola and his minister of foreign affairs, Oscar Camilión, in pursuit of his domestic political goals. Thus, while the "official" diplomats mechanically opposed following U.S. global politics, Galtieri proclaimed that Argentina marched in unity with the United States "in the ideological war that [was] being carried out in the world."[34] Working from this perspective, in a November 1981 trip to the United States Galtieri initiated the "formal" intervention of Argentine military forces in the subregion to organize and train the contras, directly contradicting the Ministry of Foreign Affairs' policy of ending Argentina's military involvement in the Central-American war. On this opportunity, Galtieri also offered to contribute Argentine soldiers to maintain the Sinai Peace Accord, a cherished project of the Reagan government, again contrary to the position of the Ministry of Foreign Affairs.

From 1983 on, the decision-making process became more unified and coherent, dominated by the presidency and those in the highest political positions in the Ministries of Foreign Relations, Economy, and, to a lesser degree, the Ministry of Defense. These ministries, especially Economics and Foreign Relations, owe much of their relevance during this period to the increased salience of economic and trade issues in the foreign-policy agenda.

This predominantly presidentialist power structure has helped limit congressional participation in foreign policymaking, although the legislature has nonetheless become more active. Congress has simultaneously played an energetic role when called upon to ratify treaties or other executive decisions. For example, it forced the executive branch of government to introduce successive changes to its original patent bill. However, its fiscal role has been less significant.

In contrast, the military's systematic influence over foreign policy diminished considerably following the defeat in the Falklands/Malvinas War, contracting even further since the initiation of the democratic process. Nevertheless, the armed forces have maintained an influence, albeit irregular, in matters dealing with defense. Furthermore, the fear that the military might utilize pending problems or conflicts with neighboring countries to recuperate lost spaces of influence did factor in various foreign policy decisions, especially during the first years of

Raúl Alfonsín's administration, when concerns about civilian control of the military were particularly intense. These policies fell within the framework of what former Radical Party Foreign Affairs Minister Dante Caputo referred to as "the defensive face of foreign policy."[35] Notable among these was the search for a prompt solution to the territorial dispute with Chile regarding the Beagle Channel in the South of Patagonia. In this instance, Argentine leaders sought to eliminate an area of conflict from the Argentine-Chilean agenda that, were it not resolved, could have encouraged greater defense spending. Along the same lines, on November 30, 1985, Argentina signed the Fox Declaration of Iguazú with Brazil, announcing a series of measures to promote economic integration and cooperation in nuclear subjects, thereby definitively depriving the military of control of nuclear policy.

As democratization has deepened, the influence of nonstate actors on the decision-making process has also increased, although it has varied depending on the case and the issue. For example, the media has played an important role in shaping the views of both the political elites and the general public. Moreover, the media has provided critical information through investigative journalism, as well as helping the government inform the public of its foreign policies regarding issues such as the Free Trade Area of the Americas, Mercosur, or debt negotiations. In contrast, the influence of nongovernmental organizations (NGOs) over foreign policy depends on such factors as their particular focus, level of organization, and the extent of international concerns and linkages. Generally, the NGOs with the greatest influence over foreign policymaking have been those concerned with human rights and environmental issues. Finally, business groups have increasingly made their voices heard by the executive branch or through Congress in order to assure that their interests would be taken into account in those areas of foreign policy that might directly affect them. Beyond this, the Ministry of Foreign Affairs has even routinized the practice of consulting business sectors when negotiating preferential trade agreements or specific issues at bilateral, subregional, regional, and multilateral levels.

As a result of this situation, civilian foreign policymakers have shown themselves to be more sensitive than their military counterparts to the interests, pressure, and influence of nonstate actors. Despite this, foreign policy continues to be mostly handled by an inner circle within the executive branch. At the same time, with respect to the content of foreign policy, the post–Cold War decision-making process has been more constrained than during the years of the Cold War as a consequence of a series of dramatic events and developments both within Argentina and internationally. On the domestic side, these included human rights violations during the 1970s, the Falklands/Malvinas War in 1982, the *carapintada* uprisings of 1987–1990 and the political and economic crises of December 2001.[36] On the international side, as discussed in chapter 2, three developments stand out: the end of the Cold War, the expansion and deepening of globalization and, within the same process, the hastening of regionalization. Together this combination of significant domestic and international changes transformed the political environment and inspired the emergence of a new foreign policy consensus about how the world works. New social practices also ensued, such as a growing proclivity toward reconciliation and bargaining, apparently internalized by most Argentine political leaders as well as much of the society.

### Presidency and Foreign Policy

The Argentine Constitution grants the president a central role in the management of the country's foreign affairs; he is both the diplomatic chief and the head of the nation's armed forces. His responsibilities are "plenary"; that is, there is nothing in this area that is inherently outside of his realm of authority.[37] Both Presidents Alfonsín and Menem used their constitutional powers extensively to define and direct—with the assistance of their cabinets—the foreign policy of the period and acted as protagonists in defining policy. They chose highly intelligent ministers of foreign affairs, but ones without independent political weight. The two presidents dedicated considerable time and attention to foreign affairs, due both to their personal interest in international affairs as well as to the conditions in which their governments assumed power. Alfonsín utilized foreign policy, among other means, to fortify the fragile and threatened incipient Argentine democracy. His external image contrasted with that of the shadowy military officers he had succeeded: it was the image of an honest political leader announcing the arrival of a new democratic era in Latin America's Southern Cone. He used his prestige to renew and deepen political ties with other countries and to disentangle complex situations.

In contrast, Menem used foreign policy to prepare the path for the great economic transformations that he instigated. If Alfonsín became the image of the new Argentine democracy, Menem stood for the new Argentine economy, open to the world and politically allied with the United States. He swiftly dispensed with his populist past to side with the West, dismantling policies perceived as dangerous by the countries of this world and initiating new policies welcomed by those countries. For this, Menem enjoyed much greater space to maneuver than Alfonsín. He was the prototypical case of a leader who found himself faced by international and domestic situations that required the introduction of changes. At the same time, he was relatively free from bureaucratic and institutional constraints, and from vetoes and pressures by nonelected actors such as the armed forces. Limited by an increasingly difficult and unmanageable political and economic situation, and with a less expansive personality than his two predecessors, De la Rúa essentially used foreign policy to procure foreign support for the depressed Argentine economy. The president soon understood that his government's fortunes depended on its capacity to reverse his country's serious economic problems. Because of this, he communicated on numerous occasions with his peers in other parts of the world, especially in the United States, Europe and Latin America, with the objective of obtaining their endorsement in Argentina's difficult negotiations with the multilateral credit organizations. Until shortly before his abrupt fall from power, these efforts helped in untangling snarled negotiations.

In the international arena, the end of the Cold War expanded the president's capacity for novel—and even audacious—initiatives, given that it helped to eliminate historically divisive and practically untouchable divisions from the Argentine foreign policy agenda, such as traditional policies of technological development and nuclear autonomy. Thus, despite the doubts of then Foreign Affairs Minister Domingo Cavallo, and Ambassador to the United States Guido Di Tella, Menem opted to participate in the Gulf War. He decided to abandon the Movement of Non-Aligned Countries, disregarding the Foreign Ministry's advice to remain within the organization in a low profile position. He championed Argentina's designation as a major non-NATO ally of the United States, surprising both those near and far. Finally, at the end of his administration, he again prompted astonishment by seeking a tighter link with NATO, following the advice of his secretary of strategic planning.[38]

On the domestic front, the intensity of the hyperinflation of May and April 1989 helped push Alfonsín to cut five months from the end of his presidential term. The consequent economic stagnation and social upheaval produced considerable uncertainty, reinforcing the general perception that the Radical government had seriously erred with respect to its economic policies, and that the exceptional circumstances in the country required rapid and innovative decisions.[39]

Menem reacted quickly, appealing to the "consensus to terminate" the prior economic and state model in order to promptly pass two laws fundamental for his extensive program of structural reform: the Administrative Emergency Law (23.696) and the Economic Emergency Law (23.697). Through these laws, approved in cooperation with the opposition, Congress delegated broad powers to the executive branch to reform the state and intervene in the economic process. Subsequently, in March 1991, Congress ratified the executive branch's Convertibility Law, which was the base of the new stabilization program originated by now Economy Minister Domingo Cavallo's team.

Endowed with these important legal instruments, Menem's government adopted a series of measures that opened the way for a new international role for Argentina. These included deregulating strategic sectors (petroleum, ports, and transportation), opening commerce and finance, and privatizing public enterprises. Specifically, Menem's economic strategy allowed the country to enter into the Brady Plan in 1993 (a U.S. program for debt relief), and permitted consider-able improvement in Argentina's relations with international banks where the United States plays a primary role.

At the same time, Menem used and abused the so-called necessary and urgent decrees like no other president in Argentine history. During the period from 1853 to 1983, only thirty-five such decrees were issued. Alfonsín issued ten decrees, while Menem issued a record total of 166 decrees between July 9, 1989 and August 24, 1994, when the 1994 constitutional reform went into effect.[40] From this date until the end of his term, he issued another three hundred such decree laws.[41]

Although the 1853 Constitution did not authorize such extensive decree pow-ers to the executive branch, the 1994 Constitution did. The decrees allowed the executive branch power to assume legislative powers rightfully belonging to Con-gress in the face of "extraordinary circumstances."[42] As Delia Ferreira Rubio and Mateo Gorretti write, "In this sense, the necessary and urgent decrees make a temporary exception to the principle of division of powers established by the Argentine Constitution in accordance with the inherited North-American mold, in that through these decrees, the executive branch dictates rules with the range and force of law, including modifying or repealing existing laws."[43]

Menem's government utilized these necessary and urgent decrees with unre-strained frequency, justifying it with the argument that the crisis could not wait for the standard, and generally slow, process of sanctioning laws. Cavallo himself, the primary brains behind the economic reforms of the early 1990s (and their modification in 2001), argued that these decrees were "indispensable to carry [the reforms] out."[44] Furthermore, the public—acutely sensitized by hyperinfla-tion, and more concerned with governability than strict respect for democratic institutions—tolerated the unusual use of this procedure without excessive dis-comfort. This was despite the fact that in many cases, the use of decrees had more to do with Menem's style of governing than the need to act quickly in the face of events or exceptional situations.[45]

Finally, Menem sought to strengthen civilian control over the military begin-ning with a two-pronged approach to insurrection: pardon for past crimes (amnesties of 1989 and 1990), and punishment for present crimes.[46] Thus, the government imposed harsh sentences on those involved in the December 1990 military insurrection—the fourth and last of the rebellions initiated by the carap-intadas in 1987. The leader of the insurrection, Mohamed Alí Seineldín, was condemned to life imprisonment, while the remaining participants were given sentences ranging from twelve to twenty years. Simultaneously, through the process of state reforms, the government privatized military enterprises and reduced the military budget, partially by cutting back the number of defense per-sonnel along with their salaries. At the same time, the system of obligatory military service, or conscription, was replaced with a system of recruiting paid volunteers. Finally, the government redefined military roles, creating positive new functions for the military in areas such as peacekeeping.

In sum, Argentina's internal state of crisis began to clear up for a time, allowing Menem to act with a degree of freedom unknown to Alfonsín. Due to this, as well as his tendency to bypass the opinions of both his party and the opposition, Menem could adopt foreign policy decisions that distanced the country from its traditional positions, and brought the government of Buenos Aires closer than ever to that of Washington, D.C. In 2001, as crisis returned to plague—and finally expel—the government of De la Rúa, some of this freedom disintegrated. However, the latest challenges seemed to further underline Argentina's need to maintain good relations with powerful foreign allies.

## CONGRESS

Like that of the United States, the Argentine Constitution assigns important responsibilities to Congress in the area of foreign affairs. For example, Congress must authorize executive declarations of war or peace and decisions to permit foreign troops to enter Argentine territory or to send Argentine troops abroad. Congress also has the power to approve or reject treaties with other nations, regulate commerce with foreign nations, legislate on customs issues, and approve the national budget.[47] Similarly, the 1994 constitutional reform gave Congress the authority to "approve treaties of integration that delegate rights and jurisdiction to international organizations based on conditions of reciprocity and equality, and that respect the democratic order and human rights."[48]

Argentina's lack of democratic continuity unfortunately impedes outlining the path of historical development in relations between Congress and the executive branch, as one might with the case of the United States. During the Cold War years, the constitutional governments were forced to deal with a Congress disinclined to collaborate with them on major foreign policy issues. More than anything, Congress was the opposition parties' privileged arena to challenge or discredit the government. Frequently, legislators contemplated external themes with one eye on domestic politics, and, consequently, their statements and actions often responded more to a "logic of opposition" than to substantive differences with the positions supported by the executive branch. This attitude was one more illustration of the precariousness of the political system during these years and, more specifically, of the weak commitment to democracy by most opposition political forces.[49] Certainly, the typical ideological disputes of the Cold War, along with the prolonged domestic debate initiated in the early 1950s regarding the limits of a domestically oriented development strategy, impeded building consensus or habits of negotiation in the legislature.

From 1983 on, despite the clear dominance of the presidency in formulating foreign policy, Congress began gaining terrain in this area. This tendency was primarily due to the strengthening of parliamentary practices within the context of institutional continuity and the fact that the legislative agenda was becoming increasingly complex and "intermestic."[50] The growing participation of Congress in foreign policy is reflected in four ways.

First, Congress was the privileged arena for the opposition to present and defend its principal objections to the executive branch's approach to certain areas of foreign affairs. It was a forum for debate and, although less important, an area of democratic control of foreign policy through congressional exercise of the rights detailed in Constitutional Article 71.[51] This article gives the two legislative houses the authority to "call the ministers of the executive branch to its house to receive explanations or information that are judged advisable."

Second, the executive branch looked to Congress to generate consensus on sensitive foreign policy themes. In particular, since 1997, it appealed to "parliamentary diplomacy" to disentangle international negotiations and to reach agreements that were presented, both within and outside of the country, as a product of government policy. The active intervention of legislators—from both the government's party and the opposition—also facilitated reaching a solution to the conflict with Chile over the border region south of the Andes known as Hielos Continentales.[52] Parliamentary diplomacy was equally key in concluding an agreement between Argentina and Great Britain on July 14, 1999 that resumed both flights between continental Argentina and the Falklands/Malvinas Islands, and visits of Argentines to the archipelago.

Third, the executive branch dodged congressional participation on various occasions to avoid legislative obstruction of the former's decisions. For example, the Alfonsín government bypassed Congress when initially attempting to draw closer to Brazil for fear that the Peronist opposition would stop the process. Thus, all the legal instruments used during this period of Argentine-Brazilian integration were the protocols. As former minister of foreign affairs Dante Caputo recalls, "They didn't require parliamentary approval, they had a certain flexibility, a certain capacity to be very rapidly arranged and, in sum, were more appropriate for the kind of things we wanted to do."[53]

Similarly, uncertainty about the position that Peronist legislators would assume with respect to ratifying the Peace and Friendship Treaty with Chile certainly influenced the Alfonsín government's July 26, 1984 decision to call a popular and nonbinding referendum regarding the terms of this agreement.[54]

President Menem used similar artifices. In January 1991, he justified his decision to send two ships to the Persian Gulf to participate in the U.S.-led multilateral force, without previously consulting Congress, alleging that this concerned a peace mission under United Nations command and, consequently, the executive branch did not require any legislative authorization.[55] This decision triggered numerous critiques by legislators from the Radicals, the principal opposition party, and from the "Group of Eight," a dissident Peronist sector. One of the harshest voices of the time was then Deputy Carlos Alvarez, who stated that "the majority of those who are here—government and opposition—feel the disdain that the executive power is demonstrating for this institutional arena. This apparent disdain toward Parliament is converting this place into a space for cathartic discourse."[56]

Along the same lines, in September 1995, conscious of the strong opposition it would face in Congress, the executive branch designated an important agreement with Great Britain regarding hydrocarbons in the water surrounding the Falklands/Malvinas Islands a "Joint Declaration on Off-Shore Activities in the Southwest Atlantic." Since the agreement did not involve an international treaty, the requirement for congressional ratification could be avoided.

On the other hand, the executive branch provoked intense debate among opposition legislators in August 1994 by simply requesting that Congress consider sending around 1,000 Argentine soldiers to Haiti as part of a multilateral force during the so-called first phase of the invasion initiated by the United States to oust the military government. The discussion became particularly intense, as Argentina was the only country of the Rio Group prepared to take things so far. However, a private survey carried out around this time demonstrated that only 14.9 percent of the population supported the idea of the intervention, and 82.3 percent opposed it.[57] Given this situation, the government decided not to involve Argentine troops in combat, and to instead participate in the "second stage" of the first phase by sending around one hundred members of the *gendarmerie* (primarily border guards). Their mission was to monitor the activities of the Haitian police and to maintain internal and police security.[58]

Finally, interest groups occasionally needed legislative support for their particular demands. The most notorious case of the 1990s occurred during the debate regarding the law concerning pharmaceutical patents (discussed further in chapter 4). The national laboratories, represented by the Industrial Center for Argentine Pharmaceutical Laboratories (Centro Industrial de Laboratorios Farmacéuticos Argentinos), through intense lobbying activity succeeded in pressuring Congress to defend the industry's interests against foreign pressures. For their part, the foreign laboratories, represented by the Argentine Chamber of Medical Specialties (Cámara Argentina de Especialidades Médicas), concentrated their actions on the executive branch, which had echoed U.S. policies in favor of protecting intellectual property rights. The U.S. ambassador in Argentina, James Cheek, adopted a high-profile role on this theme. Shortly after taking charge of the embassy in Buenos Aires, Cheek stated, "My position concerning the patents theme is that of my country: to encourage the government of Argentina to approve this law as rapidly as possible."[59] The embassy's dutiful contribution turned out to be a double-edged sword. It inspired the legislators defending the interests of the Argentine laboratories to transform the debate into a question of sovereignty and, with that, to rouse certain public sympathies in favor of those they represented.

The examples mentioned demonstrate that the executive branch could not underestimate the role of Congress. Furthermore, as the debates over borders and the law of pharmaceutical patents reveal, the legislators from the government's party did not automatically follow either the president's wishes or the course of action established by their own parties.[60] In other words, Congress holds an important potential for insubordination that the executive branch must take into account when designing policy.[61]

## BUREAUCRACY

The president and his cabinet—particularly the minister of foreign affairs and his immediate advisors (who may or may not be members of the foreign service bureaucracy)—establish the primary directions for foreign policy and play a central role in the decision-making process. At the same time, the Foreign Affairs Ministry fulfills an essentially technical function, managing different issues on the foreign policy agenda day to day, and directly participating in or offering professional advice concerning the country's international negotiations. However, other areas of the bureaucracy have also been important in Argentine foreign affairs. The Ministry of Economics has played an increasingly important role in elaborating proposals and in administering and negotiating the economic themes on the foreign policy agenda. In a varying and somewhat weaker role, the Ministry of Defense has also influenced the making of foreign policy. Finally, in the last years of Menem's second term, the Secretariat of Strategic Planning created by the president in January 1998 had a prominent role in elaborating political proposals with a powerful impact on Argentine-U.S. relations.

During the years of the *Proceso* military regime (1976–1983), the minister of foreign relations was subject to the political fluctuations of the military regime, playing only a marginal and sporadic role in decision-making. As in all military dictatorships, some career civil servants joined the regime and contributed their experience and knowledge to the conduct of foreign policy. Even more, many enthusiastically justified the military repression of those years in the most diverse international arenas. Another sector of the foreign ministry, probably the majority, appealed to a familiar logic of bureaucratic survival and, awaiting better times, confined itself to following orders. Finally, an opposition minority was either marginalized or displaced. Since 1983, the Ministry of Foreign Relations has recovered technical control of foreign policy. Nonetheless, during the governments of both Alfonsín and Menem, political leaders retained primary direction of foreign policy.

There are various areas of the Ministry of Foreign Relations that deal with relations between Argentina and the United States, either directly, through third countries, or through international institutions. Combined, these different areas of the ministry include around one hundred individuals whose principal responsibility involves managing relations with the United States. In addition to this, there are around forty-five notable diplomats in the Argentine embassy in Washington and in six consulates located in Atlanta, Chicago, Houston, Los Angeles, Miami, and New York. This clearly indicates the importance for Argentina of relations with the United States, and contrasts dramatically with the relatively limited personnel that the latter dedicates to working on Argentine affairs.

Within foreign affairs circles, since 1983 the Argentine embassy in Washington, D.C. has increased its ties with actors from diverse executive agencies and with members of Congress who deal with matters of interest to Argentina. Nonetheless, in contrast to a case like Mexico, the asymmetry of power and interest that marks bilateral relations makes it difficult for Argentine diplomats in Washington to regularly gain access to either the highest levels of the U.S. bureaucracy or to the legislature. Contacts normally occur at the level of Congressional and agency staffs. These contacts allow Argentina to communicate its concerns or positions regarding various matters of interest for the country, and facilitate meetings and interviews between bureaucrats, legislators, and politicians of the two countries that, in general, tend to have scant substantive content. In contrast, the U.S. Embassy in Argentina has preferential access to the highest levels of political power. Furthermore, the principal themes on the bilateral agenda are dealt with directly and regularly in Buenos Aires by the ambassador or chief of staff for the United States, along with the minister of foreign affairs and possible other cabinet members, depending on the case.

The growing significance of economic matters in foreign policy generated two important developments in the process of decision-making and policy execution. On the one hand, the Ministry of Economics acquired a fundamental role in managing those economic questions that constitute a relevant part of the U.S.-Argentine bilateral agenda, especially the foreign debt. On the other hand, economic/commercial themes increasingly captured the attention and daily efforts of the minister of foreign relations. Furthermore, in June 1992, the Secretariat of Foreign Commerce—previously subordinate to the Ministry of Economics— shifted to the Ministry of Foreign Affairs, thereby adding around two hundred people with training and experience in foreign trade to the latter's permanent staff.[62] Yet, if some functions were taken away from the Ministry of Economics, some economics ministers—such as Domingo Cavallo of both the Carlos Menem and Fernando De la Rúa governments—participated directly in adopting decisions that transcended the economic sphere. For example, Domingo Cavallo played an important role in the Menem government's decision to terminate the Condor II missile project.

Equally notable is that, beginning in 1987, important consulates were transformed into centers for commercial promotion; in the case of the United States, these centers were situated in three cities—Los Angeles, New York, and Miami—that were considered strategically important for Argentine-U.S. commercial relations. The three centers have close ties with the Fundación Export-Ar (Argentine Export Foundation) established under the Ministry of Foreign Relations in 1992, and with the Fundación Invertir del Banco Nación (Investment Foundation of the National Bank), which is a private organization formed by top-level Argentine business people and public officials.[63]

In contrast, the Ministry of Defense, during both military governments and democratic periods, has played a much less important role than the Foreign Affairs and Economics Ministries, or as compared with the role traditionally played by the Pentagon in the United States. The military institution's influence in foreign affairs—enormously significant until 1983—tends to be exercised through different channels, and not necessarily from the Defense Ministry. Although the newly organized ministry did enjoy a high profile during the Alfonsín administration, during Menem's first government it became overshadowed by the Ministry of Foreign Affairs, which emitted the principal ideas and policies that drastically changed Argentina's positions on issues of defense and international security.[64] Nevertheless, beginning with Menem's second term, the Defense Ministry began to carry more weight and developed a "security diplomacy" following the general lines established by the Ministry of Foreign Affairs during the early 1990s. This diplomacy was geared toward broadening and strengthening the military's international ties, and was carried out relatively independently of the Ministry of Foreign Relations; relations with NATO and bilateral defense meetings with different countries are examples of this. At the same time, the Ministries of Foreign Relations and Defense worked very closely to establish Argentina's positions for the first and second conferences of hemispheric defense ministers, or defense ministerials, carried out in Williamsburg, Virginia and Bariloche, Argentina, respectively. To the extent that these themes came to be dealt with in a more routine manner, control of the agenda gradually moved into the hands of the Defense Ministry. Thus, it was the Ministry of Defense that had the responsibility of preparing Argentina's positions for the third defense ministerial, carried out in Cartagena in 1998.

In January 1998, Menem created the Secretariat of Strategic Planning, which operated as an ideological power plant to sustain the government's short- and long-term political projects. The first of these projects was the failed effort to extend Menem's presidential mandate for a third term, despite the expressly contrary thrust of the 1994 Constitution. This was the principal goal underlying the proposal launched in January 1999 to introduce "dollarization" to Argentina (which meant adopting the U.S. dollar as Argentina's currency) and to endorse a Treaty of Monetary Association with the United States. Both of these sought to preserve Argentine economic stability in the midst of the storm unleashed by Brazil's devaluation of its currency, the real. For Menem and his collaborators, stability constituted the major political capital of the Peronist government and, for this reason alone, its loss was perceived as implying the end of the reelection project.[65] The idea, formulated in July 1999, of seeking a tighter association with NATO occurred at a moment in which Menem had already abandoned his hopes of once again being Peronism's presidential candidate, and when the opposition's triumph in the October 1999 elections had come to appear very probable. In contrast to "dollarization," this project, originated in the heat of NATO military intervention in Kosovo, was conceived with the thought of Menem's eventual return to the Argentine presidency in 2003.[66] The principal objective of its promoters was to solidify the foreign and security policies of the 1990s by fortifying ties with the West and, at the same time, reinforcing Menem's role as the principal guarantor and source of this policy orientation in Argentina.

The initiatives mentioned are of great interest to understand how the decision-making process functioned during the Menem government, especially during its final two years. According to the typology of Margaret and Charles Hermann and Joe Hagan, the Argentine decision-making process during the 1990s had as a "fundamental decision unit" a "predominant leader" sensitive to domestic and foreign circumstances.[67] As a function of his political goals, Menem established a division of labor between agencies or individuals who, on occasions, were unaware of what other top members of government were doing. This process, which irritated those at the middle and lower levels of the state apparatus, especially in the Ministry of Foreign Relations, was alternately supported, accepted, or tolerated by the members of the presidential cabinet. The practice never became so extreme as to produce angry critiques, or much less, resignation, by some minister wounded by his colleagues' incursion into areas considered his terrain. In addition, shared visions of the necessity and importance of tightening ranks with the West allowed a reasonable coexistence between the bureaucratic heads with responsibilities for foreign policy decisions.

## CONCLUSION: ARGENTINE FOREIGN POLICY IN THE 1990S

When Carlos Menem became president in July 1989, very different circumstances prevailed in both the country and the world than those that had characterized the first stage of the democratic transition, led by Raúl Alfonsín. Internationally, the Cold War had vanished, economic globalization had expanded and deepened, the democratization process—in different phases—had overtaken almost all of Latin America, the Central-American crisis had been quelled and largely resolved, and the governments of the creditor countries—along with multilateral lending organizations—had provided a new framework for negotiating foreign debts. On the domestic front, the hyperinflation crisis of 1989 accelerated the end of Alfonsín's government, and the concerns of the early years of democratic recuperation—defense of human rights and civil liberties—had moved to second place, with the country's principal social demands shaped in the heat of the economic crisis.

In this context, the Menem government defined national interest in terms of economic development, something that was much more than a mere adaptation to the end of the Cold War or the growing globalization of the economy. These processes have affected all of Latin America more or less equally, and have inspired the majority of the countries of the region to define economic and commercial themes as key in their foreign policies. Nevertheless, in the Argentine case, there were three specific variables that had an important influence on the course adopted: first, the Menem government's strong perception that it was necessary to end the oscillations of foreign policy, and more particularly, the political confrontations with the United States. Argentina's traditional opposition to the United States was considered a useless strategy, as well as an undeniable obstacle to reaching the proposed economic objectives.[68] This perspective inspired Minister of Foreign Relations Guido Di Tella to suggest a new kind of bond with the United States: "The new foreign policy is based on the need to end the traditional hostility towards Washington with respect to irrelevant problems which are neither here nor there for us in making us shine. We want carnal love with the United States; it interests us because we can extract a benefit."[69]

A second factor influencing foreign policy involved the military's very limited ability to influence foreign affairs—unlike the situation in countries like Brazil or Chile—as a consequence of its failure as a government and defeat in the Falklands/Malvinas War.[70] Both factors led to a democratic transition through collapse which made it possible to gradually subject the armed forces to civilian control. And third, the Menem government believed—along with vast parts of society—that building a strong political and economic alliance with the countries of the West was a necessary condition for Argentina's successful insertion into the post–Cold War world order. The government consistently maintained that that was the natural foreign policy orientation for a country like Argentina. Again in Di Tella's words, "What has been done from 1989 until now has been to return the country to its natural positioning, to the alliances that suit it as much due to its history as to its vocation and interest. This means cooperation with the countries of the region and firm placement in the West, sharing democratic values, respect for human rights, the market economy, and free and open trade.[71]

Economic priorities also determined the inner circle of countries that would be granted preference: the United States, the members of the European Union, and the Mercosur countries, along with Chile and Bolivia. In this way, Argentina's high profile in other areas of the world, such as its participation in the Gulf War and in the 1994 Haitian crisis, could be explained by its policies toward those countries in the preferred circles, especially the United States. Di Tella himself indicated this with respect to the decision to send two ships to the Gulf, stating, "[We] have done more than necessary to give a categorical sign of our solidarity with the Western alliance."[72] It was hoped that his solidarity would create a new and positive international reputation for the country, thereby earning Argentina the support in economic affairs—again, particularly from the United States—that it so desperately needed.

# CHAPTER 4

# DEFINING THE TERMS OF FRIENDSHIP: ISSUES IN U.S.-ARGENTINE RELATIONS

## INTRODUCTION: MENEM AND THE PREMISE OF COOPERATION

During the post–Cold War period, and especially during the administrations of Bill Clinton in the United States and Carlos Menem in Argentina, the two countries have enjoyed far more areas of friendship than friction. This is in large part due to the opportunities presented by the end of the Cold War, as well as President Menem's motivation, ability, and choice to redefine Argentine foreign policy around an alliance with the United States. In essentially all of the primary areas of foreign relations, cooperation came to characterize U.S.-Argentine relations. Parallel economic approaches formed the centerpiece and key motivation for Menem's reform, democratization provided the political base from which convergence could grow, and security cooperation became the area in which the Argentine government achieved most acclaim from the United States.

Nevertheless, even the closest of friends cannot avoid certain disagreements. While the Menem government set aside any nationalistic claims to autonomy with respect to the United States, areas of dissent arose regardless. Argentina's policy of wholehearted alignment with the United States was designed with precisely the same intent as earlier policies of resolute nationalism: both policy approaches sought to achieve and protect Argentine interests. If Menem's policies differed drastically from most of his predecessors, it was partially because of changes in both the country's needs and the means available for meeting those needs, given the transformation of the international setting. As discussed in chapter 2, the United States' increased strength in the Western Hemisphere, combined with Argentina's need for trade, investment, and support in international economic institutions, helped encourage Argentina to seek a close relationship with the United States. Yet Argentina's infamous proclamation of "carnal relations" with the United States did not entail blind love. Argentina actively sought concessions on some issues—some successfully, and others less so—and attempted to resist U.S. pressures regarding other issues.

This chapter thus explores both sides of the post–Cold War relationship between the United States and Argentina: the predominant trend toward cooperation and friendship, as well as the more troublesome realms for the two countries. Each general area of U.S.-Argentine relations has included a few of these problem areas. Issues such as Argentina's limited protection of intellectual property, the United States' application of subsidies, and Argentina's unsuccessful efforts to gain quick admittance into NAFTA have been the small clouds dotting overwhelmingly clear economic relations. Politically, Argentina gained U.S. approval for its progress toward democratization and appreciation for its support in international arenas, but the United States continued to pressure Argentina to reduce political corruption and improve human rights and the administration of justice. The two nations probably forged the strongest relationship with respect to security affairs; however, even here some areas of disappointment could be found. Argentina was forced to concede its Condor II missile project (although of questionable utility and considerable cost, anyway), to relinquish its hopes of membership in NATO, and to accept new U.S. policies on weapons sales to the region which would appear likely to favor countries with a larger military budget. Overall, however, cooperation now defined the relationship.

## Free Trade and Economic Cooperation

From his election in 1989 until the end of his second term in 1999, economic motivations drove both foreign and domestic policy for President Carlos Menem. In some respects, Menem's approach to policy inverted the military's national security doctrine from the 1960s and 1970s. This doctrine incorporated virtually all areas of policy, including economics, education, electoral politics, and domestic mobilization into "security" issues, considered the purview of the armed forces. In contrast, Menem's policies brought virtually all areas of policy—especially defense and foreign affairs—into the service of economic interests.

As Carlos Escudé and Andrés Fontana explain, Menem's foreign-policy approach used alignment with the United States as a means of furthering the government's central goal, economic development. They argue that this approach posits that "any challenge to U.S. leadership not connected to development is detrimental to development insofar as it breeds negative perceptions among potential investors and moneylenders, increasing the country risk index. . . ."[1] In other words, the Argentine government would make far-reaching cooperation with the United States a priority, unless that cooperation appeared to be problematic for economic progress. Only in those instances would the Argentine government be inclined to challenge the United States.

Argentina launched the process of improving economic relations with the United States initially through essentially unilateral economic reforms. The process of reform began during the 1983–1989 Alfonsín administration. Alfonsín's Austral and Primavera Plans (1985 and 1988) primarily sought to reduce inflation through price and wage controls, though the government also took some initial steps toward reducing government spending and selling public enterprises.[2] It was Menem, however, who truly launched neoliberal reform in Argentina. By 1990, the government had begun an extensive program of privatization, selling everything from telephone companies to airlines and military industries. Furthermore, Argentina carried out legal reforms regarding foreign investment, expanding the economically liberal orientation initiated in 1976. With these reforms, foreign investment in Argentina no longer required prior permission, and investors no longer faced any restrictions on repatriation of investments and gains. The legislation also authorized granting licenses for the exploitation and exploration of mines and petroleum and natural gas deposits, albeit without altering state ownership of these resources.[3] However, it was the 1991 Convertiability Plan, introduced by Minister of Economy Domingo Cavallo, that most dramatically redirected the Argentine economy toward free trade and a definitive U.S. orientation. The Convertiability Plan legally linked Argentina's currency to the U.S. dollar, establishing a one-to-one exchange between pesos and dollars, and requiring that all pesos be backed by dollar and gold reserves. The plan succeeded in containing Argentina's previously out-of-control inflation and establishing Argentina as a more interesting area for investors, though it did also contribute to Argentina's recession toward the end of the decade. Nevertheless, the Convertiability Plan remained firmly in place until December 2001, when an intese recession and profound political crisis finally forced the government to relinquish the fixed exchange rate.

With the Argentine economy apparently on the path toward an open economy and relative stability, Argentine and U.S. policymakers moved to solidify the relationship. Most importantly, during Menem's November 1991 visit to the United States, presidents Menem and George H. W. Bush signed a treaty "Concerning the Reciprocal Encouragement and Protection of Investment."[4] According to President Bush, this was "the first bilateral investment treaty with a Latin American country to be transmitted since the announcement of [his] Enterprise for the Americas Initiative in June 1990."[5] The treaty, which became active on October 20, 1994, was designed to protect investors from each country who chose to invest in the other.[6] It guarantees that foreign investors from either country would be treated at least as favorably as citizens, and even better if advantages had already been granted to investors from a third country.[7] In addition, the treaty seeks to prevent nationalization of foreign-owned enterprises, although with the caveat that this could occur "for reasons of public utility." Nevertheless, in the event of expropriation, the treaty mandates that this would occur in a "nondiscriminatory manner" and that investors would be compensated promptly and in accordance with the real market value of their investments.[8] The treaty thus sought to imbue Menem's economic reforms with permanence, formally and openly welcoming U.S. investors, and offering potential investors some assurance that their investments would be safe, regardless of who might follow Menem in the presidency.

Other measures taken to encourage trade and investment between the United States and Argentina included the establishment in 1994 of a Business Development Council, with ongoing meetings to share information and facilitate cooperation on trade issues.[9] The United States also sought to further strengthen its increasingly important economic partner by helping to restructure the substantial Argentine debt; this was negotiated through the Brady Plan in April 1992.[10] Following Brazil's 1999 devaluation, which naturally hurt Argentina's exports, Argentine representatives again approached U.S. and World Bank officials to seek help with a new budgetary crunch.[11] The problem of the debt reached new heights in December 2001, when Argentina's government was forced to default on its debt.

In 1999, representatives of the two countries also began negotiating an Open Skies agreement that would allow airlines to compete more openly for Argentine routes, opening up new possibilities for U.S. carriers such as Delta and Continental.[12] After some early complications, in August 1999, delegations from the two countries reached an agreement in Buenos Aires for an Open Skies accord. However, fears that the increased competition might prove fatal to Argentina's struggling airline, Aerolineas Argentinas, led the new administration of Fernando De la Rúa to suspend the pact in February 2000.[13] Renegotiating the agreement became a central issue in President De la Rúa's first official visit to the United States in June 2000. While U.S. leaders continued to insist on a rapid move toward open competition (likely to favor the stronger U.S. carriers), De la Rúa proposed a slower transition, placing a few checks against potentially devastating fare wars.[14] The Argentine government also sought to modify other aspects of the agreement that could conceivably limit outside investment in national airlines. For some U.S. observers, De la Rúa's position on the Open Skies issue indicated a potentially troublesome tendency toward greater protectionism, and a possible step back from Menem's pro-Americanism.[15]

Nevertheless, Argentina's overall trend was toward economic reform during the 1990s, and thus contributed to changing U.S. business practices in the region. In response to economic globalization and liberalization in the region, new investment patterns came to replace the traditional practice of establishing miniature replicas of U.S. factories to sell to protected markets. Thus, U.S. investments in Argentina during the 1990s were inspired by two principal goals: obtaining access to natural resources with important comparative advantages (mining or hydrocarbons) and assuring access to the Argentine and regional markets (Mercosur). This last element became especially evident in certain manufacturing industries (automotive, food, drink, and tobacco) and in the service sector (banks, insurance, telecommunications, and energy). In some cases, the process was driven by the configuration of large holdings by the financial sector.[16]

**Table 4.1**

**United States' Foreign Direct Investment in Argentina and Latin America (in millions U.S. dollars)**

|  | 1980–89 (average) | 1991 | 1993 | 1995 | 1997 |
|---|---|---|---|---|---|
| Argentina | 123 | 367 | 1079 | 2048 | 1774 |
| Latin America | 1474 | 5411 | 8560 | 15350 | 17825 |
| Argentina as % of Latin America | 8.3% | 6.8% | 12.6% | 13.3% | 10% |

Source: Comisión Económica para America Latina y el Caribe, "La inversión extranjera en América Latina y el Caribe," *Informe 1998* (Santiago, Chile: 1998), 207.

Consequently, both investment and trade expanded considerably between Argentina and the United States during the Menem decade. With respect to the first of these, foreign direct investment (FDI) expanded from an average of $123 million per year during the 1980s to over $1 billion during 1993—the year before the treaty regarding Reciprocal Encouragement and Protection of Investment went into effect; FDI almost doubled again two years later (see table 4.1). This increase did accompany a dramatic overall increase in U.S. foreign direct investment in Latin America as a whole during this period; however, the Argentine share of U.S. FDI also rose notably.

Trade between Argentina and the United States followed a similar pattern to that of U.S. foreign direct investment. According to the Argentine International Relations Council, during the first five years of Menem's presidency (1989-1994), trade expanded 154 percent.[17] Again, though, this increase in U.S.-Argentine trade followed an overall increase in trade between the United States and Latin America during this period, as it more than doubled between 1990 and 1998 (see table 4.2). The greatest benefactor in the region was Mexico, which more than tripled its exports to the United States, and came close to that with imports. While Argentine trade with the United States also increased, the balance clearly favored the latter. For example, in 1998, Argentina tallied an approximately four-billion-dollar trade deficit with the United States.[18] Some of this imbalance was due to Argentina's need for capital goods to aid in development, with machinery constituting much of the imports from the United States between 1996 and 1999.[19] Other factors involved Argentina's relatively rapid liberalization and its expensive currency, which made Argentine goods fairly costly for foreign buyers. Nevertheless, after controlling for the influence of Mexico, Argentina still shows a slight upward trend in its share of U.S. imports from Latin America during the 1990s. Argentina's share of U.S. exports to Latin America does increase much more dramatically, from 2.4

**Table 4.2**

**United States' Trade with Latin America, 1990–1998**

| | U.S. Imports (in millions of U.S. dollars) | | | | | U.S. Exports (in millions of U.S. dollars) | | | | |
|---|---|---|---|---|---|---|---|---|---|---|
| | 1990 | 1992 | 1994 | 1996 | 1998 | 1990 | 1992 | 1994 | 1996 | 1998 |
| Total U.S.* | 495311 | 532665 | 663256 | 795289 | 913828 | 393592 | 448164 | 512626 | 625075 | 682977 |
| Argentina* | 1511 | 1256 | 1725 | 2279 | 2252 | 1179 | 3223 | 4462 | 4517 | 5885 |
| Argentina as % of U.S. total | 0.3% | 0.2% | 0.3% | 0.3% | 0.2% | 0.3% | 0.7% | 0.9% | 0.7% | 0.9% |
| Latin America | 59981 | 70582 | 85625 | 111529 | 139371 | 49360 | 71464 | 87914 | 103861 | 135735 |
| Latin America as % of U.S. total | 12.1% | 13.3% | 12.9% | 14.0% | 15.3% | 12.5% | 15.9% | 15.5% | 18.6% | 19.9% |
| Argentina as % of Latin America | 2.5% | 1.8% | 2.0% | 2.0% | 1.6% | 2.4% | 4.5% | 5.1% | 4.3% | 4.3% |
| Mexico | 30157 | 35211 | 49494 | 74297 | 94709 | 28279 | 40592 | 50844 | 56792 | 79010 |
| Mexico as % of Latin America | 50.3% | 49.9% | 57.8% | 66.6% | 68.0% | 57.3% | 56.8% | 57.8% | 54.7% | 58.2% |
| Latin America *minus* Mexico | 29824 | 35371 | 36131 | 37232 | 44662 | 21081 | 30872 | 37070 | 47069 | 56725 |
| Latin America-Mexico as % of U.S. total | 6.0% | 6.6% | 5.4% | 4.7% | 4.9% | 5.4% | 6.9% | 7.2% | 7.5% | 8.3% |
| Argentina as % of Latin America-Mexico | 5.1% | 3.6% | 4.8% | 6.1% | 5.0% | 5.6% | 10.4% | 12.0% | 9.6% | 10.4% |

*U.S. Census Bureau, *Statistical Abstract of the United States* (Washington, D.C., 1999), 805–807; 823–26.

percent in 1990 to 4.3 percent in 1998; and, controlling for Mexico, from 5.6 percent to 10.4 percent over this period.

The United States' 1997 policy change toward Argentine beef was an important symbol of the changing relationship. Within Argentina, many had suspected that the true reason for excluding the beef was not foot-and-mouth disease, but a desire to protect the U.S. cattle industry. Even following the decision to resume U.S. purchases, imports of Argentine beef into the United States remained limited by quota, initially set at 20,000 metric tons (slightly less than 6 percent of Argentina's total beef exports).[20] By 1999, U.S. demand for Argentine beef was high enough that sales surpassed the quota, with the surplus subject to a substantial tariff.[21] However, around a year later, a resurgence of the disease in both Great Britain and South America placed a damper on this new development, and U.S. imports of fresh Argentine beef were temporarily halted.

Protectionism thus remained a problem in U.S.-Argentine economic relations, and one of the few areas where Argentina found it necessary to pressure the United States. In particular, Argentines complained of the United States' Export Enhancement Plan (EEP), initiated in 1985. Purportedly to counter subsidies elsewhere, the EEP authorized government subsidies for a number of products, including wheat (the largest recipient), other grains, poultry products, and cattle.[22] The subsidy program clearly conflicted with the United States' declared principles of free trade, as well as the principles of such international organizations as the General Agreement on Tariffs and Trade, or GATT. Argentina, along with other countries, thus appealed to GATT in the 1994 meetings and achieved some limitations on the use of the subsidies.[23]

Complaints of protectionism have also come from the other side, however. Less central in U.S.-Argentine negotiations, but also of interest, have been U.S. critiques of protectionist policies by Argentina. While recognizing that Argentina has made enormous progress in reducing trade barriers, the U.S. State Department has nonetheless complained of such issues as Mercosur tariffs, duties applied to textiles and footwear, and quotas and tariffs on automobiles.[24]

Regardless of which party may or may not be at fault, these disputes emphasize a basic underlying difficulty in molding a symbiotic relationship between the United States and Argentina. As in earlier eras, the two countries still have far too similar economies to avoid competition. Both countries remain major producers of such agricultural products as grains and beef. Differing levels of industrialization have had some impact on compatibility, with the United States selling more manufactured goods and Argentina more agricultural products, but similarities in the climates and lands of the two countries still make some overlap inevitable.

An issue that generated even more tension between Argentina and the United States during the 1990s was the question of intellectual property, especially in the area of pharmaceutical patents, as mentioned in chapter 3. According to the 1988

Omnibus Trade Act of the United States, the Office of the United States Trade Representative must issue an annual report indicating which countries do not adequately protect intellectual property. Countries that are reported to be in violation become subject to sanctions by the United States. After considerable debate, in 1995, the Argentine Congress did succeed in passing a patent law (Law 24572), which committed Argentina to begin paying royalties to foreign pharmaceutical patent holders beginning in October 2000.[25] According to Argentina's position, the patent law sufficed to put Argentina in compliance with intellectual property agreements previously negotiated in the context of GATT.[26] Even after further protective legislation in 1996, the U.S. government and U.S. pharmaceutical companies remained dissatisfied, expressing concerns that the law did not "provide exclusive protection for confidential data submitted by pharmaceutical and agrochemical companies for approval of new products by regulatory authorities."[27] Thus, in 1997, Argentina lost around a quarter of a million dollars in trade benefits after the U.S. government deemed its protection of pharmaceutical patents to be inadequate.[28] As the October 2000 deadline approached, the debate intensified, with U.S. officials arguing that the existing law still contained too many loopholes. Many members of Argentina's Congress, however, saw the law as potentially too harsh on local pharmaceutical companies, and sought legislation which might either postpone when the law would go into effect, or otherwise protect the Argentine companies.[29]

In 1998, Argentina also came under fire by the United States for a different intellectual property issue, this time for failing to protect computer software makers. According to the *Wall Street Journal*, a February 1998 decision by the Argentine Supreme Court "effectively [made] the pirating of software legal" in Argentina, by proclaiming software exempt from Argentine copyright laws.[30] However, a new Argentine Intellectual Property Law, No. 25.036, which passed in October 1998, essentially nullified the earlier decision. Along with granting protections to numerous forms of intellectual property, the law gives special attention to computer software, proclaiming that users only have the right to "reproduce a single backup copy" of licensed software, and that this copy could only be used to replace the original.[31] This legislation thus effectively resolved the software dispute with the United States.

Perhaps one of the most interesting aspects of the intellectual property dispute concerns the role played by actors outside of the executive branch, in both countries. Argentina's failure to protect pharmaceutical and software patents seemed to conflict with Menem's efforts to make his country an enthusiastic member of an international economic community and, in particular, a partner of the United States. Argentina's lapses in this regard appear to have occurred despite Menem's efforts rather than because of them. In the United States, the initiative in sanctioning Argentina came initially from the pharmaceutical companies, which claimed losses of "up to $200 million a year in Argentina because of pirating of [their] patents."[32] Yet the Argentine government was prevented from reforming its laws extensively, in part because of opposition from its own pharmaceutical industry. The Menem administration repeatedly sought to pass a more stringent patent law, but could not find sufficient congressional support due to "a powerful Argentine pharmaceutical industry with sales of more than $2 billion that has exerted broad influence on Congress."[33] After U.S. complaints about the moderate 1995 patent law, Menem—resorting to a common practice of his administration—issued a March 1996 decree modifying the patent legislation, albeit still not enough to satisfy the United States. The conflict between the Argentine Congress and the executive regarding pharmaceutical patents even continued into the De la Rúa administration. Ironically, the executive found itself confronting legislators from the president's own Alliance Coalition when the latter sought to rescind some of the 1995-96 patent protections.[34] The complex struggle between private and public players in both countries continued on the issue of intellectual property.

Despite these areas of conflict, U.S.-Argentine economic relations progressed in a generally positive direction. In particular, Argentina continually sought to deepen and institutionalize the relationship throughout Menem's administration. Argentina did not succeed in its efforts to be the second Latin-American country admitted to the North American Free Trade Agreement—Chile was promised that honor, if NAFTA were to expand. However, the United States did negotiate an agreement with Mercosur as a group to improve trade conditions between the U.S. and the four Mercosur countries (see chapter 5).

It was toward the tail end of his administration that Menem advanced the most radical proposition for economic integration with the United States. Following Brazil's January 1999 devaluation, and speculation that Argentina might need to follow suit, the Argentine government sought to dispel these concerns by proposing a directly contradictory path: Argentina's adoption of the U.S. dollar as its national currency.[35] The topic was not entirely new in Argentine circles, as "dollarization" had begun to emerge as a topic of debate as far back as 1989, in the midst of Argentina's inflation crisis.[36] During the 1989–1990 period, inflation in consumer prices soared to around 1086 percent annually;[37] Argentine currency had become so unstable that simply making it to the end of the month required immediately trading one's *australes* (then Argentina's currency) for U.S. dollars. Dollarization, however, was still a highly sensitive topic in 1989. Following a few years of Cavallo's Convertibility Plan, de facto dollarization became increasingly more of a reality for Argentina, and the idea of taking this process to its conclusion began to be somewhat more politically palatable. Nevertheless, opposition to dollarization remained strong in both countries. For Argentina, it would mean giving up important control of the country's finances, including forfeiting the ability to use monetary policies to alter interest rates.[38] U.S. officials, especially Deputy Treasury Secretary Lawrence Summers and Federal Reserve Chairman Alan Greenspan, also expressed some concerns about the proposal, and the possibility that such a reform could lead to increased pressures on the United States for emergency aid or regarding decisions on monetary policies. In the wake of the Peronists' 1999 electoral defeat, however, the topic of dollarization seemed to fade from the headlines.

## DIPLOMACY, DEMOCRACY, AND JUSTICE

For the Argentine government, improving the national economy was the key motivation for expanding cooperation with the United States. However, attracting the support of the U.S. government and the interest of U.S. investors required establishing a favorable political climate, as well. In part, this occurred naturally, as Argentina had elected a democratic government in 1983, several years before the end of the Cold War and Menem's post–Cold War reformulation of Argentine foreign policy. However, during Menem's administration, the government did seek to ensure that Argentina remained cooperative and in line with U.S. political priorities in both diplomacy and domestic politics. From its side, the United States sought to build on Argentina's base, pushing for further political reforms seen as necessary to strengthen and deepen democratization.

Many of Argentina's initiatives to advance a shared political agenda and support political liberalism took place in the international arena, rather than directly within a bilateral framework. As these will be dealt with further in chapter 5, we will mention these only briefly at this point. One of the first indicators of Menem's new approach to foreign policy was to revise a wide range of Argentine positions within the United Nations, transforming Argentina into an open supporter of the United States. Argentina thus adopted such positions as condemning Cuba's human-rights policies, and withdrew from prior critiques of Israel. Subsequently, Argentina continued to support the United States in the international arena, for example, backing both the 1994 occupation of Haiti and the 1991 war against Iraq in the Persian Gulf.

The United States sought to further this political compatibility by encouraging political reforms within Argentina. Through the United States Agency for International Development, the U.S. government provided support to nongovernmental organizations in an effort to build up civil society in Argentina.[39] The United States also pressured Argentina from early in Menem's presidency to fight corruption in the government. The process of privatization carried particular risks of corruption, given the amount of money changing hands, but eventually did help diminish the problem simply by reducing the size of the public sector. One area seen as particularly inclined toward corruption in Argentina has been the judiciary, which the U.S. State Department's 1998 *Report on Argentina's Human*

*Rights Practices* described as "subject to political influence at times and to inordinate delays."[40] The United States thus also provided aid to help reform the justice system, although with indeterminate results.

One case that attracted considerable U.S. attention involved the July 1994 bombing of a Jewish community center (the Asociación Mutual Israelita Argentina, or AMIA). The attack killed eighty-six people and wounded around another three hundred,[41] with no apparent motive beyond blatant anti-Semitism.[42] Since anti-Semitism runs deep in some Argentine sectors, especially the armed forces and police,[43] many immediately suspected involvement by state officials. Furthermore, according to Patrice McSherry, evidence existed to support this theory, including the excessively incompetent police investigation and phone calls to victims' families apparently using "sophisticated telephone surveillance technology."[44]

While Argentine officials tended to portray the AMIA bombing as a case of terrorism,[45] U.S. officials portrayed the event more in terms of possible human-rights violations, and clearly as an indication of problems with the Argentine justice system.[46] Following President Clinton's trip to Buenos Aires in October 1997, during which he "met with relatives of the victims and promised U.S. support," the United States stepped up pressure on Argentina to solve the case.[47] Argentine officials subsequently began to make some headway; by December 1997, four police officers had been charged and a congressional deputy was being investigated. In August 1998, the FBI—which had become involved through its investigations of property and bank deposits in Florida—announced that officials from the Iranian Embassy in Buenos Aires were also suspected to have been involved.[48] The case remained unresolved at the end of Menem's presidency, leaving the De la Rúa administration with the challenge of finding an answer and administering justice. In September 2001, not long after the U. S. terrorist attacks, twenty men were brought to trial for the AMIA bombing.

## SECURITY COOPERATION

Despite Menem's overriding interest in economic matters, security cooperation emerged as the strongest area of convergence with the United States, and the area that gained Argentina the most recognition from its North American ally. During the 1970s and early 1980s, Argentina had earned a very negative reputation in security affairs. The military was known first for its repression, and second for its international aggression, invading the nearby British-held Falklands (or Malvinas) Islands in 1982 and very nearly initiating a war with Chile in 1978. Argentina's refusal to subscribe to nuclear nonproliferation agreements, and apparent efforts to develop its own potential as a nuclear power, further contributed to U.S. distrust.

Yet by the end of the 1980s, not only had the international system changed radically, but so had Argentina's domestic political context. The military had finally left office, nearly completely devoid of legitimacy after its multiple failures in both politics and war, yet still with considerable residual power.[49] Thus, a central challenge for both postauthoritarian governments was to subordinate the armed forces. While Alfonsín sought control through confrontation, initiating human rights trials and legislation to limit military roles, Menem pursued control through a different approach—co-optation. Menem continued Alfonsín's practice of shrinking the armed forces' budget, but pardoned them for their violations of human rights. In a sense, this continued the gradual backtracking forced upon the Alfonsín government in the face of military pressures. The legislature first passed a *punto final*, or endpoint, law in 1986, which set a deadline after which no further human rights cases could be initiated.[50] When the courts responded with an intensive push and an enormous quantity of new cases, however, military tensions increased instead of diminishing. Thus, in 1987, a "due obedience law" followed, which freed most of the younger officers of responsibility for their actions.[51] Menem completed the process, however, in a series of decrees from 1989 to 1990 with which he pardoned virtually all those who had been convicted or accused of human rights violations—including the junta members—and even those members of the military who had rebelled against Alfonsín's government.[52] The only officers who remained jailed were those who had rebelled during the Menem administration, in 1990.

Menem also designed new and positive roles for the armed forces to replace the repressive and interventionist missions of the past. These new roles fit cleanly with his broader agenda of internationalization and cooperation with the United States: now the Argentine armed forces would keep the peace rather than making violence. From 1990 on, Argentina began actively contributing to a range of multilateral military missions and in fact made peacekeeping a central role for the armed forces. This participation in international missions directly coincided with U.S. interests for two reasons. First, following the end of the Cold War, the United States became more interested in cooperative security, at least in part as a means of reducing the need for the United States to unilaterally assume the responsibility and costs of policing. Second, while some of the military missions in which Argentina participated were "truly" international and led by the United Nations, others were more authentically U.S. operations with a multilateral veneer.

Two episodes stand out with respect to Argentine participation in U.S.-led military missions: the Gulf War and the occupation of Haiti. The Gulf War, often portrayed as the model for post–Cold War conflict—multilateral and highly technological—also marked the beginning of Argentina's military partnership with the United States. Argentina contributed two ships to the multilateral force; however, what made this contribution particularly significant was the choice involved. Since 1984, Iraq had secretly been helping finance Argentina's intermediate range missiles program, known as the Condor II project, in exchange for missile technology.[53] Thus, Argentina's decision to join the United States against this erstwhile ally implied an important shift in allegiances. Argentine support of the 1995 proposed invasion and occupation of Haiti, which will be discussed more extensively in chapter 5, further underscored the Menem government's new commitment to the United States. In this instance, "Argentina stood alone among Latin American states in offering its support to such an invasion" and in participating in the UN's blockade.[54]

Argentina also shifted its position in line with the United States in the area of nuclear nonproliferation. By the time Menem was elected in 1989, the Condor II missile project had become a major area of contention with the United States. According to Rut Diamint, Menem's government initially attempted to defend the project, "denying the danger of the missile" and claiming that the project "did not have military ends and the technology would not be disseminated."[55] However, this did not diminish U.S. concerns, or the likelihood that the continuation of the Condor II project would result in some form of sanctions by the United States. Although no longer linked to U.S.-Soviet competition, nonproliferation remained a clear priority for the United States during the post–Cold War period. In particular, the U.S. Congress had stipulated that virtually no technology could be transferred to missile producing countries.[56] Retaining Condor II could thus potentially nullify the Argentine government's substantial efforts to regain international confidence, foreign investment, and hopefully economic growth; consequently, in May 1991, Argentina agreed to dismantle the project and to relinquish or destroy its components. Argentina then followed this decision with further efforts to become a leader in nonproliferation, subjecting itself "to the strictest nonproliferation constraints accepted by any member of the international community."[57]

The results of Argentina's new efforts toward nonproliferation were not long in coming. In February 1993, before Argentina had yet even dispensed with all Condor II parts, the United States and Argentina signed a Memorandum of Understanding that would regulate, and thus permit, the transfer of strategic technology to Argentina.[58] In April 1994, representatives of the U.S. Department of Energy and Argentina's National Atomic Energy Commission signed a further agreement to enhance cooperation "on research, development, testing, and evaluation" of nuclear technology and procedures, presumably with peaceful intentions.[59] Argentina's nonproliferation posture also created the possibility for collaboration with the United States in the area of space exploration. During a February 1996 visit to Buenos Aires, U.S. Secretary of State Warren Christopher signed two accords dealing with Space and Nuclear Energy which, according to Christopher, underscore[d] Argentina's growing and important role in non-proliferation.[60] Thus, while the decision to dismantle the Condor II project unquestionably created some friction at home (particularly with the U.S. Air

Force), relinquishing the right to pursue a nuclear weapons capability did bring some clear rewards for Argentina.

Achieving convergence with respect to fighting narcotics trafficking has been somewhat more problematic for the United States and Argentina, although perhaps also less essential. Throughout the Americas, the United States has traditionally concentrated on eliminating and interrupting the supply of drugs before they could enter U.S. territory. Beyond requesting that others comply with U.S.-led efforts, the United States has essentially demanded that others cooperate. According to a 1986 law, countries that the United States does not "certify" as adequately fighting narcotics trafficking lose their eligibility for most U.S. aid.

Given its climate and rather remote location, Argentina is neither a major drug producer nor the most important transit country for drugs on their way to the United States. According to the U.S. State Department, Colombian heroin and cocaine from Bolivia, Peru, and Colombia do, however, pass through Argentina.[61] The United States has thus pushed the country to adopt an increasingly active role in combating narcotics trafficking, in order to help the United States deal with its drug use problem, which has historically been considerably more severe than that of Argentina. As an indicator, in the United States, approximately 9.9 percent of people twelve to seventeen years old are estimated to be active drug users (based on use in the month prior to the interview), along with around 5.8 percent of adults eighteen and above.[62] In contrast, drug use in Argentina is relatively low, though it does appear to be increasing. According to 1999 data, around 2.9 percent of Argentines between sixteen and sixty-five years of age are estimated to use illegal drugs, along with approximately 12 percent of children between twelve and fifteen years.[63] To deal with the problem (at least on the supply side), the United States has provided Argentina with aid for fighting the narcotics industry, including "a wide variety of training programs [for] Argentine law enforcement officials" and "information technology equipment to better coordinate police counternarcotics efforts."[64] The United States also helped to develop a task force of Argentine law enforcement officers working on the border with Bolivia.

Although Argentina has certainly cooperated, its government officials have traditionally approached the narcotics issue from a somewhat different perspective. To begin with, Argentine officials have sought a more balanced approach to combating narcotics, one that would pay relatively more attention to the demand for narcotics.[65] Furthermore, the United States' aggressive approach potentially brought a certain risk to Argentine security, with some expressing concern that strong actions against drug production in nearby countries could encourage the narcotics traffickers to move their processing operations elsewhere, possibly even to Argentina.[66] This concern undoubtedly enhanced the military's reluctance to become directly involved in fighting narcotics, a task already seen as both potentially corrupting and as rightfully the terrain of police officers. Nonetheless, in

1990, the army incorporated "logistical support . . . in the fight against narcosubversion" to its list of secondary missions.[67] The Argentine military did continue to avoid substantial involvement in counternarcotics operations, however, while the government focused on issues such as corruption and reorganizing existing law enforcement organizations—areas more amenable to compromise with the United States. At the same time, during the 1990s, the U.S. approach to combating drugs became moderately more cooperative and multidimensional, which further helped facilitate collaboration in this area.

In spite of these moderate disagreements, U.S.-Argentine relations have been overwhelmingly positive with respect to security affairs. One sign of the two countries' convergence in this area is the extent to which discussion and cooperation have been institutionalized. Both the U.S. State Department and the Department of Defense have regularly scheduled meetings with their counterparts from Argentina. Officials from the State Department, including the Americas Region (now Western Hemisphere) Office and the Office of Political-Military Affairs have been meeting annually with representatives of Argentina's Foreign Relations Ministry since 1993 to discuss security and arms control issues.[68] Similarly, the Inter-American Affairs Office in the Pentagon initiated a bilateral working group (BWG) with Argentina in 1995, which has also met annually. The BWG initially established three purportedly ongoing committees, related to politics and strategy, military cooperation, and technology, each of which would be tasked with following up agreements or queries from the annual meetings.[69] More than any concrete accomplishments, however, the BWGs established the pattern of regular cooperation and communication between officials at the lower, less visible levels of the U.S. and Argentine bureaucracies.

For Argentina, some of the more concrete payoffs for security cooperation have come in the form of weapons sales. Acquiring weapons has been a problem for Argentina for some time. During the military regime, Argentina could not purchase arms from the United States due to U.S. legislation that banned sales to countries with human rights problems.[70] Before Argentina could overcome that obstacle, the military regime's leaders led the country into the 1982 war with Great Britain, which in turn inspired an arms embargo by the British and their allies. The embargo essentially remained in place until December 1998, at which point the British government authorized weapons exports to Argentina on a case-by-case basis. The British foreign office explained the policy change as a response to "the change in circumstances since the embargo was established."[71]

However, Argentina's new role as a democracy and a "good citizen" in the world community encouraged the United States to sell the Argentines sophisticated machinery well before Great Britain considered lifting the embargo. For example, in 1994, the United States authorized the sale of thirty-six Skyhawk fighter planes, equipped with limited radar power.[72] As the British opposed including any radar, the United States did not sell Argentina the more advanced radar systems that it sought; however, the compromise position adopted by the United States did indicate a shift away from adhering to the British embargo. The United States also adopted a mediating role between the Argentines and the British, seeking to overcome the rift between its two allies.

Yet most U.S. gestures toward Argentina, including weapons sales, have been explicitly in recognition and support of Argentina's contributions to international peacekeeping. Following Menem's January 1999 visit to the United States, the Office of the Press Secretary announced that "we have supported Argentina's peacekeeping capability through funding and equipment assistance. The President was pleased that the United States would provide a Coast Guard patrol boat, a Coast Guard buoy tender and a TA-4J flight simulator. The Administration is also notifying Congress of its intent to make available from excess U.S. military stocks 900 Light Anti-Tank Weapons (LAWS) for force protection use by Argentine peacekeepers."[73] This decision to provide Argentina with this equipment followed a symbolically important decision in 1997 to grant Argentina the status of "major non-NATO ally" again, explicitly on the basis of Argentina's contributions to international peacekeeping. By most accounts, the label has little substantive meaning, primarily allowing Argentina access to surplus military equipment, as well as further training and shared exercises.[74] However, the symbolism of MNNA was much more significant. Argentina was only the seventh country to be granted such status, and the first in the Western Hemisphere.[75] Furthermore, Argentina was the first country to be designated a major non-NATO ally based on participation in peacekeeping, another indicator of the United States' new priorities following the end of the Cold War.

Naturally, with respect to both alliances and weapons, Argentina did have some disappointments. The "non" was an important part of Argentina's status as a "major non-NATO ally," as Menem had initially sought Argentina's admittance into NATO itself.[76] Once it became clear that this was not an option, the Menem administration shifted its aims, seeking instead the more modest goal of non-NATO ally to the United States. With respect to weapons, Argentina first suffered a lack of weapons for purchase, and subsequently, from a surplus. In 1997, not long before Argentina's MNNA designation, the Clinton administration announced that it would no longer universally restrict the sale of advanced weapons to Latin America.[77] Given its difficulty in acquiring weapons in the past, Argentina's strong opposition to the policy change may have seemed surprising. However, Argentina's military budget was severely limited, while that of neighboring Chile was not. Argentina thus feared an arms race in the region, which they would most certainly lose. The potential disruption of the strategic equilibrium in South America was also seen as posing a threat to the confidence-building process that had been so successful in the region during the democratic period.

Consequently, Argentine leaders became increasingly interested in expanding transparency in weapons sales, in the hopes that this would facilitate continued communication and peace in the region. Nevertheless, once the policy change had already been implemented, some members of the military did begin to see things in a more positive light, hoping that Chile's increased firepower might give them more leverage with their own government regarding their own potential equipment purchases.

## CONCLUSION

Argentine President Carlos Menem was the first Latin American president to pay an official visit to newly inaugurated U.S. president Bill Clinton in 1993. Yet this was only the beginning of the new era of friendship between the United States and Argentina. Argentina adopted economic policies in line with U.S. traditions of economic liberalism, embraced political democracy and U.S. political positions abroad, and contributed wholeheartedly to international military missions and the pursuit of cooperative security. Areas of friction unavoidably did emerge during this period, simply because even the best intentions could not eliminate all areas in which the interests of the two countries conflicted. Yet, compared to past U.S.-Argentine relations, the extent of friction was remarkably limited, and the extent of cooperation remarkably broad.

One of the more interesting facets of the post–Cold War relationship between the United States and Argentina has to do with the extent to which it reflects the changes in both the international system and U.S. priorities. The United States rewarded Argentina with MNNA status at least as much for Argentina's role in the international community as for Argentina's loyalty specifically to the United States. In terms of economic relations, not only did newly international norms of economic liberalism shape Argentina's economic policies, but a new regional bloc influenced how Argentina would pursue its objectives of free trade and increased investment. In sum, as will be discussed in the next chapter, Argentina and the United States developed a strong bilateral relationship during the post–Cold War period, but did not do so in isolation. Instead, the relationship between the United States and Argentina fell within a larger web of international and regional institutions that in some ways tied the two countries even more closely together.

# INTERNATIONAL INSTITUTIONS AND THE BILATERAL RELATIONSHIP: AN ACCOMMODATION WITH LIMITS

## INTRODUCTION

From the beginning of the Cold War until the mid-1980s, three principal factors affected the Argentine-U.S. relationship in international institutions: the course of U.S. policies toward Latin America, which centered around the containment of communism; Argentina's political instability, which gave rise to cycles of advances and withdrawal between both countries' diplomats; and Argentina's internally focused strategy of economic development through much of this period. The prior tradition of diplomatic rivalry between Argentina and the United States also influenced this aspect of the relationship.[1]

The political and economic changes that occurred both in the global order and in Argentina during the 1990s had a strong impact on the relations between the United States and Argentina within international institutions. The major factors guiding these relationships during the Cold War years began disappearing one by one, to be replaced by a new, more propitious context. Furthermore, in contrast to earlier administrations, the Menem government considered the rivalry with the United States to be not only dysfunctional for Argentina's interests in the 1990s, but also saw it as a primary cause of the country's decline since the Second World War. The administration thus changed the direction of the country's ties to some international institutions, and lowered its profile in others or directly abandoned them—as was the case with the Movement of Non-Aligned Countries in 1991— in large measure to embrace a tighter relationship with Washington. For the same reason, the country joined numerous international regimes, particularly in the area of international security. Nevertheless, Argentina did not always automatically follow the United States' policies, wishes, and preferences. On the contrary, Argentina maintained numerous differences with the United States in various important themes in the global and hemispheric agenda, just as occurred with the bilateral agenda (see chapter 4).

This chapter analyzes relations between Argentina and the United States during the 1990s in global, hemispheric, and subregional international institutions, through the analysis of various themes including security, politics, and economics. This approach facilitates identifying the two countries' concurrences and differences in the multilateral arena regarding the questions with the greatest impact on the relationship. The concept of "international institution" is utilized in the broad sense to include both formal international organizations and regimes as well as those systems that bind governments with some degree of regularity.

The United Nations Security Council, General Assembly, and Geneva Conference of Disarmament, the Organization of American States (OAS) and the Conferences of the Defense Ministers of the Hemisphere were the principal international institutions in which Argentina and the United States expressed their national positions, almost always close, in security and international politics themes. More specifically, the two countries tended to coincide on issues of disarmament, nonproliferation of weapons of mass destruction, peacekeeping operations, collective security, transparency of defense policies, civilian control of the armed forces, and defense and promotion of democracy and human rights. These areas defined Argentina and the United States' principal political and security interests following the Cold War.

In economic affairs, areas of agreement and disagreement between Argentina and the United States during the 1990s can be demonstrated in three principal multilateral arenas: the Uruguay round of the General Agreement on Tariffs and Trade (GATT); its successor, the World Trade Organization (WTO); and the numerous hemispheric meetings carried out from 1994 regarding the formation of the Free Trade Area of the Americas.

## GLOBAL AND HEMISPHERIC SECURITY: AN UNUSUAL COINCIDENCE OF INTERESTS AND PERSPECTIVES

During 1994–95 and 1999–2000, Argentina occupied a seat as a nonpermanent member of the United Nations Security Council. Previously, the country had held this position on five opportunities, the last time during 1987–88, at the end of Raúl Alfonsín's government.[2] The end of the East-West rivalry provoked a substantial transformation in the activities of the Security Council, as much in qualitative terms as quantitative. Its agenda became more elaborate, with both formal and informal meetings occurring with a previously unknown frequency.[3] The number of resolutions nearly quintupled the average of approximately fourteen resolutions annually from the 1946–1989 period, rising to an average of sixty-four during the 1990–99 period. From a qualitative perspective, the Security Council adopted the practice of searching for positions of consensus in order to have its resolutions approved by the greatest number of votes possible. This new practice, combined with Argentina's shift toward greater convergence with U.S.

positions, allowed a fluid, intense, and close connection to develop between these countries' foreign policies, a connection that was further strengthened by the excellent personal relations between the countries' respective ambassadors to the United Nations. When significant differences arose in the heart of the council, Argentina systematically supported the North American positions.

The United Nations' Geneva Conference on Disarmament was another multilateral space in which Argentina and the United States supported the same causes.[4] The conference, an independent entity within the United Nations, is the only multilateral bargaining organization to elaborate legally binding instruments in the security area. Until the 1990s, Argentina formed part of the Group of Non-Aligned and Neutral Countries within this forum, known as the "Group of Twenty-One," which traditionally maintained positions contrary to those of the United States-led "Western Group." Since 1991, Argentina began taking positions so similar to those of the Western countries that, on March 1, 1995, it became a member of the latter group.

At the same time, Argentina's participation in United Nations peacekeeping operations helped change the direction of the relations between the Argentine and U.S. militaries, and was a determining factor in gaining Argentina the designation of a "major non-NATO ally" of the United States on January 26, 1998. Like the Security Council, United Nations peacekeeping operations expanded dramatically from the end of the 1980s, both in quantity and in magnitude. Between 1948 and 1987, the United Nations approved only fourteen operations; between 1988 and 1999, the number grew to around forty.[5] This process granted the Menem government an extraordinary opportunity to demonstrate to the world the Argentine military's growing integration in the democratic system and the country's commitment to collective security mechanisms. Furthermore, it allowed Menem to assign new roles to the military, who embraced the opportunity to travel abroad and to enhance their relationships with professionals from other, especially developed, countries.

Argentina's participation in United Nations peacekeeping missions has a long tradition. Since the first dispatch of four observers to Lebanon in 1958, its contributions have been constant, but still limited to military observers and logistical support. Only in the 1990s did Argentina begin to assume a leading role: the sixty men participating in these missions in 1990 ballooned to more than seventeen hundred in 1994, finishing the decade with around seven hundred participants. With this many forces involved, Argentina became one of the eight countries of the world contributing the greatest number of troops to peacekeeping operations, and by far the largest contributor in Latin America. Argentina's involvement followed the same ascending and descending curve that characterized the total deployment of United Nations forces in the 1990s. From an average of 7,000 troops prior to 1990, deployment expanded to an average of 60,000 between 1991 and 1995, descending to less than 15,000 at the end of the decade. Regardless, Argentina's contribution to total peacekeeping forces rose from 2.5 percent in December 1993 to 4.5 percent in December 1999.[6]

Argentina also followed the general tendencies of the 1990s with respect to the nature of its contributions. Along with the "classic mandate" (truce observers and interjecting forces), the Argentine forces carried out, among others, functions of protecting shipments of humanitarian aid, reconstructing infrastructure, demining, attention to refugees, and supervision of political elections.[7] With respect to geographic deployment, the peacekeeping missions encompassed such diverse countries and regions as Angola, Bosnia, Cambodia, Croatia, Cyprus, Ecuador, Haiti, Iran-Iraq, Kuwait, the Middle East, Peru, Rwanda, and the Western Sahara.[8]

Within the context of the United Nations, the Menem government found clear U.S. support for one of its most prized initiatives: the creation of national volunteer corps ("White Helmets") to carry out humanitarian aid functions.[9] The White Helmets, like the Blue Helmets, are composed of national contingents whose activities are coordinated under the auspices of the United Nations.[10] The two forces differ in that the White Helmets are composed of civilians, while the Blue Helmets are composed of members of the armed forces; furthermore, the latter are financed by the United Nations budget, while the former are supported by voluntary contributions of governments, and multilateral and private organizations.[11] The volunteers may come from nongovernmental organizations or from public institutions capable of offering humanitarian assistance, such as universities, hospitals, and community support organizations. They may also be individuals spontaneously inspired by a humanitarian vocation.

Argentina's diplomats feverishly sought U.S. government support for the creation of the White Helmets from the moment that Menem first launched the idea in October 1993. Finally, the Argentine proposal was approved in the United Nations in December 1994, through General Assembly Resolution 49/139B.[12] In his speech before this forum, President Bill Clinton declared, "Let me suggest that it is time for the members of this Assembly to consider seriously President Menem's suggestion for the creation of a civilian rapid response capability for humanitarian crises."[13] The support of the U.S. executive branch for the White Helmets was repeated on other occasions, particularly during President Clinton's visit to Argentina in October 1997. Nevertheless, given congressional opposition to expending resources on the United Nations, the executive branch's support stayed at the political plane; neither financial donations nor contributions of U.S. volunteers followed.[14]

The affinity of Argentine and U.S. interests and perspectives in the international security area reached its highest point in hemispheric affairs. The two countries promoted the development of confidence-building measures, transparency in defense policies, civilian control of the armed forces, implementation of cooperative security schemes in the region, and participation in peacekeeping operations. At the same time, disarmament and arms control measures promoted by the United States coincided with the Argentine goal of seeking regional equilibrium at a low level of conventional forces.

Since the beginning of the 1990s, Argentina—along with Canada—led the process of revising the conceptions and presuppositions on which the security of the region had historically been based. The first expression of this vocation for change emerged during the Eleventh Ordinary Period of Sessions of the General Assembly of the OAS (Organization of American States), carried out in June 1991. This meeting produced a critical political declaration entitled the Santiago Commitment to Democracy and the Renovation of the Inter-American System. This document demonstrates the decision of the Latin American countries to "initiate a joint process of reflection regarding hemispheric security in light of the new world and regional circumstances, from a current and integral perspective of security and disarmament, including the theme of all forms of weapons proliferation and instruments of mass destruction."[15] The Santiago Commitment gave the initial impetus to the innovations in the region with respect to defense doctrines, threat perceptions, and new roles for the armed forces. As Andrés Fontana writes, "Although with marked intra-regional differences, the security process introduces the notions of cooperation and confidence-building as basic elements in regional security. Little by little, it opens the way—above all in the sub-region composed of those belonging to and associated with Mercosur—to more 'global' visions of security, first in matters of non-proliferation of weapons of mass destruction and, gradually, in matters of global and international security."[16]

In order to put the Santiago Commitment into action, the OAS approved the creation of a working group that in 1992 established the Special Committee on Hemispheric Security. Argentina presided over this forum until its 1995 transformation into the Permanent Committee on Hemispheric Security. Once again, Argentina and Canada were the countries in the vanguard in creating this organism and, with it, the incorporation of the security theme into the institutional system of the OAS. The United States, albeit from a lower profile, strongly supported this process, which some Latin American countries, especially Brazil and Mexico, strongly criticized.

Subsequently, Argentina and Canada sought unsuccessfully to include the analysis of hemispheric security questions in the agenda of the first Summit of the Americas (Miami, Florida, 1994). In particular, they sought to carry out periodic meetings of defense ministers, establish mutual confidence measures, and implement other measures oriented toward strengthening civilian control of the armed forces. Some months later, the U.S. Department of Defense retook the initiative and invited the defense ministers of the continent to meet in the city of Williamsburg, Virginia. The goal of the July 25–26, 1995, meeting was to exchange ideas about defense and security issues, and, more specifically, about the new role of the armed forces in the hemisphere in the context of the end of the Cold War and the democratization of Latin America. Argentina not only enthusiastically endorsed the idea, but also assumed an active lobbying role to defeat the then strong Brazilian resistance to join this first ministerial summit.

On the vast majority of themes discussed in Williamsburg, Argentina and the United States spoke with practically a single voice, something that was repeated in the subsequent two meetings of the defense ministers (in Bariloche, October 1996, and Cartagena, November 1998). Nevertheless, the repeated U.S. proposal that the militaries of the larger Latin American countries should become more committed to the fight against narcotics trafficking raised doubts on the part of the Argentine government. The Southern Cone countries, led by Argentina, Brazil, and Chile, stood firm in the three hemispheric summits against authorizing military intervention for this purpose, reserving the armed forces for logistical support only. The Bariloche meeting in particular put these differences in evidence. Argentina, along with the other Southern Cone countries, rejected two important projects initiated by Washington: the creation of a Panama-based air traffic control center to fight against Latin American narcotics trafficking; and the establishment of a regional institute to train civilian leaders in security themes, financed by the United States and based at the National Defense University at Fort McNair. In the first case, Argentina supported the idea conceptually, but was opposed to having this center solely under U.S. control, rather than allowing each country the right to carry out its own inspection of so-called strategic air traffic.[17] With respect to the second theme, and along similar lines, Argentina objected to having this institute controlled by the United States and instead proposed the creation of a training center "of a regional character, neither financed nor organized by a single country," which would be incorporated into the OAS framework.[18]

The Menem administration's opposition to involving the armed forces beyond the threshold of logistical support was based on Argentina's defense and internal security laws, which prohibit the military's involvement in matters which, like narcotics trafficking, are considered to be internal security.[19] A second factor also contributed to Argentina's position: the fear, shared by the majority of countries in the region, that a new national security doctrine could be re-created—this time to fight against narcotics trafficking instead of communism—which could encourage not only different forms of U.S. intervention in Latin America but also military involvement in functions of intelligence and internal repression.

Nonetheless, the Menem government believed that limits on the military's counternarcotics actions should be strongly related to the extent that narcotics trafficking threatened the country's security. Thus, given the advances of this scourge throughout the nineties, along with terrorism and organized crime, Argentina proved prepared, as demonstrated in Minister of Interior Carlos

Corach's June 1999 speech to the OAS General Assembly, to rethink "what the role of the armed forces must be in the battle against these phenomena."[20]

In the same meeting, the members of the OAS unanimously approved the creation of the Inter-American Committee against Terrorism, an idea initiated by Argentina with strong support from the United States during the OAS's Second Special Inter-American Conference on Terrorism carried out in the city of Mar del Plata on November 23–24 of 1998.[21] The terrorist attempts suffered by both Argentina and the United States in the 1990s resulted in shared interests in this area of security, as well.[22] Both countries considered it indispensible to have an organization within the OAS charged specifically with promoting inter-American cooperation for preventing and combating terrorism.

On similar lines, defining a hemispheric strategy to fight against drugs inspired demanding meetings within the OAS. Throughout the decade, significant advances occurred that helped delineate the differences between Latin America and the United States on two fundamental questions: the burden of responsibility and the system of evaluating the counterdrug policies pursued by the countries of the hemisphere regarding the drug problem. The first aspect was dealt with in the so-called Anti-Drug Strategy of the Hemisphere, approved in October 1996 during the Twentieth Ordinary Period of the Inter-American Drug Abuse Control Commission (CICAD).[23] The principles of "shared responsibility" and "equilibrium," recognized in the Rio Action Plan of 1987, constituted the basis of the strategy negotiated in Buenos Aires.[24] In effect, the document recognizes that the problem includes supply as much as demand and, as a consequence, that the drug problem should be dealt with in a balanced manner, suppressing supply (production, trafficking, and sale) and reducing demand (preventing consumption). In this way the United States set aside its perspective of the 1980s, which had focused on combating supply, and gradually drew nearer to the Latin-American position, which Argentina had always shared. Nonetheless, in practice, the proportion of U.S. resources assigned to the fight against narcotics trafficking in the 1990s continued to be clearly slanted toward the supply side, reflecting a similar distribution to that of the prior decade (approximately 65 to 70 percent).[25]

The consensual definition of a joint antidrug strategy soon demonstrated the need to seek a similar agreement regarding the method of evaluating the efforts of OAS members in the fight against drugs, both individually and collectively. Following numerous debates, especially in the arena of the CICAD, a hemispheric agreement emerged to create a multilateral evaluation mechanism, encouraged by the "decertification" policies practiced by the United States. This unilateral mode of evaluating whether or not countries cooperate in the battle against drugs—established in law by the U.S. Congress in 1986—received serious criticism in Latin America, including Argentina. Along with providing a source of tension in inter-American relations, the law was perceived as not only unjust and discriminatory (the United States is the major drug consumer and the primary money-laundering center in the world), but also as an anachronistic manifestation of imperial power.

The multilateral evaluation mechanism (MEM) was approved in October 1999, during the Twenty-Fifth Ordinary Period of Sessions of the CICAD in Montevideo, Uruguay, and began functioning in 2000. Argentina, along with various countries in the region, decidedly and systematically defended the formation of the MEM. Latin America's united front regarding this theme pushed the United States to accept its creation, but the United States reserved the right to continue the practice of certification, in part due to the fact that the new mechanism still lacked the power to impose sanctions. U.S. diplomats were, of course, also constrained by their inability to alter congressional legislation. During the debates regarding the creation of the MEM, Mexico, accompanied by Brazil and Colombia, demanded that the United States' 1986 law be repealed—again, something that U.S. diplomats would be powerless to carry out. Argentina, on the other hand, did not demand this measure.

## ARGENTINA AND THE UNITED STATES IN THE INTERNATIONAL SECURITY REGIMES

Argentina's insertion in diverse regimes for controlling exports of dual use materials and for nonproliferation of weapons of mass destruction was another decisive step toward strengthening U.S.-Argentine relations. With firm U.S. support, in December 1992, Argentina became a full member of the Australia Group, which establishes controls over chemical and biological substances. In November 1993, Argentina joined the Missile Technology Control Regime, whose goal is to control the proliferation of missiles and related technology by means of rules regulating their export.[26] Argentina also adhered to the group of Nuclear Supplier Countries, or the Club of London, in March 1994, by virtue of incorporating in the country's internal legislation the guidelines of this group for controlling sensitive exports. Finally, in March 1996, Argentina joined the Wassenaar Accord in Vienna, which promotes international and regional security by encouraging transparency in the transfer of conventional arms, sensitive materials, and technologies.

Perhaps most important were the ratification of the Treaty of Tlatelolco and Argentina's commitment to the Nuclear Non-Proliferation Treaty which definitively eliminated conflict over nuclear proliferation from the U.S.-Argentine agenda. The Treaty of Tlatelolco and the Non-Proliferation Treaty (NPT) were approved by the Argentine Congress on November 10, 1993 and December 22, 1994, respectively. At the moment when Argentina formalized its new adhesion to the NPT in Washington, on February 10, 1995, the government expressed its support for the U.S. position in favor of an indefinite extension of the treaty. Argentina actively defended this position during the Conference on Revising and

Extending the NPT, carried out in New York between April and May of 1995. At this time, Argentina joined the United States in the Friends of NPT Group of Countries and presided over the working group of nuclear weapons-free zones.

With these steps, the Menem government dramatically abandoned Argentina's traditional opposition to a treaty that it had always considered "asymmetric and discriminatory," a position that was "the axiom within Argentine nuclear policy."[27] To demonstrate the necessity of this change to the Argentine Congress, the government argued both on the basis of principle and interest. First, it was claimed that adhering to the NPT would be the culmination of the growing transparency in Argentine nuclear policy, increase the country's credibility, and secure its commitment to peace and world security. Second, the government asserted that following the nuclear agreements with Brazil and the ratification of the Treaty of Tlatelolco, joining the NPT would not imply additional obligations. Finally, the administration also proposed that ratifying the treaty would open up new possibilities for cooperation with the developed countries in the nuclear field.

With respect to the last point, as a result of Argentina's new policies in this area, the United States eliminated all restrictions impeding the transfer of technology to Argentina, and kept Argentina off the list of countries with limitations regarding the acquisition of nuclear and sensitive materials. Furthermore, the two countries signed important agreements on nuclear affairs and on the civilian use of outer space. Argentine businesses also began to find a much smoother ground for carrying out foreign enterprise.

Along the same lines, Argentine and U.S. diplomats collaborated closely in the two most important debates in the Conference on Disarmament, which concluded with the signing of a Convention on Chemical Weapons and the Comprehensive Nuclear Test Ban Treaty. The negotiations on the Convention on Chemical Weapons concluded in September 1992, following more than a decade of complex discussions. The United States originated the document in February 1983, when then President Ronald Reagan presented a complete proposal to the Conference on Disarmament for a convention seeking the complete and verifiable prohibition of the development, production, storage, and transfer of chemical weapons.

In the final phase of negotiations, Argentina carried out a very active role in the Southern Cone as well as in Geneva. With respect to the first, Argentina pushed the countries of the region to make a firm commitment to the prohibition of chemical weapons one year before negotiations were completed in Geneva. In September 1991, Argentina signed the Declaration of Mendoza with Chile and Brazil. With this declaration, the three countries made a commitment not to develop, produce, or store chemical weapons and, at the same time, to become original parties to the Convention on Chemical Weapons. Argentina simultaneously played an important role in Geneva in the negotiations regarding protections against chemical weapons and the destruction of nuclear arsenals.[28]

Later on, Argentina actively participated in the negotiations on the Comprehensive Nuclear Test Ban Treaty. Following more than two years of discussions in the Conference on Disarmament, the treaty was adopted by the United Nations General Assembly through Resolution 50/245 of September 9, 1996. The resolution, sponsored by 128 countries, including Argentina and the United States, obtained 158 votes in favor, 3 opposed (Bhutan, India, and Libya) and 5 abstentions (Cuba, Lebanon, Mauritius, Tanzania, and Syria). Argentina was one of the first countries to ratify the treaty, doing so on December 4, 1998. In contrast, in the United States, the process of ratification produced a wide debate. Despite President Clinton's personal campaign to gain approval, the U.S. Senate defeated the Comprehensive Nuclear Test Ban Treaty on October 14, 1999, when the Republican majority blocked it in a vote of 51 to 48.[29]

## POLITICAL ISSUES IN INTERNATIONAL INSTITUTIONS

One of the most eloquent demonstrations of Argentina's accommodation to U.S. positions was the change in the former's voting profile in the United Nations General Assembly beginning in 1991. From a traditional position of few convergences, Argentina shifted to a position considerably closer to that of Washington, albeit without automatically mirroring U.S. postures. During the second half of the 1980s, Argentina's convergence with the U.S. position varied between a minimum of 10 percent (1988) and a maximum of 16.4 percent (1985).[30] Nevertheless, the level of overlap between Buenos Aires and Washington, D.C. was much higher on issues considered a priority by the United States, fluctuating between 40 percent and 60 percent.

From 1991 on, Argentina deliberately advanced toward the U.S. positions, moving from approximately 12.5 percent convergence in 1990 to 41 percent, arriving at a peak of 68.8 percent agreement in 1995. The end of the Cold War and, with that, the conclusion to many strongly controversial themes in the UN General Assembly, facilitated carrying out this considerable change. To be sure, other countries in the region also moved closer to the U.S. position, but not to the same extent (see table 5.1). Like other decisions of the Menem government, the decision to modify the voting profile in the General Assembly was adopted for the purpose of visibly demonstrating Argentina's firm cooperation with the Western Alliance.[31]

The fiftieth UN General Assembly (1995) was the moment of greatest bilateral agreement. The principle differences between the two countries arose in the case of the U.S. economic, commercial, and financial blockade of Cuba, on questions regarding the verification of weapons and disarmament limits, and on diverse issues tied to the Arab-Israeli conflict. Since 1996, the degree of convergence began to decline, arriving at 44.4 percent in 1999, although it remained at 70 percent on the votes which the United States considered most important.[32] The

**Table 5.1**

## Convergence of Argentine and U.S. Votes in the U.N. General Assembly, 1989–99

| Year | Argentina | Brazil | Chile | Mexico |
|------|-----------|--------|-------|--------|
| 1989 | 13.3% | 11.8% | 23.7% | 12% |
| 1990 | 12.5% | 14.9% | 16.5% | 15.2% |
| 1991 | 41% | 22.7% | 25% | 20.6% |
| 1992 | 44.4% | 22.7% | 28.4% | 20.3% |
| 1993 | 53.8% | 28% | 33.9% | 28.3% |
| 1994 | 67.9% | 39.1% | 46.3% | 33.3% |
| 1995 | 68.8% | 41.1% | 45% | 41.6% |
| 1996 | 60.7% | 42.4% | 46.6% | 38.8% |
| 1997 | 56.1% | 42.6% | 44.8% | 37.5% |
| 1998 | 50% | 41.7% | 40.7% | 32.8% |
| 1999 | 44.4% | 38.9% | 40.3% | 30% |
| 2000 | 44.2% | 39.7% | 41.9% | 34.4% |

Source: U.S. Department of State: *Report to Congress on Voting Practices in the United Nations* (Washington D.C.: U.S. Government Printing Office, 1989–2000).

government of Fernando De la Rúa has displayed a practically identical voting profile to that of Menem's last year; the level of convergence with the United States in 2000 was 44.2 percent. The major explanation for the greater relative distance between the two countries' positions was the stalled peace process in the Middle East after Benjamin Netanyahu's coalition took control of the Israeli government. The United States maintained an almost solitary position of firm support to the Israeli positions while Argentina adopted a critical position, coinciding with the stance maintained by, among others, the countries of the European Union, Australia, Canada, and New Zealand.[33] Argentina and the United States also repeated their differences regarding the U.S. embargo of Cuba and regarding complete and general disarmament.

Certainly, the most symbolic change in Argentina's voting profile during the 1990s involved the human rights situation in Cuba. Since March 1991, Argentina set aside its traditional position of abstention to vote in favor of the resolutions condemning Cuba, both in the Commission on Human Rights in Geneva as well as in the Third Commission of the UN General Assembly (Social, Cultural, and Humanitarian).[34] The remaining Latin American countries represented in this committee—with the exception of Panama—either abstained or voted against the resolution.

In the other two most conflictive cases regarding human rights, those of China and Iran, again Argentina and the United States held different positions. From

1990 on, the European Union presented the resolution to condemn China for seven consecutive years with consistently negative results, since the Chinese diplomats managed to impede it through a vote of "no action."[35] During all these years, the European Union and the United States voted against the "no action" motion, while Argentina abstained. In 1998, the European Union decided against raising the Chinese question in the Commission on Human Rights. In addition to the successive defeats suffered by the resolution, the EU took into account the Beijing government's positive steps in subscribing to the two big international pacts on human rights (the International Pact on Economic, Social, and Cultural Rights, and the International Pact on Civilian and Political Rights), as well as the decision to permit the president of the Working Group on Arbitrary Detentions to visit China. The following year, the United States presented the condemnatory resolution unsuccessfully; once again, China resorted to a procedural maneuver of a "no action" vote, blocking treatment of the issue for the eighth time. Argentina maintained its position of abstention while the United States voted against the motion.[36]

In contrast to the Chinese case, Argentina's position on the human rights situation in the Islamic Republic of Iran varied significantly. The United States, in contrast, maintained a continuous position of condemnation. From 1991 to 1993, Argentina's representatives managed to be absent at the times when both the Commission on Human Rights and the United Nations General Assembly voted on resolutions condemning Iran. These momentary absences occurred for economic reasons: Argentina's need to preserve an important commercial relationship, strongly in its favor. Between 1991 and 1993, Argentina's exports to Iran, composed principally of oil and cereals, surpassed $895 million, while imports from Iran were less than $2 million.[37] In addition, the Menem government considered the decision to miss the votes to be a means of compensating Iran for its unilateral decision to conclude nuclear cooperation programs with that country, which undeniably did not fit within the new parameters of Argentina's international security policy.

The alleged involvement of Iranian diplomats in the bombing of AMIA decisively influenced Argentina's changed position beginning in 1994. From then until 1998 in the General Assembly, and following Argentina's readmission into the Commission on Human Rights in 1997, Argentina began voting with the United States in favor of condemning Iran for massive human-rights violations.[38] Nevertheless, Argentina again modified its position in 1999, shifting from condemnation to abstention, in light of the "positive changes" perceived to have occurred in Iran's domestic politics that year.[39] Economic considerations again influenced Argentina's arguments. During the first half of 1998, the Iranian authorities decided to cancel all their imports from Argentina in response to official declarations charging Iran with responsibility for the 1994 terrorist attack, something that had not been proven. The figures on bilateral trade between these two countries roughly reflect Iran's decision, with trade descending from more than $659 million in 1997 to $468 million in 1998 and less than $157 million in 1999.[40] Following the vote change in the Human Rights Commission and the General Assembly, Iran gave orders to resume purchases from Argentina. Thus, Argentine exports to Iran in 2000 increased to $348.5 million.[41]

The reform of the United Nations Security Council and the creation of an International Penal Court (IPC) were two other important themes on which Argentina and the United States demonstrated differences. The end of the Cold War created the possibility for the debate initiated in the 1970s on greater democratization of the Security Council to take place formally within the General Assembly. Resolution 48/26 of the General Assembly, approved by consensus on December 3, 1993, addressed the necessity of revising the composition and operations of the Security Council, and ordered the creation of a Working Group on Open Composition to examine this theme.

From the moment that this debate was initiated in the United Nations, the United States promoted incorporating Germany and Japan as new permanent members, to reinforce the council's capacity to act and to share the burden of managing threats to global peace and international security. The United States also accepted the eventual incorporation of three other permanent members to represent the developing countries and backed expanding the council up to a maximum of twenty or twenty-one members. The United States opposed, however, any expansion involving only nonpermanent members, as well as any change in the status, obligations, or privileges of the existing five permanent members. Regarding the representation of the developing world, the U.S. position has been flexible, open to the possibility of having fixed countries, rotating seats or some other criteria. The United States also did not define a position regarding the degree of veto power these new members might have.

In contrast, Argentina has sought more extensive reform of the Security Council, both in procedures and membership. Diplomats have dedicated considerable effort to reforming practices and procedural norms of the organization in order to guarantee more transparency in its efforts. Regarding membership, Argentina supported expanding the number of nonpermanent members, favoring a total council size of twenty-four. Argentina opposed adding fixed permanent members, supporting instead expansion through a system of open regional rotation, in which each region (Latin America, Asia, Africa, and Eastern Europe) would have one or two seats.[42] According to the Argentine Ministry of Foreign Affairs, this design would assure more democratic representation, versus the traditional, power-based criteria. Thus, Argentina proposed the following criteria for new rotating permanent members of the Security Council: respect for the principles and propositions of the UN Charter; support in the form of finances and personnel for peacekeeping operations; financial contributions to the United Nations; and democratic government and respect for human rights. In addition to assuring Argentina a rotating seat on the council, this approach sought to halt Brazil's aspirations to become the permanent member for Latin America. Brazil, following the traditional criteria, favored the "2 + 3" formula, meaning that Germany and Japan would join the council as permanent members, along with three developing countries from Latin America, Asia, and Africa, to be chosen principally based on "capabilities." According to the Brazilian Ministry of Foreign Relations, Brazil would be a "natural candidate" to occupy the Latin American seat, due to its history and economic potential.[43]

With respect to the creation of an International Penal Court, Argentina and the United States maintained opposite positions on the central theme of the debate, the degree of autonomy to be conceded to the Court and the prosecutor. Since 1995, Argentina played a leading role in preparations to establish the International Penal Court in accord with General Assembly Resolution 50/46, which actively backed it. The Resolution was inspired by a perceived growing need for an international tribunal that could judge crimes of war, crimes against humanity, genocide, and aggression when the justice systems of the affected countries could not or would not judge these crimes in an impartial manner. The supranational organization would thus substitute for the absences or defects of these national justice systems, as well as the "temptation towards unilateralism" by any particular country's justice system that "sought to assume the right to investigate offences committed in another."[44]

In the United Nations' Diplomatic Conference of Plenipotentiaries to conclude the Statute of the IPC, carried out in Rome in June and July 1998, Argentina, as well as the majority of the countries of the European Union, sought to grant both the tribunal and the prosecutor considerable autonomy. Argentina's diplomats emphatically demonstrated their support for the creation of a "solid, independent and responsible prosecutor" with "power to pass judgments." Although the Argentines envisioned a high level of cooperation between the Court and the Security Council, they nonetheless argued that it would be "inadmissible to create an International Penal Court which depended on the Security Council's authorization to act."[45] In contrast, the United States, along with Russia, China, and France, argued in favor of precisely this dependence. According to the U.S. Ambassador to the United Nations, Bill Richardson, the idea of an autonomous court and prosecutor was unrealistic: "We do not want an international tribunal or its prosecutor to become a guarantee to anyone coming up with any kind of complaint or accusation."[46] The Rome conference concluded with a broad defeat for the United States; in the end, the Statute of the International Penal Court, granting broad autonomy to both the tribunal and the prosecutor, was approved by 120 votes in favor, including that of Argentina; 7 opposed; and 21 abstentions.[47]

These differences in Argentine and U.S. perspectives and interests in the multilateral plane did not obscure the high level of agreement reached in the hemispheric context for the defense of democracy and human rights. On both issues, the two countries took the same tone, unmatched by the rest of Latin America. Along with Chile and Canada, Argentina and the United States composed a group of activist states favoring the formation of a strong regime in defense of democracy on the continent. Argentina, furthermore, situated itself "at the most interventionist end of the spectrum."[48] During the Eleventh General Assembly of the OAS, carried out in Santiago, Chile, in June 1991, Argentina actively supported the historic resolution 1080 on "representative democracy," which consecrated an automatic safeguard mechanism to deal with any "abrupt interruption" in the democratic process of any OAS nation.[49] At the insistence of Argentina, which presided over the meeting, the OAS General Assembly subsequently adopted the Washington Protocol, which added a new article to Chapter III of the OAS Charter.[50] This article allows the suspension of a country in which a democratic government has been overthrown by force from participating in OAS deliberations and decisions, until such time that democracy is reestablished.

Finally, Argentina cooperated enthusiastically with the United States, in the OAS as well as in the UN, in resolving the Haitian political crisis that occurred as a consequence of the September 30, 1991 coup d'etat that ousted Haitian president Jean Bertrand Aristide. The Argentine government strongly condemned the coup, imposed sanctions against its perpetrators and, in addition, was the only Latin American country to participate in the embargo and naval blockade that the UN Security council imposed on the island.[51] More important, Argentina was the only Latin American country involved in the multinational force that the UN Security Council authorized (through the June 1994 Resolution 940) to intervene in Haiti in order to restore democracy and the elected government. Argentina's contribution to the U.S.-led multilateral force consisted of around one hundred gendarmes engaged in monitoring the Haitian police.

Menem's government also maintained a high profile in defense of democracy in all the political crises that threatened Latin American democratization in the 1990s: Peru and Venezuela (1992), Guatemala (1993), and Paraguay (1996 and 1999). Beyond this, at the subregional level, Argentina played a decisive role in Mercosur's incorporation of a "democratic clause" that makes membership and even association contingent on having democratic institutions. Without a doubt, Paraguay's April 1996 political crisis helped vanquish Brazil's initial resistance to assuming this kind of commitment.

The Paraguayan crisis occurred after General Lino Oviedo, then commander of the Paraguayan Army, retreated to his barracks with his troops to resist retirement from active service, mandated by President Juan Carlos Wasmosy. In the meantime, the power struggle between the president and the leader of the Army brought back memories of the blackest periods of recent Latin American history and created numerous uncertainties over the future of the still weak Paraguayan democracy. Thus, the Argentine, Brazilian, and Uruguayan governments reacted immediately and energetically. They warned that they would not allow any rupture of democratic stability and that they would expel Paraguay from Mercosur should the rebellion succeed.[52] The opposition political parties in the three countries clearly supported this position, demonstrating the high level of commitment to democratization existing in the subregion. All agreed that the Paraguayan crisis could not be seen as merely a domestic problem, given that it affected Mercosur's credibility and, as a consequence, the external relations of all member countries by endangering agreements reached with other blocs or countries.

Following the Paraguayan crisis, on July 25, 1996, Mercosur adopted a first "democratic commitment" proclaiming that any interruption of the constitutional order in countries belonging to, or associated with, this block "constitutes an unacceptable obstacle for the continuation of the process of integration."[53] Later, during a Mercosur summit meeting carried out in Ushuaia, Argentina, in June 1998, Mercosur's members, along with Bolivia and Chile, formally approved Mercosur's "democratic clause" indicating that "in the event of a rupture in the democratic order" of a participating state, the remaining states could suspend that state's rights to "participate in the distinct organs of the respective processes of integration," as well as "their rights and obligations emerging from those processes."[54]

## THE MULTILATERAL AND HEMISPHERIC ECONOMIC AGENDA

Since its 1947 creation until 1994, the General Agreement on Tariffs and Trade (GATT) regulated international trade, promoting the liberalization of commerce through eight rounds of negotiations. Argentina subscribed to the agreement only in 1967. Its nearly twenty-year absence can be explained by its low participation in world trade, due to an internally oriented development strategy carried out from the mid-1930s to the end of the 1970s. Beginning in the 1980s, and particularly in the 1990s, multilateral economic negotiations acquired a growing importance for Argentina, due to the country's opening to international trade and the constitution of Mercosur.

Within GATT, Argentine diplomats dedicated the bulk of their efforts toward bringing agriculture into the negotiations. Outside GATT, Argentina worked assiduously to construct alliances that would augment its negotiating power on this theme. The most important of these alliances was the Cairns Group, founded in Cairns, Australia, in 1986, shortly before the Uruguay Round of GATT negotiations (1986–1994). The Cairns Group, composed of Argentina, Australia, Brazil, Canada, Colombia, Chile, the Philippines, Indonesia, Malaysia, Thailand, South Africa, New Zealand, Fiji, Paraguay, and Uruguay has, despite its obvious diversity, both a common objective and a common situation. The group seeks to liberalize agricultural trade, and lacks the resources to compete with the richest countries through subsidies to agricultural products.

The group's great initial success was to achieve the inclusion of agriculture in the Uruguay Round of GATT negotiations, which, up until this time, only regulated commerce in industrial products. As stated by Jorge Campbell, former secretary of international economic relations of the Argentine Ministry of Foreign Affairs, "Agriculture was seen as an exception to the rules of the market economy and as a theme that could not be subject to the general norms of the system, since the countries resistant to its liberalization insisted, and still insist, on characterizing this sector as a highly sensitive activity with unmanageable political consequences."[55] The temporary alliance between the Cairns Group and the United States during the Uruguay Round was fundamental in obtaining an Accord on Agriculture, despite strong confrontations with the European Union. The accord established modest reductions in subsidies and tariffs, albeit also affirming the necessity of renewing the negotiations on January 1, 2000, in order to achieve greater advances in this area.

With the initiation of the Word Trade Organization in 1995, Argentina and the United States exhibited some important discrepancies, while still remaining allied within the group of efficient producer countries. Argentina, one of the most active and resolute countries of the Cairns Group, had promoted the widespread liberalization of agricultural trade and the elimination of subsidy policies both in production and in exports.[56] In contrast, the United States had favored the gradualist focus adopted by the Uruguay Round, which included new tariff reductions, a cutback on export subsidies, and the implementation of restrictions to programs of domestic support.

The U.S. policy on subsidizing exports and "food aid" was the principal theme separating the United States from Argentina and the remainder of the Cairns Group.[57] Nonetheless, these differences were considerably milder than the conflicts between these two countries, on the one hand, and the group formed by nations whose agricultural production relies on subsidies and other forms of support. Members of this group include the European Union (plus other, associated countries, like Switzerland and Norway), Japan, and South Korea. This latter group of countries, along with others greatly influenced by them, managed to maintain the particularity of the agricultural theme by employing diverse arguments summarized by the so-called multifunctionality of agriculture and noncommercial concerns.[58] Through these concepts, the group asserted that agriculture generates a series of positive externalities of a demographic nature (such as avoiding an excessive population concentration in the cities caused by uprooting producers), scenic (maintaining certain landscapes valued by the society), and environmental (improving the air and the ecology), which justify different mechanisms to protect this sector.

In the third ministerial meeting of the World Trade Organization carried out in Seattle (November 30–December 3, 1999), the Cairns Group and the United States acted as "objective allies," supporting a shared position in favor of carrying out fundamental reforms in agricultural trade. In addition, these countries arrived at an agreement on a document of consensus with the European Union and Japan regarding the terms for a future negotiation, although this could not be concluded due to the meeting's general failure (for reasons unrelated to the agricultural theme). The document incorporated issues of considerable interest to Argentina, such as the elimination of export subsidies, lowering tariffs on agro-industrial products, and the reduction of internal subsidies. The United States and the Cairns groups accepted the inclusion of the issues encapsulated in the term *multifunctionality* in exchange for avoiding the use of this term as well as preventing these issues from being transformed into arguments for distorting commerce.[59]

Closely tied to the agricultural theme, trade in products containing genetically modified organisms gained importance in the late 1990s due to differing criteria for "scientific evidence" and "consumer protection," stipulations included both in Article XX of GATT as well as the Sanitary and Phytosanitary Agreement that resulted from agricultural negotiations in the Uruguay Round. This agreement limits member countries' freedom to impede trade for unilaterally invoked reasons of sanitation, requiring that such barriers be based on a scientific foundation.[60] Various countries, led by the European Union, supported reopening this accord, arguing that the agreement does not permit countries to satisfy the concerns of consumers—intensified following the "mad cow" disease crisis—regarding the composition and production process of foodstuffs. In the face of these arguments, which without a doubt had a basis in important economic concerns, Argentina and the United States tightened ranks and defended their right to put genetically modified products on the market, arguing that "there is no scientific proof that they are harmful."[61] Again, common interests united the two countries. The United States and Argentina are the two principal producers of genetically modified products, with 74 percent and 15 percent of world output, respectively.[62]

This example of "noncommercial concerns," which has generated strong disputes within the World Trade Organization, has also been carried into other multilateral battlefronts. Thus, this was the nucleus of the March 1999 debate over eventually incorporating a Protocol on Biosecurity into the Agreement on Biological Diversity.[63] The firm opposition from a group of temperate climate grain producing countries, including Argentina, Australia, Canada, Chile, Uruguay, and the United States (which was not party to the agreement), managed to block the protocol, which would have severely restricted trade in genetically modified grains and their derivatives.[64]

At the same time that Argentina and the United States developed their respective positions on international commerce within the global arena, first in the

Uruguay Round and later in the World Trade Organization, commercial and financial questions were generating previously unheard-of interest within the Western Hemisphere. The economic agenda of the 1980s, dominated by the foreign debt crisis and, consequently, marked by negativity, was replaced by an essentially positive tendency as a result of three principal factors. First, from the Latin-American side, the adoption of externally oriented trade and investment practices, programs to privatize state enterprises, and the economic growth experienced by the region throughout the 1990s, opened up new opportunities in trade and investment for Latin America's primary foreign partners, which naturally included the United States. As an example of this positive transformation, U.S. exporters nearly tripled sales to Latin America between 1990 and 1997. On average during the 1990s, the Latin American countries imported eleven times more goods from the United States than from China, twice as many as from Japan, and the same amount as from the European Union. Even without counting Mexico, the countries of South and Central America were nearly as important for U.S. exporters as Japan. Along the same lines, the United States' sales to Mercosur doubled exports to Australia, while Argentina and Chile were more important markets for the United States than countries of the size and importance of India and Russia.[65] With respect to direct investment, Latin America absorbed approximately one-fifth of U.S. cash flow, while capital stock from the United States surpassed that in Canada and tripled the corresponding investment in Japan. Thus, the United States was the primary foreign investor in the Mercosur countries, as well as in Mexico, Central America, and the countries of the Andean Community.[66]

The second positive factor was the "revival" of regionalism, reflected in the considerable increase in preferential trade pacts throughout the world. This regionalism nonetheless exhibited important qualitative differences with similar processes of the past. In the 1990s, GATT was notified of nearly one hundred preferential agreements carried out under its Article XXIV, in contrast to only seventy during the period from 1947 to 1990. Furthermore, these agreements included two novel characteristics: they went beyond the goods market, and some of them included unprecedented free trade practices between developed and developing countries.[67]

The third factor, tightly linked to the last, was the United States' changed position on the role of preferential trade agreements in the promotion of its commercial interests. During the Cold War, commercial discrimination was alternately promoted or tolerated by Washington more for strategic than commercial reasons, since nondiscrimination (manifested in the principle of most-favored nation) was the core of U.S. trade policy.[68] Nevertheless, this position was modified during the second half of the 1980s, due principally to two considerations. Initially, U.S. concerns were defensive, fearing discrimination from the European and Asian blocks at a moment when the Uruguay Round negotiations seemed that they might fail. In this context, preferential trade agreements were perceived as both insurance against an eventual increase in European and Asian protectionism, and as a means of pressuring other countries to seriously commit themselves in multilateral trade negotiations.[69] Second, the growing complexity of the multilateral agenda, which has traditionally come to include internal areas such as intellectual property, policies on unfair competition, and labor and environmental standards, has encouraged most countries to pursue their interests in narrower arenas, given the difficulty of succeeding in multilateral negotiations. Thus, for the United States and other large countries, regionalism has acquired a strategic value because extensive integration at this level could serve as a prior step toward multilateral negotiations.[70]

In addition to these strictly commercial reasons, security interests also encourage regional integration. In the words of Stuart E. Eizenstat, Undersecretary for Economic, Business, and Agricultural Affairs, "The trade agreements of the post–Cold War era will be equivalent to the security pacts of the Cold War—binding nations together in a virtuous circle of mutual prosperity and providing the new frontline of defense against instability. A more integrated and more prosperous world will be a more peaceful world—a world more hospitable to American interests and ideals."[71]

The Initiative for the Americas, announced by President George H. W. Bush in 1991, and the later project for a hemispheric free trade agreement were the regional expressions of this new U.S. world trade strategy. According to an agreement from the first Miami Summit of thirty-four presidents and heads of state of the Western Hemisphere, this free trade area was to be defined by the year 2005. With respect to this issue, Argentina gradually came to define its positions in conjunction with the countries of Mercosur (the proposed common market of South America including Argentina, Brazil, Paraguay, and Uruguay, which was created by the Treaty of Asunción in 1991), and particularly with Brazil.

The Latin American countries' reaction to these projects was enthusiastic in some cases and cautious in others. Argentina initially fell into the first category; the country's principal incentive to reach a free trade agreement with the United States was to lock in economic reforms and lower the country risk. The Minister of Economy, Domingo Cavallo, even suggested that if Argentina were invited to form part of the Free Trade Area of the Americas (FTAA), it would have to accept, even if forced to do so independently of its Mercosur partners.[72] Nevertheless, Argentina's expectations of reaching a preferential trade agreement with the United States quickly became diluted due to President Clinton's difficulty in obtaining fast-track negotiating authority from the U.S. Congress.[73] As Scott Otteman writes, "As fast-track flagged, Argentina gradually abandoned its ambition to be the next country in line to join NAFTA after Chile, in favor of supporting Brazil's vision of a strengthened Mercosur."[74]

Following the first Miami Summit, Argentina's positions increasingly tended to mesh with those of Mercosur, giving rise to the formation of a unified block in hemispheric negotiations. Mercosur thus constituted the United States' principal interlocutor in Latin America, somewhat balancing the enormous negotiating power of the United States in the hemisphere. Progressively, FTAA negotiations became inserted within a nearly bipolar framework, far from the simple process of the gradual incorporation of Latin American countries into NAFTA that many observers predicted when the hemispheric dialogue was formally initiated in 1994.[75]

The United States and Mercosur exhibited their first differences in the Miami Summit when defining the agenda for the hemispheric meeting. The U.S. sought to include those themes known as part of the "new multilateral economic agenda" (services, investments, intellectual property), with the goal of adopting deeper commitments in the hemisphere than those reached in the Uruguay Round. For Argentina, and for Mercosur in general, the FTAA agenda was only interesting if it permitted a complete hemispheric discussion, which would also encompass themes of the "old multilateral agenda" (agriculture, subsidies, and access to markets). For the Southern Cone countries, these issues had not been totally or satisfactorily resolved in the WTO agreements, whether for problems of definition or due to the difficulty of putting agreements into practice.

Once a general agenda had been accepted, the differences between Mercosur and the United States shifted into the rhythm of negotiation. The United States proposed simultaneously launching negotiations on all themes, with interim approval of any agreements, leading toward a final agreement in 2005. Undoubtedly, the issues for which interim agreements were possible complied with U.S. interests such as investments, service matters, and transparency in public purchases. From its side, Mercosur supported a gradual and all-inclusive method of negotiation, supporting the principle of a "single undertaking" on the basis that "nothing is agreed until all has been agreed," and consequently opposed approving interim accords that could affect the overall equilibrium in negotiations. Mercosur's focus tended to incorporate regional interests (always more difficult to negotiate) as an inseparable part of the negotiating package. Another goal of gradualism was to gain time to adapt national producer sectors to the expanded market that FTAA would offer. The discussion on interim sectoral agreements reappeared when analyzing the "concrete advances" of the process exhibited in the year 2000, as stipulated by the Miami Summit. Thus, while the United States claimed that interim sectoral agreements did constitute concrete progress, Mercosur only recognized as such the approval of measures to facilitate negotiations; this latter was the criteria which was finally approved in the December 1998 meeting of the Committee on Trade Negotiations in Surinam.

In sum, Mercosur succeeded in consolidating a common negotiating position vis-à-vis the United States, despite the different national interests within the block, especially between Argentina and Brazil. This task was facilitated in the

1990s due to the fact that negotiations made it no further than various prepara-
tory phases without delving deeply into any substantive theme. In the future,
maintaining Mercosur as a decisive actor in hemispheric negotiations will depend
principally on its capacity to deepen its own commercial agenda, a challenge that
is far from simple.

## Conclusions

The Menem government made extensive use of international institutions to
demonstrate its firm commitment to change the direction of Argentine-U.S. relations. The unusual situation of the ending of a world order offered Menem,
especially during his first administration, an extremely favorable external context
for reaching this objective. Due to pragmatic considerations and, in most cases,
also conviction, the Menem government adapted Argentina's positions in international institutions to the political and international security interests of the
United States and the Western alliance in the post–Cold War era. Participation in
the Gulf War, and joining the Non-Proliferation Treaty were the emblematic cases
of this transformation of traditional positions in security matters. In political
affairs, this space was occupied by Argentina's changed voting profile in the
United Nations' General Assembly, which had the admitted purpose of avoiding
economic costs for political differences with Washington perceived as relatively
irrelevant to the country's central interests.

On the hemispheric plane, Argentina and the United States saw most security
problems in the same light, as with matters regarding the defense and the promotion of democracy. Here, too, the end of the Cold War created an extraordinary
opportunity to expand the inter-American system's capacity for collective action,
now without the risk of being a mere instrument of the White House in its global
political and security competition with other great powers. In this new context,
important advances occurred in matters of security (i.e., the Conferences of the
Ministers of Defense of the Hemisphere) and in the defense and promotion of
democracy (such as OAS Resolution 1080 on "representative democracy").

In addition, the United States assumed a more genuine commitment to democracy than in the years of the East-West rivalry, during which time the defense of
democracy was often subordinated to other goals considered more valuable to the
fight against international communism. In the 1990s, the democratization of Latin
America coincided closely, perhaps more than ever, with the United States' value
system and political, economic, and security interests. For its part, Argentina also
had a clear interest in countering attacks against democracy in Latin America, perceived as an indirect threat to the process of democratization of the country itself,
whose fortunes remained uncertain. Furthermore, the Menem government considered democracy to be a necessary condition in maintaining a fluid relationship
with the Western world and with the international financial organizations where

the requirement for democracy grew increasingly more prevalent.[76] Thus, the country's actively prodemocratic role during the Menem years cannot be explained solely by the government's intent to adapt to Washington, D.C.'s preferences.

In sum, the rapprochement between Argentina and the United States in matters of international security and policy responded to various factors that united moral reasons with convenience. At the same time, Argentina demonstrated important differences with Washington on various international or hemispheric matters, as demonstrated by the former's voting patterns in the United Nations' General Assembly and in the Geneva Commission on Human Rights, as well as in issues regarding the fight against narcotics trafficking. Certainly, the major differences occurred in the economic sphere, due to circumstances or simply to the existence of conflicting national interests. For example, the lack of fast track, combined with the "mercantilist" benefits Argentina obtained upon gaining preferential access to the Brazilian market through Mercosur, helped forge a strong domestic political consensus that the block should occupy a privileged place in Argentina's foreign relations. Nevertheless, and for fear of an excessive dependence on Brazil, the Menem government appeared increasingly supportive of constructing a hemispheric free trade area, in which Mercosur and FTAA should both complement and counterbalance each other, instead of seeking a trade strategy limited to South America.

The same perception influenced the foreign policy of Fernando De la Rúa's government. In its first declarations, the new government identified Mercosur and FTAA as the first and second priorities in the area of multilateral negotiations.[77] Beyond this, on the occasion of the First Summit of the Presidents of South America, convoked in Brazil at the end of August 2000, the Argentine Ministry of Foreign Affairs clearly expressed its desire that this meeting of twelve countries not be interpreted as an attempt to create a South American bloc. Instead, it should be seen as a move toward Latin American integration and greater hemispheric cooperation that should continue through numerous already established inter-American, regional, or subregional mechanisms.[78] A similar perspective characterized the Ministry of Foreign Affairs' policies toward Mercosur until the end of the De la Rúa government.

# CONCLUSION

CHAPTER 6

IN 2OO1, A SERIES OF DEVELOPMENTS OCCURRED THAT WOULD seriously challenge the new relationship between Argentina and the United States. First, both countries found themselves facing economic difficulties, albeit of different intensities. For the United States, this meant that the record period of economic growth characterizing the 1990s finally ended. By the latter half of the year, the recession could no longer be denied, as unemployment began to creep up, and productivity declined. The U.S. recession was spurred on by the brutal terrorist attack of September 11, 2001—a date now firmly etched in the memory of every American—when hijackers commandeered four commercial airplanes, crashing one into the Pentagon and two others into the World Trade Center; a fourth never made it to its target. The Twin Towers of the World Trade Center collapsed, leaving thousands dead in its wake. Following this, the United States gained a new level of consensus about both foreign and domestic policy. Fighting terrorism became the government's primary concern, and even reviving the stagnating economy paled in comparison. Defense spending soared, and a once substantial budget surplus quickly disappeared. With this, U.S. interest in benign Latin American neighbors— far from Afghanistan or any other countries seen as partially or potentially culpable for terrorism against the United States—diminished considerably. If before, post–Cold War U.S. foreign policy had seemed somewhat without direction, now the focus had become all too clear.

Developments in Argentina were no less dramatic. The U.S. slow-down seemed mild indeed compared to Argentina's years-long recession, complete with double-digit unemployment. As the De la Rúa government floundered, trying unsuccessfully to escape the monetary prison born of Domingo Cavallo's once miraculous convertibility plan, the country exploded in violence. Riots broke out, both in Buenos Aires and provincial towns, with supermarket looting by poor and unemployed Argentines, and a rampage of destruction from many others who had become furious and exasperated with the government's policies.

On December 20, 2001, De la Rúa abruptly resigned, and the economic crisis immediately merged with an equally profound political crisis. None could, or would, govern this apparently ungovernable country. Between De la Rúa's resignation and the beginning of the new year, three different men were named president, none of whom would govern more than a few days. Finally, the Peronists—the majority party in Congress—settled on Eduardo Duhalde, a well-known political leader, to (hopefully) fill the remainder of De la Rúa's term, with new elections to be held in 2003. The new president's mandate was clear: fix the economy and restore security in the country, and quickly.

Nevertheless, these new challenges could not entirely erase the progress that had occurred in Argentine-U.S. relations during the 1990s. Relations between these countries were never as close and intense as during this period. From the Argentine side, a fluctuating combination of necessity, conviction, audacity, opportunity, and opportunism gave way to a foreign policy that placed the country throughout the decade as the United States' most solicitous ally in Latin America. Furthermore, Argentina's past hostility toward Washington, D.C., to which Peronism had certainly contributed, and the more recent history of domestic political and economic stability, convinced the government of Carlos Menem that constructing a linkage based on mutual confidence imposed the burden of proof on Argentina. Furthermore, it was considered necessary to demonstrate ostentatiously that this will to change was authentic. The aspiration to maintain "carnal relations" with Washington, at the level of discourse, and the decision to send ships to the Gulf War, in practice, were the most forceful expressions of this perceived need to demonstrate the new foreign policy to the United States.

These exaggerated gestures toward Washington, as Minister of Foreign Affairs Guido Di Tella described them himself, helped delineate a new paradigm of foreign policy, but cannot themselves be considered paradigmatic. To fairly assess the elements in the new pattern of bilateral relations established by the Menem government, it is necessary to leave aside these particular gestures. At its most basic level, this model constituted a response to a new world situation—globalization, and the post–Cold War era—and a new domestic situation, democratization, and the final crisis in a internally oriented development strategy. It presumed, to use the words of President Fernando De la Rúa's Minister of Foreign Affairs, that "the best interests of the United States are analogous to those of Argentina."[1] Nonetheless, this does not imply that Argentina would follow a policy of automatic alignment, due to differences on particular questions that are unavoidable in an intense relationship.

This mode of linkage with the United States emanated from a focus on convergences between the two countries, including values, common viewpoints, and objectives, and was sustained by an unprecedented degree of institutionalization at multilateral, hemispheric, and bilateral levels. In the bilateral arena, during the

Menem era, Argentina signed fifty-seven accords with the United States, a considerable statistic if compared to the scarcely one hundred nineteen agreements the two countries had subscribed to during the prior 136 years.[2] The agreements of the 1990s included a wide range of issues, such as counternarcotics and counterterrorism, defense, exchanges of military personnel, transfer and protection of strategic technology, peaceful use of nuclear energy, civilian use of space, air transport, commerce development, reciprocal promotion and protection of investments, environmental protection, development of tourism, management and protection of national parks, public health, and education.

As the prior chapters have demonstrated, the Menem government did not automatically adhere to the wishes and interests of Washington. The very idea of "carnal relations" and Menem's inclination to systematically support the United States in different global and regional causes tended to obscure the differences that arose on various themes, in both the bilateral and multilateral arenas. Argentina frequently concurred with the United States due to common interests and conviction. In smaller measure, Argentina also did so for reasons of complacency, submissiveness, or opportunism. This was principally due to Menem's personal style, following which Argentina tended to be "more Catholic than the Pope" on certain issues, for example, issuing fiery critiques of Fidel Castro's government. Menem's declarations toward the end of his administration—soon moderated—that Argentina was prepared to send troops to intervene in Colombia's internal war or that it would quickly dollarize the economy offered further evidence of his approach. At the same time, Argentina maintained distinct or even opposing positions to those of the United States in a wide range of areas. These ranged from agricultural subsidies, intellectual property rights and methods of negotiation in the World Trade Organization and the proposed Free Trade Area of the Americas, to Argentina's rejection of the United States' Helms-Burton Law,[3] the level of autonomy of the International Penal Court, the United States' unilateral "certification" on narcotics trafficking, and human rights in China and Iran.

This situation, which combined close relations with numerous differences, invites a more nuanced contemplation of the standard international relations' concept of autonomy, especially in Latin America. The level of autonomy of a Latin-American country vis-à-vis the United States tends to be evaluated based on the extent to which this country opposes Washington's preferences. As a first step in another direction, the Menem government proposed defining autonomy in terms of the relative costs to a weak country of opposing or confronting a powerful state. Thus, Carlos Escudé indicates "It is necessary to know how to distinguish between autonomy in itself, and the use which is given to this. At the same time, this use can be conceived as the *inversion of autonomy*, when it aims (correctly or not) to nourish the base of power or well-being of the country, or as the *simple consumption of autonomy,* when it aims toward the exhibitionist demonstration that one is not under the tutelage of anyone."[4]

Following this, if autonomy is defined (and measured) as a country's capacity to determine its own national interest without foreign interference, and to put in practice policies serving its own interests (in the sense of the "inversion of autonomy"), then it is insignificant whether or not these policies coincide with the interests of the United States or other countries. Rather, a high level of autonomy could converge with a high level of agreement with the United States. Once again, it is not the high or low level of opposition or confrontation that characterizes autonomy, but the capacity to establish or execute policies that best serve the national interest, in accordance with how each government may define that.

With globalization and the end of the Cold War, expanding national autonomy would not easily result from policies of isolation, self-sufficiency, and low involvement in cooperative arrangements and international regimes. Rather, autonomy should be construed "within a context of relations more than in opposition to them."[5] As Celso Lafer indicates, referring to the new challenges in Brazil's foreign policy, "if the country was previously able to construct, with reasonable success, its possible degree of autonomy through a relative distancing from the world, then at the turn of the millenium this autonomy, necessary for development, can only be achieved through active participation in the elaboration of norms and codes of conduct for the governance of world order."[6]

According to this perspective, the relationship between the Menem government and the United States should not be seen as simply "alignment," which encompasses the idea of renouncing autonomy in the traditional sense. Instead, it should be seen as seeking a "pragmatic accommodation" to a new internal and international context, aided and sustained by a system of beliefs that emphasized the shared values between Argentina and the West, and flavored with strong elements of audacity and opportunism. In many themes in the bilateral, hemispheric, and multilateral agenda, Argentina acted on its own convictions and worked with the United States—not for the United States—in order to achieve or defend shared objectives.

The idea of finding a modus vivendi with the United States functional to Argentina's interests—particularly economic—was by no means novel, although it had never taken the shape it did during the Menem years. In the Cold War era, this reached its pinnacle during the governments of Arturo Frondizi and Raúl Alfonsín. Both constructed substantially similar conceptual schemes that separated the "basic consensus" on values from the "instrumental differences" for realizing it. In the two cases, the objective was to demonstrate that the inevitable divergences of the bilateral relationship did not touch—or at least *should* not touch—fundamental questions that constituted the permanent base of the U.S.-Argentine relationship. The Menem government deepened this approach, taking advantage of the opportunities offered by the end of the Cold War, economic and financial globalization, and a democratic process that—unlike in Frondizi's and Alfonsin's governments—had begun to show unequivocal signs of consolidation by the time the administration took office. Menem's recognized pragmatism and political sense led him almost instinctively to opt for a particular form of "bandwagoning" with the United States that was contrary both to his own history and that of his party. Other governmental actors and some academics, more sophisticated than the president, took charge of giving this policy approach its intellectual support.

Without recognizing it, the route chosen largely followed that laid out in the two prior periods mentioned. Its detractors also failed to perceive these common elements. Thus, the relationship with the United States again came to be seen as having two distinct levels. At one level could be seen the macrorelationship, which required constructing a general framework of fundamental agreements and in turn necessitated eliminating the "useless confrontations" with Washington. At a second level, the microrelationship involved the multiple interactions between public and private actors of the two countries in which authentic interests come into play and, consequently, where concessions cannot be made.[7]

This scheme helps explain a substantial part of Menem's foreign policy toward the United States, especially during his second administration when the exaggerated gestures waned. In Di Tella's words, "In the beginning, we needed to affirm clearly and categorically our alignment with the West, but this period has passed. Now we can criticize the United States."[8] Menem's dramatic gestures shortly before the conclusion of his administration, such as the failed attempt to enhance ties with NATO in July 1999, had little to do with those of the period referred to by Di Tella. Instead, these were decayed expressions of the original scheme, peculiar to the end of the period and oriented toward an eventual return to government in 2003.

The effect of the initial gestures and those during the degenerative phase, the continual exhibitionism and opportunism of the president and the diplomatic style of his government veiled the fact that the U.S.-Argentine relationship in the 1990s in many respects followed a general tendency in Latin America of greater approximation to the United States. The impact of Argentina's policy change, however, was stronger than in any other case due to its source (a country that had traditionally been a rival, and was governed by Peronism), and because of the extreme form in which it was implemented. Even more important, these factors also obscured the level of consensus forged among Argentina's leadership since 1983 regarding the mode of relating to the United States. A careful analysis of the debate in the 1990s regarding U.S.-Argentine relations reveals widespread agreement that Argentina needed to maintain a strong relationship with the United States.

This agreement is the product of both experience and necessity. Most Argentines, to one degree or another, experienced during the past twenty-five years a process of "social learning" nourished by state terrorism, the Malvinas/Falklands War and hyperinflation. In the specific case of Menem's government, the good and

**Table 6.1**

**Evaluations of Menem's performance in different policy areas, rated from 1 to 10.**

| Policy Area | Average rating |
| --- | --- |
| Argentina's relations with the world | 6.4 |
| Inflation | 6.1 |
| Civil liberties | 5.4 |
| Housing | 4.8 |
| Economy | 4.7 |
| Education | 4.4 |
| Health | 4.3 |
| Standard of living of Argentines | 4.0 |
| Justice | 3.6 |
| Work | 3.3 |
| Security/Crime | 3.0 |
| Corruption | 2.8 |

*Source*: Gallup Polls, *La Nación*, July 4, 1999, 5.

bad experiences of the first phase of the transition to democracy can be added to this. This "social learning" contributed to more open and less ideological attitudes and a better understanding of the country's place within the international system, and perhaps stopped Argentines from overestimating the country's capabilities.

Certainly Menem's government contributed to the construction of consensus because of the various measures that resulted in reducing the scope of the debate. The government produced cultural shocks, confronted head on a series of taboo themes (such as the ratification of the Treaty of Tlatelolco and adhering to the Non-Proliferation Treaty) and embarked on paths with no return (such as deactivating the Condor II missile project). In this way the government attacked the core of many issues until then considered untouchable, actions that had a decisive impact on the relationship with the United States. Recognizing that these policies had merit in themselves, it is nonetheless the case that the end of the Cold War strongly influenced adopting some of these decisions.

Necessity also played a fundamental role in narrowing the scope of the domestic debate regarding relations with the United States. Few disputed that overcoming Argentina's serious economic problems, within a context of economic opening and an increasingly globalized economy, required a high level of political and economic accord with the United States and the West as a whole. This was true both when Menem took office and at the beginning of Fernando De la Rúa's presidency, and became even more evident at the inception of Peronist Eduardo Duhalde's transition government, which took office on January 1, 2002 in a context marked by a grave political, economic and social crisis, precipitated by the December 20th resignation of President De la Rúa. In his first written communication to President Bush, the new Argentine executive, after reaffirming "the fundamental principles and values that inspire our two democracies" solicited rapid financial aid from the United States, in coordination with the countries of the Group of Seven.[9]

Practical reasons also explain the changes that occurred in Argentine public opinion during the 1990s regarding the countries with which Argentina should expand ties. From the beginning of the decade, with an agenda largely dominated by economic issues, most Argentines placed the developed countries at the top of their list of preferred partners, and put the United States in first place.[10] The economic and technological benefits that these countries could offer Argentina clearly influenced these preferences. Beginning in 1996, with the first commercial successes from Mercosur, interest in regional integration increased, but not sufficiently to detract from support for a broad international opening and, especially, for ties to the West. In a 1998 poll regarding which countries Argentina should look to for the closest relations, Brazil and the United States occupied the first and second places, with 51 percent and 34 percent of support, respectively[11]. In January 2002, following the crisis that brought down the De la Rúa government, a survey carried out by Gallup Argentina revealed that 70% of Argentines surveyed considered it "very" or "fairly important" for Argentina to maintain good relations with the United States, while 59% thought the country needed financial help from Washington.[12] Respondents indicated that the countries they expected to aid Argentina's government most in the immediate future were Spain (47%), followed by Brazil (40%) and, in third place, the United States (33%).[13] Thus, maintaining close and cooperative relations with the United States remained a priority for Argentines, as it had during Menem's presidency.

Throughout Menem's administration, foreign policy turned out to be the policy area that garnered the highest public opinion ratings (see table 6.1). According to a Gallup poll carried out in the first half of 1999, respondents gave Argentina's relations with the world an average rating of 6.4 on a scale of 10. This was followed closely by control of inflation, which achieved a score of 6.1.[14] Toward the end of Menem's presidency, 44 percent of those surveyed still gave a positive evaluation of his foreign policy over the course of his administration.[15] This positive evaluation is another interesting demonstration of the extent of consensus regarding relations with the United States. This consensus also included the deepening and expansion of Mercosur within a scheme of open regionalism, Argentina's progressive opening to international trade, and the creation of a political and economic association between Mercosur and the European Union that includes the gradual liberalization of trade.

The consolidation of international ties with the United States was naturally accompanied by a considerable expansion of contacts and interactions between the civil societies of the two countries. Bilateral trade and U.S. investments in Argentina reached unprecedented magnitudes. Politicians and legislators exchanged visits, becoming more familiar with each other's countries. As Marc Falcoff writes, " for the first time in all its history, Argentina enjoys contact and access to the two parties."[16] In addition, relations with nongovernmental organizations were strengthened in the area of human rights, environmental protection, promotion of democratic values, transparency of public administration, education, and citizen responsibility. Cultural and academic ties were also strengthened; in 1999, as many as 3,500 Argentine students could be found in the United States (54.8 percent at the postgraduate level, 34.5 percent in college, and 10.8 percent carrying out other studies).[17] Scholarship funds from the Fulbright Commission quadrupled between 1991 ($1,018,996 for 67 students) and 2000 ($3, 756, 398 for 207 students).[18] Furthermore, several Argentine universities established agreements with U.S. universities for cooperation at the undergraduate and graduate levels that allowed regular exchanges of professors and students from these countries. Finally, around 500,000 Argentines traveled to the United States in 1997, primarily visiting the states of California and Florida, and the cities of Chicago, Las Vegas, New York, and Washington, D.C. From the other side, U.S. travelers visiting Argentina increased from 110,050 in 1990 to 375,046 in 1997, and spent around $739,000,000 in the latter year.[19]

This varied combination of links between private actors gave the relationship between the United States and Argentina a density and complexity never before reached, although still far from the levels recorded by countries such as Mexico and Brazil. The size and quality of this societal support base is one of the fundamental elements in considering the likely future of the relationship and anticipating opportunities and obstacles. Yet, these linkages also seem likely to pose some difficulties for the government. The strong pressures that private groups from both countries exercise over the Argentine government on two of the issues of greatest concern to the United States regarding trade with Argentina—intellectual property and the agreement on "open skies"—constitutes the clearest example of the growing weight of nongovernmental interests in determining government policies at the "micro" level of the relationship.

A second key point regarding the future of the relationship concerns the two countries' foreign policies. This is a theme that has provoked considerable anxiety both within and outside of Argentina: the extent to which the Menem government's foreign policy model—specifically, the extensive ties to the United States—could be sustained. The question became particularly salient after both countries elected new presidents, Argentina in 1999, and the United States in 2000. In both cases, not only were these leaders different from those who had initiated the period of friendship, but they also represented different political parties.

The question became even more important following the abrupt conclusion of the De la Rúa government, which generated fears in the United States regarding the possibility of a reversal in Argentine policies. Those in Washington worried that incoming Peronists might lean towards more populist international positions, thereby abandoning the market line in favor of protectionist solutions.

In the case of the De la Rúa government, this uncertainty was rapidly cleared up. A few days after taking over as Minister of Foreign Relations, Adalberto Rodríguez Giavarini declared, "We not only want to maintain the optimal level of the relationship with the United States, but increase it."[20] Faithful to these words, he put into practice a policy toward Washington that followed almost to the letter the premises of the paradigm initiated by Menem, although the President and his Minister of Foreign Relations had to face considerable criticism from within their own ranks, especially from the Radical party. The new government exhibited a voting profile in the United Nations similar to Menem's final years, cooperated closely with the United States in defense and the promotion of democracy in Latin America and continued to condemn Cuba on human rights issues. De la Rúa also acted as a loyal ally to the United States following the September 11th terrorist attacks, even offering in December 2001 to send troops to participate in the peace-keeping forces designed to sustain the new Afghan government.[21] This was all carried out in a much more sober and discreet style than Menem's, as audacious gestures were not characteristic of De la Rúa. In his words, "We have an excellent relationship with the United States, mature, affectionate and trusting. Only the word alignment does not fit."[22] In sum, the relationship fit within the framework laid by Menem, but without the drama.

On the other hand, upon taking charge of government, De la Rúa reaffirmed the importance of Mercosur for regional growth, and his minister of foreign relations, Adalberto Rodríguez Giavarini, spoke of the necessity of strengthening ties with Europe. This reflected the government's decision to further diversify Argentina's foreign relations in a context of a greater global diffusion of power.[23] Yet these declarations did not indicate an intent to qualitatively alter the place that the United States occupied within the country's external priorities.

With respect to both Mercosur and the relationship with Europe, more continuity than change occurred. The Menem government developed an active foreign policy toward Europe, producing important advances that, again, were obscured by the policies toward the United States. The failures and lack of success in many areas had more to do with European policies than with disinterest or ineptitude on the part of Argentine diplomats.[24] For its part, Mercosur experienced various vicissitudes, for both internal and external reasons. Its two primary partners, Argentina and Brazil, shared responsibility for both the advances and declines. Undoubtedly, the diplomatic style of the Menem government did not help create the confidence that a process of regional integration requires. As Lucio García del

Solar points out, "the episode of the "non-NATO" bestowal would not have stung our neighbors so much if it were not preceded by sensitivity provoked by our "carnal" relations with the United States. It is the impression of the Latin American governments in general that Argentina tends, when it can, to go off on its own and that it looks at the world through Washington's eyes; and if, to be sure, its solidarity with members of Mercosur is reasonably present with regard to economic objectives, the same does not occur in the political sphere."[25] This reading, voiced by Argentina's ambassador to Washington during the Alfonsín government, was shared by President De la Rúa and his government team. Thus, after taking office, the new authorities demonstrated their intent to relaunch Mercosur, smooth the mechanisms of policy coordination with Brazil, and take some measures to counteract the negative impact of Menem's postures on the confidence of Argentina's neighbors. Nevertheless, the De la Rúa administration coincided with the period of Mercosur's stagnation, which, though originating in 1997, intensified following the January 1999 Brazilian devaluation. From the Argentine side, this was aggravated by serious problems of governability, an acute economic recession of more than three years, and Minister of Economy Cavallo's ambivalence, if not opposition, toward the regional integration project. Despite these problems, in the June 2001 meeting of Mercosur presidents, carried out in Asunción, Paraguay, Argentina and Brazil's presidents reiterated Mercosur's strategic importance for their respective countries, and made a commitment to negotiate as a bloc with the United States and the European Union.

The Clinton administration, for its part, celebrated the transition from Menem to De la Rúa, in that it also implied alternating the political party in government. Menem's attempts to achieve a second reelection would never have received U.S. approval. If the United States did value the role carried out by the ex-President in strengthening the bilateral relationship and as an ally, U.S. leaders nonetheless perceived the presidential change as a necessary condition for the consolidation of democracy in Argentina. Following De la Rúa's triumph, President Bill Clinton expressed, in a friendly communication, his desire to "deepen the association" between the two countries and, furthermore, qualified the presidential elections as "a model of civic participation and testimony to the force of democracy in Argentina."[26]

It is worth emphasizing that the elections of October 1999 occupied little space in U.S. newspapers. Neither did the elections trigger much interest among North American officials responsible for Latin America or in the relevant academic circles. At the same time, neither of Argentina's principal presidential candidates felt it necessary to visit Washington and to establish contacts with North American officials and politicians during the campaign.[27] The relationship with the United States was also absent from the debate between the candidates, since it is not a theme that divided Argentines or that could help capture votes; its absence in the debates constitutes a particularly striking example of the consensus indicated above.

These points are not minor. The absence of interest in public and private North American arenas in the Argentine elections, which were characterized as "boring" in both countries, was good news. The greater interest of other periods was defined in essentially negative terms due to the uncertainties and perplexity of a country marked by long years of violence and political and economic instability, a situation that unfortunately returned in a serious form toward the end of 2001. At the same time, the lack of interest in the elections demonstrated that the United States correctly expected the new Argentine government to differ more in style than in substance from its predecessor.

At the time, the Clinton administration perceived De la Rúa as a less solicitous ally than Menem, but perhaps much more reliable with respect to certain U.S. priorities in Latin America on which the ex-President was not graded as highly: juridical security, governmental transparency, and combatting corruption. These themes, along with the battle against unemployment—which reached 13.8 percent in Argentina in October 1999[28]—constituted the core of the Alliance's electoral campaign and the primary reason for its victory of 48.5 percent of the votes, in contrast to 38.1 percent for Peronism and 10.1 percent from Acción por la República (Action for the Republic), the party led by Domingo Cavallo.

Formed by the union of Radicalism and a center-left front known as FREPASO (Frente País Solidario), the Alliance incarnated better than Peronism—spent after ten years in government—the citizens' expectations for answers to the major issues of concern since the mid-1990s. These included unemployment, control of corruption, and a change in the style of carrying out politics toward more balanced power, austerity, transparency, clear respect for institutions and democratic methods. Of course, the Argentine political agenda also included other, equally far-reaching themes, such as reclaiming greater social equality and reformulating the role of the state on issues of education, health, justice, and security.

As explained in the preceding chapters, the Menem government carried out important reforms of the economy and public administration that were indispensable, but also very difficult to actualize in practice. At the same time, the government managed to defeat the great scourge of many decades—inflation. This is a merit that the great majority of Argentines recognizes. Nonetheless, the Menem administration was unable to avoid the undesirable effects of these reforms, which emerged in a painful and brutal form in terms of insecurity and social exclusion. As Susana Torrado points out, "The extremely high unemployment, the shrinking of real salaries and the regressive distribution of income induced never-before known levels of critical poverty: the number of poor people (the population whose incomes do not suffice to buy a basket of basic goods and services at minimum cost) went from 21.5% in 1991, shrank significantly in the initial years following convertability, began to increase suddenly in 1995 to end close to 26 percent in 1998. The volume of indigents (those whose incomes do not suffice even to cover the costs of food) jumped from 3 percent to 7 percent, between the first and last years."[29]

Within this context, most Argentines saw in the Alliance an important opportunity not only to bring fresh air into Argentine politics, but also to overcome the negative legacies of the Menem government. Thus, on December 10, 1999, 71.6 percent of Argentines believed that there would be less corruption, 61.2 percent that there would be more work and 58.2 percent that there would be more security.[30]

Unfortunately, these hopes were quickly frustrated. The electoral coalition that permitted the victory over Peronism failed to transform itself into an effective government coalition. The miscommunications and disputes at its center culminated in the resignation of Vice-President Carlos "Chacho" Alvarez in October 2000, as a result of his poor relationship with the President and a series of scandals that jolted the Argentine Senate, having to do with well-founded suspicions of bribes from a sector of the executive to various Senators in exchange for their support for a questioned labor law.[31] The fracture of the Alliance, which fell apart following Vice President Alvarez's resignation, generated a growing crisis of governability that, of course, had a negative impact on the country's economy, deepening the crisis. Within this context, in March 2001, President De la Rúa named Domingo Cavallo as his Minister of Economy, since the latter was perceived both within and outside of the country as the only storm pilot capable of rescuing the country from its economic stagnation and of reversing the distinctly pessimistic expectations of Argentine society. With Cavallo's appointment, a new government coalition was created; from then on, the President tied his fortune to that of his Minister of Economy who, just as during the Menem years, obtained extraordinary powers for managing the country's economy. Nevertheless, this time he could not escape gracefully from the government's increasingly difficult situation. The back-and-forth policy shifts on economic issues, the president's slow and vacillating style, and his own party's lack of support and even opposition contributed to gloomy visions of Argentina's future by those both within and outside of the country.

To make things worse, two external factors acted against De la Rúa's government. First, Brazil's 1999 devaluation hit Argentina's economy hard. As Pastor and Wise point out, "In contrast to the Mexican, Asian, and Russian crises, the Brazilian devaluation hit Argentina not through its financial flows but through trade."[32] The fact that the Argentine peso was pegged to the dollar meant that the majority of Argentina's products were too expensive for the country's Mercosur partners as well as for the rest of the world, sinking the country further into recession. The Argentine economy was also incapable of increasing its competitiveness through a significant increase in efficiency and productivity.

The second key negative external factor for the De la Rúa government was the model introduced by the George W. Bush administration regarding rescuing emerging nations in situations of economic crisis. Geared toward promoting a more prudent use of the IMF's resources, this new vision held that the international community should not always divert large scale financing to countries that cannot resolve their own problems.

To its misfortune, Argentina went from being an example of the economic reforms that the United States had promoted in Latin America during the 1990s, to a test case of this new policy. After having supported important aid packages to Argentina through the multilateral credit organizations, in December 2001, the United States government decided to lower the boom on the country by opposing the IMF's distribution of a previously agreed upon disbursement of 1,264 million dollars. Washington's reading was that the costs for North-American interests would be small, there would not be a contagion effect on other emerging nations, especially on neighboring countries of the Southern Cone, and that the markets already considered the cessation of payments and a devaluation inevitable for Argentina.

In this way, a potentially explosive situation began growing, which combined domestic political weakness and a lack of external support with depression, deflation, hyper-unemployment (20 percent of the active population), extreme poverty (14 million people), high external debt (142,000 million dollars), a combined national and provincial fiscal deficit that reached 16,500 million dollars in 2001, and a country risk rate that surpassed 4,000 points.[33] Cavallo's decision, supported by the president, to freeze salaries and Argentines' savings deposits in the banks, in order to avoid major capital flight, was the trigger for the final social explosion toward the end of December, which finished the Alliance government in a painful and bloody manner. The convertibility plan was also terminated and Argentina, finally, fell into default.

With the majority in the Senate and the House of Deputies, the Peronists regained control of the national government. In a strange twist of history, Eduardo Duhalde inherited the remainder of the governmental term—until December 2003—from the man who defeated him in the 1999 elections. In accordance with the Argentine Constitution, he was elected by the two Houses of Congress, with strong support from a Peronist-Radical coalition, with 262 votes in favor, 21 against, and 18 abstentions.[34]

This strong support is simultaneously Duhalde's greatest strength and his greatest weakness, given that he comes from a political class profoundly rejected by the Argentine people. This rejection has its immediate antecedents in the high percentage of blank and null votes characterizing the legislative elections of

October 14, 2001, known as the "anger vote" in Argentina. The social explosion at the end of December and the spontaneous empty pot protests, in which protesters banged on empty pots to indicate frustration with the economy and a political class perceived as corrupt and inefficient, constituted the most striking expression of the end of a political cycle. Demands were not limited to asking for the end of De la Rúa's government, but also for the end of the vices and abuses by the overall political leadership. Thus, Argentina faces complex challenges of gigantic dimensions. In the short term, the government must restore public order, reform the political system, put the economy in motion and recover internal and external confidence.

The crisis of December 2001 has left various important lessons that are key in considering the future course of Argentine-U.S. relations and, more generally, Argentina's foreign policy and its priorities in foreign relations. First, Argentina will undoubtedly seek a new equilibrium between policies inclined toward the country's greater integration into the world, something that is perceived as inevitable, and those which would seek to protect Argentina from the negative effects of globalization, without reverting to anachronistic protectionist or statist prescriptions.

In contrast to the end of the 19th century, when Argentina successfully opened its economy to the world under the wing of Great Britain, most Argentines consider the country's return to the world scene in the 1990s, in this new phase of globalization, to be a failure. This perception may not lead to a predominance of antiglobalist postures, but neither does it leave space for policies of unconditional adhesion to the neoliberal principles sustaining the "Washington consensus."

In second place, the search for this new equilibrium seems likely to be accompanied by greater diversification in foreign relations and an increase in the relative importance of the strategic alliance with Brazil, within the scope of Mercosur. The political and security alliance with the United States, often charged with excessiveness, did not save the country from default and created a world of jealousy and intrigue with respect to Brazil. Market and political reasons led Argentina to revive its ties to South America's largest country. The end of dollarization and the devaluation—two big measures applauded in Brasilia—opened up the possibility for Mercosur to progress in the medium term toward a common currency, following the example of the European Union. Furthermore, the upcoming tough negotiations with the United States to create the Free Trade Area of the Americas should naturally unite Argentina and Brazil's negotiating positions with respect to the United States, on the basis of strong shared interests.

Third, and this is a repeated lesson, there is an enormous difference between being a friend and ally of the United States, and being a country that falls within the sphere of Washington's vital interests. The Bush government allowed Argentina to fall because the country has neither the economic importance of

Mexico nor the strategic importance of Turkey. This decision has helped Argentines to understand better their country's place within the United States' hierarchy of foreign interests, and the limits of the alliance shaped in the 1990s. At the same time, this enlightenment has encouraged Argentines to reconsider their own hierarchy of interests.

Nevertheless, it seems unlikely that Argentina would regress to the confrontational positions of other eras, described in the previous chapters. More than in any other phase of its history, the country needs the economic support of the United States, especially its favorable vote in the multilateral credit organizations. The first economic program launched by the Duhalde government in February 2002 was formulated elbow to elbow with officials from the International Monetary Fund, under the close watch of the United States Treasury.

Certainly, the bond with the United States surpassed considerably the scope of mere economic necessities. There are shared principles, values and interests that continue uniting the two countries and that constitute a fundamental pillar in the bilateral relationship. One point worth emphasizing is that Argentina survived one of its most grave and intense crises without democracy coming into question. In the words of Natalio Botana, "Nobody, for now, questions out loud the legitimacy of the democratic Republic. What are, in fact, questioned are those who represent this legitimacy, not its constitutional principle. This is small consolation in the midst of the disaster."[35] In place of the coup d'etats of other periods, the country experienced what has been called a "civil coup" within which no anti-American slogans have stood out.[36] The major demands and complaints were directed toward the inside the country.

The relationship with the United States, the most powerful country in the region and the world, continues to be essential for Argentina. Although far from "carnal relations," the country seems likely to maintain close relations with Washington. Overall, the level of convergence reached in the bilateral relations is lodged in common values and long-range interests that should resist the challenges from complex and difficult situations. Within the U.S.-Argentine agenda there is no matter of a political-strategic nature that could translate into the kind of major conflicts produced during the Cold War years. The traditional economic themes (tariffs, export subsidies, open markets) and other newer issues (formation of the Free Trade Area of the Americas, protection of intellectual property, copyrights, trademarks, the Open Skies agreement) may give rise to differences, but do not threaten the general framework of the bilateral relationship. With respect to the new themes in the negative agenda of the United States in the regions—such as corruption, environment, narcotics trafficking, and citizen security—the two countries seem to be on the same track, or at least fairly close.

In a work from September 1941 entitled "Speaking of the United States to the Argentines," Federico Pinedo indicated that the estrangement that existed between the two countries, "more than deliberate acts of men, came from real circumstances that had in their time an invincible force."[29] Although Pinedo himself advocated closer relations with the United States, he found little support for this position among the Argentine elites. Furthermore, as this book has demonstrated, the circumstances at the time did little to facilitate closer relations between both parties. Only as recently as the early 1980s, with the recuperation of democracy, and finally in the 1990s, with the end of the Cold War and the expansion and deepening of regionalism, did Argentina have the opportunity and will to define an essential part of its national interests in the terms proposed by Pinedo some five decades earlier. With this redefinition, the historical oscillations and rivalries became part of a past to which it would be difficult to return.

## INTRODUCTION

1. See Deborah Norden, *Military Rebellion in Argentina: Between Coups and Consolidation* (Lincoln: University of Nebraska Press, 1996).

2. Guillermo O'Donnell, "Delegative Democracy," *Journal of Democracy* 5, no. 3 (July 1994), 55–69.

3. "Cuarenta pasos más cerca de Washington," *Clarín* (October 30, 1991), 13.

4. Import-substituting industrialization was a popular development program in Latin America beginning in the mid-1900s. Countries following this model set up protectionist barriers (i.e. tariffs) to protect infant industries while importing the capital goods required by those industries. The goal was to gradually move from producing consumer goods to developing a deeper level of industrialization, at which point manufacturing equipment would also be domestically produced. Such policies proved problematic, however, in that countries tended to acquire enormous debt, and the newly manufactured goods were rarely competitive on the international market.

5. Inflation based on the consumer price index, from Felipe A. M. de la Balze, *Remaking the Argentine Economy* (New York: Council on Foreign Relations, 1995), 71.

6. In early 2001, Menem's former Minister of Economy, Domingo Cavallo—subsequently Minister of Economy to De la Rúa, began exploring means of pegging the peso simultaneously to the dollar and the Euro.

7. Francis Fukuyama, "The End of History?" *The National Interest* 16 (summer 1989), 3.

## CHAPTER I: AUTONOMOUS ARGENTINA

1. Carlos Escudé, *Patología del nacionalismo: El caso argentino* (Buenos Aires: Instituto Torcuato di Tella, 1987), 11.

2. Joseph Tulchin, *Argentina and the United States: A Conflicted Relationship* (Boston: Twayne, 1990), 3.

3. Thomas McGann, *Argentina, the United States, and the Inter-American System, 1880–1914* (Cambridge: Harvard University Press, 1957), 85.

4. Ibid.

5. Arturo O'Connell, "La fiebre aftosa, el embargo sanitario norteamericano contra las importaciones de carne y el triángulo Argentina-Gran Bretaña-Estados Unidos en el período entre las dos guerras mundiales," *Desarrollo Económico* 26, no. 101 (1986), 21.

6. Quoted in Peter H. Smith, *Talons of the Eagle: Dynamics of U.S.-Latin American Relations* (New York and Oxford: Oxford University Press, 1996), 20.

7. Tulchin, *Argentina and the United States*, 8.

8. Armando Alonso Piñeiro, *La trama de los 5.000 Días: Orígenes de las relaciones argentino-norteamericanos* (Buenos Aires: Ediciones Depalma, 1986), 144–45.

9. Tulchin, *Argentina and the United States*, 9.

10. Andrés Cisneros and Carlos Escudé, ed. *Historia general de las relaciones exteriores de la República Argentina*, part 2, vol. 8, *Las relaciones exteriores de la Argentina consolidada, 1881–1943: Las relaciones con Europa y los Estados Unidos, 1881–1930* (Buenos Aires: Grupo Editor Latinoamericano, 1999), 19–20.

11. Quoted in Smith, *Talons of the Eagle*, 99.

12. Smith, *Talons of the Eagle*, 99.

13. McGann, *Argentina, the United States, and the Inter-American System*, 70.

14. Andrew Hurrell, "Regionalism in the Americas," in *Latin America in a New World*, ed. Abraham Lowenthal and Gregory Treverton (Boulder: Westview Press, 1994), 168.

15. Cisneros and Escudé, *Las relaciones con Europa y los Estados Unidos, 1881–1930*, 64–67.

16. Carlos Escudé, *Realismo Periférico: Fundamentos para la nueva política exterior argentina* (Buenos Aires: Grupo Editorial Planeta, 1992), 241.

17. McGann, *Argentina, the United States, and the Inter-American System*, 75.

18. Escudé, *Realismo Periférico*, 241.

19. Yrigoyen was first elected in 1916, benefitting from the 1912 Saénz Peña electoral law. He was reelected in 1928, but many perceived him to be too senile to govern effectively at this point.

20. David Rock, *Argentina, 1516–1987: From Spanish Colonization to Alfonsín* (Berkeley and Los Angeles: University of California Press, 1987), 217.

21. General José Uriburu, the first president in this regime, did favor a more closed, corporatist approach. However, this sector lost influence when coup leader Uriburu was overthrown in 1932. See David Rock, *Authoritarian Argentina: The Nationalist Movement, Its History and Its Impact* (Berkeley and Los Angeles: University of Cali-

fornia Press, 1993), 92–94. Sympathies for corporatism would remain in the army, however, to be developed more fully during the Peronist years.

22. José Paradiso, *Debates y trayectoria de la política exterior argentina* (Buenos Aires: Grupo Editor Latinoamericano, 1993), 82; and Rock, *Argentina 1516–1987*, 224–25.

23. Andrés Cisneros and Carlos Escudé, ed., *Historia General de las Relaciones Exteriores de la República Argentina*, part 2, *Las Relaciones Exteriores de la Argentina Consolidada, 1881–1943*, vol. 9, *Las Relaciones Exteriores, 1930–1943* (Buenos Aires: Grupo Editor Latinoamericano, 1999), 213–24.

24. Alberto Conil Paz and Gustavo Ferrari, *Politica Exterior Argentina, 1930–1962* (Buenos Aires: Editorial Huemul, 1964), 41.

25. See Harold F. Peterson, *Argentina and the United States, 1810–1960* (Albany: State University of New York Press, 1964). In 1936, Carlos Saavedra Lamas was awarded the Nobel Peace Prize for his role in mediating the Paraguay-Bolivia conflict.

26. Mario Rapoport, *Aliados o Neutrales: La Argentina frente a la Segunda Guerra Mundial* (Buenos Aires: Editorial Universitaria de Buenos Aires, 1988), 16.

27. Michael Francis, *The Limits of Hegemony: United States Relations with Argentina and Chile during World War II* (Notre Dame, Ind.: University of Notre Dame Press, 1977), 59.

28. Carlos Escudé, "U.S. Political Destabilisation and Economic Boycott of Argentina during the 1940s," in *Argentina between the Great Powers, 1939–46*, ed. Guido Di Tella and D. Cameron Watt (Pittsburgh: University of Pittsburgh Press, 1990), 58.

29. Andrés Cisneros and Carlos Escudé, et al., *Las Relaciones Exteriores, 1930–1943*, 250.

30. Quoted in Rapoport, *Aliados o Neutrales*, 16.

31. Ronald Newton, "Disorderly Succession: Great Britain, the United States and the 'Nazi Menace' in Argentina, 1938–1947," in *Argentina between the Great Powers, 1939–46*, ed. Guido Di Tella and D. Cameron Watt (Pittsburgh: University of Pittsburgh Press, 1990), 120–21.

32. Escudé, "U.S. Political Destabilisation," 59.

33. Whitaker, *The United States and Argentina*, 113.

34. Tulchin, *Argentina and the United States*, 85.

35. Tulchin, *Argentina and the United States*, 87; Whitaker, *The United States and Argentina*, 127.

36. Rapoport, *Aliados o Neutrales*, 20.

37. Selections from *Libro Azul*, in Rapoport, *Aliados o Neutrales*, 284.

38. Callum A. MacDonald, "The Braden Campaign and Anglo-American Relations in Argentina, 1945–6," in *Argentina between the Great Powers, 1939–46*, ed. Guido Di Tella and D. Cameron Watt (Pittsburgh: University of Pittsburgh Press, 1990), 150.

39. Juan D. Perón, *Libro Azul y Blanco* (Buenos Aires: 1946), 3.

40. Ibid., 127.

41. Mario Rapoport and Claudio Spiguel, *Estados Unidos y El Peronismo* (Buenos Aires: Grupo Editor Latinoamericano), 225.

42. Tulchin, *Argentina and the United States*, 111.

43. David Pion-Berlin, "The National Security Doctrine, Military Threat Perception, and the 'Dirty War' in Argentina," *Comparative Political Studies* 21, no. 3 (October 1988), 385.

44. Tulchin, *Argentina and the United States*, 117. The Frondizi government cannot be considered entirely democratic, however, as the military prohibited Peronist participation during the 1958 and 1963 elections. See Guillermo O'Donnell, *Modernization and Bureaucratic-Authoritarianism* (Berkeley: University of California-Berkeley Institute of International Studies, 1973).

45. Proceso de Reorganización Nacional, "Acta fijando el propósito y los objetivos básicos para el Proceso de Reorganización Nacional" in *Medio siglo de proclamas militares*, ed. Horacio Verbitsky (Buenos Aires: Editora/12), 146.

46. The fourth military president of this period, General Augusto Bignone, naturally adopted more of a "third world" orientation, as his administration immediately followed Argentina's loss of the 1982 Falklands/Malvinas War, in which the United States supported Great Britain.

47. Comisión Nacional Sobre la Desaparación de Personas, *Nunca más* (Buenos Aires: Editorial Universitaria de Buenos Aires, 1986).

48. The Carter administration's efforts to veto credits to Argentina was, however, largely frustrated by the U.S. State Department's "pragmatic" sectors who believed that the White House's "principled" approach could affect U.S. political and economic interests in Argentina. See Andrés Cisneros and Carlos Escudé, ed., *Historia general de las relaciones exteriors de la República Argentina*, part 3, *Las relaciones exterior de la Argentina subordinada, 1943–1989*: vol. 14, *Las relaciones políticas, 1966–1989* (Buenos Aires: CARI/Grupo Editor Latinoamericano, 2000), 295.

49. Mark Falcoff, *A Tale of Two Policies: U.S. Relations with the Argentine Junta, 1976–1983* (Philadelphia: Foreign Policy Research Institute, Philadelphia Papers, 1989), 21.

50. Roberto Russell, "Proceso de toma de decisiones en la Política Exterior Argentina (1976–1989)," in *Política exterior y toma de decisiones en América Latina*, ed. Roberto Russell (Buenos Aires: GEL, 1990) 17–25.

51. Falcoff, *A Tale of Two Policies*, 24.

52. Robert Pastor, "The Reagan Administration: On its Own Petard," in *United States Policy in Latin America: A Decade of Crisis and Challenge*, ed. John D. Martz (Lincoln: University of Nebraska Press, 1995), 8.

53. Falcoff, *A Tale of Two Policies*, 34–35.

54. Reagan's policies followed the ideas developed by Jean Kirkpatrick in "Dictators and Double Standards," *Commentary* 68 (November 1979), 34–45.

55. Pastor, "The Reagan Administration," 8.

56. Ariel Armony, *Argentina, the United States, and the Anti-Communist Crusade*

*in Central America, 1977–1984* (Athens, Ohio: Center for International Studies, Ohio University, 1997), 15.

57. According to Armony, around fifteen members of the Argentine Ejército Revolucionario del Pueblo participated in the final stages of the Sandinista revolution against Somoza. Ibid., 79.

58. Falcoff, *A Tale of Two Policies*, 43.

59. Armony, *Argentina, the United States, and the Anti-Communist Crusade*, 107; Falcoff, *A Tale of Two Policies*, 42.

60. Armony, *Argentina, the United States, and the Anti-Communist Crusade*, 94.

61. Deborah Norden, *Military Rebellion in Argentina: Between Coups and Consolidation* (Lincoln: University of Nebraska Press, 1996), 68–76.

62. Rock, *Argentina, 1516–1987*, 382–83.

63. Gary Wynia, *Argentina: Illusions and Realities* (New York: Holmes and Meier, 1986), 97–98.

64. Tulchin, *Argentina and the United States*, 156; Norden, *Military Rebellion in Argentina*, 73.

65. Falcoff, *A Tale of Two Policies*, 51.

66. *La Prensa* (Buenos Aires, September 23, 1984).

67. See Norden, *Military Rebellion in Argentina*.

CHAPTER 2: THE NEW INTERNATIONAL ORDER

1. Francis Fukuyama, "The End of History?" *The National Interest* 16 (summer 1989): 3.

2. John Gaddis, "The Cold War, the Long Peace, and the Future," in *Beyond the Cold War: New Dimensions in International Relations*, ed. Geir Lundestad and Odd Arne Westad (Oslo: Scandanavian University Press, 1993), 7–32.

3. Samuel P. Huntington, "Clash of Civilizations," *Foreign Affairs* 72, no. 3 (summer 1993): 22–49; and Zbigniew Brzezinski, *Out of Control: Global Turmoil on the Eve of the Twenty-First Century* (New York: Charles Scribner's Sons, 1993).

4. For example, Ikenberry has observed that the end of the Cold War has essentially left intact a "liberal democratic order" that was established in the wake of World War II. See G. John Ikenberry, "The Myth of the Post–Cold War Chaos," *Foreign Affairs* 75, no. 3 (May/June, 1996): 79–91.

5. Ibid., 81.

6. Roberto Russell, "El contexto externo de la política exterior argentina: Notas sobre el 'Nuevo Orden Mundial,'" in *La política exterior: Argentina en el Nuevo Orden Internacional*, ed. Roberto Russell (Buenos Aires: GEL, 1992), 16.

7. Stanley Hoffman, "The Crisis of Liberal Internationalism," *Foreign Policy*, No. 98 (spring 1995): 166.

8. James Rosenau, *Along the Domestic-Foreign Frontier: Exploring Governance in a Turbulent World* (Cambridge: Cambridge University Press, 1997).

9. Hoffman, "The Crisis of Liberal Internationalism," 175.

10. Brzezinski, *Out of Control*; Atilio Borón, "Las Transformaciones del Sistema Internacional y las Alternativas de la Política Exterior Argentina," in *La política exterior argentina*, ed. Roberto Russell (Buenos Aires: Grupo Editorial Latinoamericano, 1992); Dani Rodrik, "Sense and Nonsense in the Globalization Debate," *Foreign Policy* 107 (summer 1997): 19–37.

11. Rosenau, *Along the Domestic-Foreign Frontier*.

12. Samuel Huntington marks the beginning of the "third wave" of democratization with Portugal's 1974 transition to democracy. Notably, at this time Argentina had not yet even begun its latest bout with authoritarian rule, and Uruguay and Chile had only just initiated military rule. Huntington thus argues that the third wave in Latin America begins somewhat later, toward the late 1970s. See Samuel P. Huntington, *The Third Wave: Democratization in the Late Twentieth Century* (Norman: University of Oklahoma Press, 1991), 3, 22.

13. See Guillermo O'Donnell and Philippe Schmitter, *Transitions from Authoritarian Rule: Tentative Conclusions about Uncertain Democracies* (Baltimore: Johns Hopkins University Press, 1986); Karen Remmer, *Military Rule in Latin America* (Winchester, Mass.: Unwin Hyman, 1989); Gerardo Munck, *Authoritarianism and Democratization: Soldiers and Workers in Argentina, 1976–1983* (University Park, Penn.: Pennsylvania State University Press, 1998); Andrés Fontana, "Political Decision-Making by a Military Corporation," Ph.D. dissertation, University of Texas, 1987.

14. Huntington, *The Third Wave*, 46.

15. Fukuyama, "The End of History?" 3.

16. Brzezinski, *Out of Control*, 88.

17. Nevertheless, others have argued that following the Cold War, the United States stood "as the single most powerful entity in the world, arguably its only superpower," and that it held this status on *all* fronts, including the economic front. See Richard Haass, "Fatal Distraction: Bill Clinton's Foreign Policy," *Foreign Policy* 108 (fall 1997), 2; Geir Lundestad, "Beyond the Cold War: New and Old Dimensions in International Relations," in *Beyond the Cold War: New Dimensions in International Relations*, ed. Geir Lundestad and Odd Arne Westad (Oslo: Scandanavian University Press, 1993).

18. Raimo Vayrynen, "The Nature of Conflicts in Future International Relations," in *Beyond the Cold War: New Dimensions in International Relations*, ed. Geir Lundestad and Odd Arne Westad (Oslo: Scandanavian University Press, 1993), 109.

19. Organization for Economic Cooperation and Development, "Gross Domestic Product" table, online at http://www.oecd.org/std/gdp.htm.

20. Andrew Hurrell, "Regionalism in the Americas," in *Latin America in a New World*, ed. Abraham Lowenthal and Gregory Treverton (Boulder: Westview Press, 1994), 167.

21. Jorge Castañeda, "Latin America and the End of the Cold War: An Essay in Frus-

tration," in *Beyond the Cold War: New Dimensions in International Relations*, ed. Geir Lundestad and Odd Arne Westad (Oslo: Scandanavian University Press, 1993), 206.

22. See Larry Rohter, "Driven by Fear, Colombians Leave in Droves," *New York Times*, March 5, 2000, 8.

23. Aldo Vacs, "A Delicate Balance: Confrontation and Cooperation between Argentina and the United States in the 1980s," *Journal of Interamerican Studies and World Affairs* 31, no. 4 (winter 1989): 45.

24. Bruce Weinrod, "The U.S. Role in Peacekeeping-Related Activities," *World Affairs* 155, no. 4 (spring 1993), 148–155.

25. Ashton B. Carter, William J. Perry, and John D. Steinbrunner, "A New Concept of Cooperative Security," Brookings Occasional Papers (Washington, D.C.: Brookings Institutions, 1992), 6.

26. See Charles Krauthammer, "The Lonely Superpower: How to Bear America's New World Burden," *New Republic* 205, no. 5 (July 29, 1991), 23–26.

27. The U.S. Congress resisted granting Clinton the fast-track authority necessary to create the FTAA, originally proposed by George H. W. Bush. However, George W. Bush took up the matter with renewed determination from the beginning of his administration.

28. Davide G. Erro, *Resolving the Argentine Paradox: Politics and Development, 1966–1992* (Boulder: Lynne Rienner, 1993): 154.

29. Deborah Norden, *Military Rebellion in Argentina: Between Coups and Consolidation* (Lincoln: University of Nebraska Press, 1996).

30. Roberto Russell, "Las relaciones argentino-norteamericanas: reflexiones sobre la experiencia reciente," in *Estados Unidos y la transición argentina* , ed. Roberto Bouzas and Roberto Russell (Buenos Aires: Editorial Legasa, 1989), 347.

31. Roberto Russell and Laura Zuvanic, "Argentina: Deepening Alignment with the West," *Journal of Interamerican Studies and World Affairs* 33, no. 3 (fall 1991): 121.

32. Felipe A. M. de la Balze, *Remaking the Argentine Economy* (New York: Council on Foreign Relations, 1995).

33. Deborah Norden, "Keeping the Peace, Outside and In: Argentina's United Nations Missions," *International Peacekeeping* 2, no. 3 (autumn 1995): 330–349, and Norden, "The Transformation of Argentine Security," in *Beyond Praetorianism: The Latin American Military in the Post–Cold War Period*, ed. Richard Millett and Michael Gold-Bis (Miami: North-South Center, 1996): 241–60.

34. Jorge Shvarzer, "Mercosur: The Prospects for Regional Integration," *NACLA Report on the Americas* 31, no. 6 (May-June 1998), 25–27.

35. Thomas Andrew O'Keefe, "The Evolution of European Union-MERCOSUR Relations and Diminishing U.S. Business Dominance in South America's Southern Cone," *Latin American Law and Business Report* 7, no. 1 (January 31, 1999), 2.

36. "Sour Mercosur," *Economist* 352, no. 8132 (August 14, 1999), 13.

37. Mónica Hirst, "Security Policies, Democratization, and Regional Integration in the Southern Cone," in *International Security and Democracy: Latin America and the Caribbean in the Post–Cold War Era*, ed. Jorge I. Domínguez (Pittsburgh: University of Pittsburgh Press, 1998), 113–14.

CHAPTER 3: THE MAKING OF FOREIGN POLICY

1. See, for example, David Rock, *Argentina: 1516–1987: From Spanish Colonization to Alfonsín* (Pittsburgh: University of Pittsburgh Press, 1987).

2. David Pion-Berlin, *Through Corridors of Power: Institutions and Civil-Military Relations in Argentina* (University Park: Pennsylvania State University Press, 1997).

3. Guillermo O'Donnell, "Delegative Democracy," *Journal of Democracy* 5, no. 1 (January 1994): 55–69.

4. David Pion-Berlin argues that many issues that would naturally reside in the Ministry of Defense have instead been taken up by the now more powerful Ministry of Foreign Affairs. See Pion-Berlin, "Civil-Military Circumvention: How Argentine State Institutions Compensate for a Weakened Chain of Command," in *Civil-Military Relations in Latin America: New Analytical Perspectives*, ed. David Pion-Berlin (Chapel Hill: University of North Carolina Press, 2001), 135–60.

5. See, for example, Eugene Wittkopf and James McCormick, "The Institutional Setting," in *The Domestic Sources of American Foreign Policy: Insights and Evidence*, ed. Eugene Wittkopf and James McCormick (Lanham, Md.: Rowman and Littlefield, 1999), 109.

6. See, for example, Graham Allison, *Essence of Decision: Explaining the Cuban Missile Crisis* (Boston: Little, Brown, 1971), and Jerel Rosati, ed., *The Politics of United States Foreign Policy* (Fort Worth, Tex.: Harcourt Brace, 1993) for different models of the foreign policy process.

7. Glenn Hastedt and Anthony J. Eksterowicz, "Presidential Leadership and American Foreign Policy: Implications for a New Era," in *The Domestic Sources of American Foreign Policy*, ed. Eugene Wittkopf and James M. McCormick (Lanham, Md.: Rowman and Littlefield, 1999), 123.

8. Donald Snow and Eugene Brown, *Puzzle Palaces and Foggy Bottom: U.S. Foreign and Defense Policy-Making in the 1990s* (New York: St. Martin's Press, 1994), 32.

9. Hastedt and Eksterowicz, "Presidential Leadership."

10. Ibid., 133.

11. Robert Lieber, "Eagle without a Cause: Making Foreign Policy without the Soviet Threat," in *Eagle Adrift: American Foreign Policy at the End of the Century*, ed. Robert Lieber (New York: Longman, 1997), 19.

12. Geoffrey Kemp, "Presidential Management of the Executive Bureaucracy," in

*The Domestic Sources of American Foreign Policy: Insights and Evidence*, ed. Eugene Wittkopf and James McCormick (Lanham, Md.: Rowman and Littlefield, 1999), 159.

13. Kevin Mulcahy and Harold Kendrick, "The National Security Advisor: A Presidential Perspective," in *Executive Leadership in Anglo-American Systems*, ed. Colin Campbell and Margaret Jane Wyszomirsky (Pittsburgh: University of Pittsburgh Press, 1991), 259–79.

14. Kemp, "Presidential Management," 162.

15. See, for example, Wittkopf and McCormick, "The Institutional Setting," 111.

16. George Szamuely, "The Imperial Congress," *Commentary* (September 1987): 27–32. Reprinted in *The Politics of United States Foreign Policy*, ed. Jerel Rosati (Fort Worth, Tex.: Harcourt Brace, 1993), 244–45.

17. Hastedt and Eksterowicz, "Presidential Leadership," 125.

18. Ibid., 126.

19. Eugene Wittkopf and James M. McCormick, "Congress, the President, and the End of the Cold War," *Journal of Conflict Resolution* 4 (August 1998), 440.

20. Luis Pablo Maria Beltramino, "El Congreso de los Estados Unidos de América: Su participación en la política exterior. Implicancias para la Argentina." Instituto del Servicio Exterior de la Nacion, Argentina (August 1999), 19.

21. Ibid., 17, 19.

22. James M. Lindsay, "End of an Era: Congress and Foreign Policy after the Cold War," in *The Domestic Sources of American Foreign Policy: Insights and Evidence* , ed. Eugene Wittkopf and James McCormick (Lanham, Md.: Rowman and Littlefield, 1999), 181.

23. The Cold War organization of the policy offices in the Defense Department, Office of the Secretary of Defense, divided regionalists into two offices: International Security Affairs (ISA) and International Security Policy (ISP). ISA included the countries of NATO, Latin America, Africa, and Asia—potentially friendly countries. ISP, on the other hand, combined regional specialists on the Soviet Union (subsequently Russia, Ukraine, and Eurasia), as well as specialists in nuclear weapons issues (U.S. Department of Defense, Directorate for Organizational Planning, Office of the Secretary of Defense, "Department of Defense Key Personnel Location," September 1996). A 1998 reorganization drastically pared the number of offices at the assistant secretary level, leaving only ISA, SOLIC, and Strategy and Requirements beneath the Undersecretary of Defense for Policy.

24. William Perry continued to advocate increased security cooperation between the United States and Latin America even after ending his tenure as secretary of defense, as revealed in an October 1999 draft of a Center for Strategic and International Studies policy report for which Perry served as project principal.

25. U.S. Department of Agriculture, Animal and Plant Health Inspection Service, "94–106–5 Importation of Beef from Argentina," *Federal Register* 62, no. 123 (June 26, 1997), 34385–94.

26. U.S. Department of Justice, Office of the Attorney General, "Memorandum for all United States Attorneys," October 16, 1997; online at www.usdoj.gov:80/ag/readingroom/interextra.htm.

27. "FBI Report Cites Iran in Argentine Bombing," *New York Times*, August 8, 1998, A5. See also the speech by Louis J. Freeh, Director of the FBI, Buenos Aires, May 12, 1998. FBI Press Room—Director's Speeches.

28. Deputy Treasury Secretary Lawrence H. Summers. Text of speech delivered to Senate Banking Committee, Subcommmittee on Economic Policy and Subcommittee on International Trade and Finance, April 22, 1999. *Treasury News*, Office of Public Affairs, RR-3098.

29. Quoted in Richard Haass, "Fatal Distraction: Bill Clinton's Foreign Policy," *Foreign Policy* 108 (fall 1997), 112–23.

30. John Stremlau, "Clinton's Dollar Diplomacy," *Foreign Policy* 97 (winter 1994), 18–35; and Snow and Brown, *Puzzle Palaces and Foggy Bottom*.

31. Lindsay, "End of an Era," 176.

32. For more details about the right known as the "shared veto," see Joseph Tulchin, "Régimenes autoritarios y política exterior: el caso de Argentina," in *Entre la autonomía y la subordinación: Política exterior de los países latinoamericanos*, ed. Heraldo Muñoz and Joseph Tulchin (Buenos Aires: Grupo Editor Latinoamericano, 1984), 366.

33. Regarding the process of decision making during the years of the military dictatorship, see Andrés Fontana, "Political Decision-Making by a Military Corporation: Argentina 1976–1983," Ph.D. dissertation, University of Texas at Austin, May 1987; and Roberto Russell, "El Proceso de Toma de decisiones en la Política Exterior Argentina (1976–1989)," in *Política exterior y toma de decisiones en América Latina*, ed. Roberto Russell (Buenos Aires: GEL, 1990), 17–25.

34. "Reunión de Galtieri con el Presidente de Panamá," *Clarín*, (August 17, 1981), 2.

35. See Roberto Russell, "Los ejes estructurantes de la política exterior argentina," *América Latina/ Internacional* 1, no. 2 (autumn-winter 1994), 8.

36. *Carapintada* means "painted face," in reference to the camouflage makeup worn by the 1987 military rebels. See Deborah L. Norden, *Military Rebellion in Argentina* (Lincoln: University of Nebraska Press, 1996).

37. Juan Vicente Sola, *El manejo de las Relaciones Exteriores. La Constitución y la Política Exterior* (Buenos Aires: Editorial Belgrano, 1997), 49.

38. This request was rejected by NATO at the end of July 1999, causing a strong diplomatic setback. The proposal was also strongly rejected by the two leading presidential candidates of the time, Fernando De La Rúa and Eduardo Duhalde.

39. H. Gaggero, A. Iriarte, and H. Roitberg, *Argentina, 15 años después. De la transición a la democracia al menemismo (1982–1997)* (Buenos Aires: Oficina de Publicaciones del CBC; Universidad de Buenos Aires, 1997), 76.

40. The number 166 is acknowledged by the executive branch. Rubio and Goretti

believe that another 170 unacknowledged decrees, included in the category of "need and urgency," should be added to the above statistic. See Delia Ferreira Rubio and Mateo Goretti, "Cuando el presidente gobierna solo: Menem y los decretos de necesidad y urgencia hasta la reforma constitucional (julio 1989–agosto 1994)," *Desarrollo Económico* 36, no. 141 (April-June 1996): 443–474.

41. "Decretos de necesidad y urgencia," *La Nación*, May 25, 2000; 8.

42. Since the 1994 Constitution went into effect, the necessary and urgent decrees ceased to be extraconstitutional, as this authority was incorporated into Article 99, Section 3. There are different opinions regarding the effect of making these decrees constitutional on the division of powers. Among others, see: María Angélica Gelli, "Relación de poderes en la Reforma Constitucional de 1994," *La Ley* 58, no. 186 (1994); Humberto Quiroga Lavie, "Decretos de necesidad y urgencia en la Reforma de la Constitución Nacional," *La Ley* 58, no. 168 (1994); and Gregorio Badeni, *Reforma Constitucional e instituciones políticas* (Buenos Aires: Ad-Hoc, 1994).

43. Ferreira Rubio and Gorretti, "Cuando el presidente gobierna solo," 450. Translated by Deborah L. Norden.

44. "Los decretos son una herramienta indispensable," *La Nación*, August 3, 1993, 1, 5.

45. Actually, numerous decrees concerning deregulation, commerce, transport, the public debt, and taxes were issued in order to deal with the economic emergency, while others had no relation to situations of "extreme gravity." The most prominent cases involved approving a direct contract to issue new Argentine identification documents (decree 603/91), the donation of asphalt to Bolivia (decree 1809/91), and the commitment to renegotiate the contracts of those who owned the rights to broadcast soccer games on television (decree 1563/93).

46. See Gaggero, Iriarte, and Roitberg, *Argentina, 15 años después*, 88–90, 119.

47. This final authority is enormously important. Congress's capacity to control the budget converts it into a relevant foreign policy actor, as is the case in the United States. Nonetheless, during the 1990s, this congressional power was not utilized in Argentina as a tool for defining domestic public policy, much less foreign policy.

48. Article 75, Section 24 of the 1994 Constitution; translation by Deborah L. Norden.

49. For more on this topic, see Gary Wynia, *La Argenitina de posguerra* (Buenos Aires: Editorial de Belgrano, 1986), 145–46; 176. During the Frondizi presidency, critiques from the opposition forced the president to increasingly avoid the parliamentary process. On the other hand, the style of Frondizi's government allowed Congress little participation in key areas, such as petroleum policy. See Catalina Smulovitz, *Oposición y gobierno: Los años de Frondizi* (Buenos Aires: Centro Editor de Américo Latino, 1988), 75ff.

50. "Intermestic" refers to the overlap between domestic and international affairs.

51. Miguel Danielan, *Constitución de la Nación Argentina: antecedents, leyes*

*constitucionales, derechos humanos. Reseña hisórica y comentario* (Buenos Aires: A-Z editoria, 1996), 27.

52. For further details regarding the role of Congress in this issue, see Carlos Cherniak, "El acuerdo sobre Hielos Continentales como modelo de construcción de una política de Estado." Master's Thesis in International Relations (Buenos Aires: FLACSO Argentina, May 2000).

53. Interview by Roberto Russell with former Minister of Foreign Affairs Dante Caputo. Translation by Deborah L. Norden.

54. Russell, "El Proceso de Toma de Decisiones en la Política Exterior Argentina," 53–58.

55. This argument was difficult to defend given that the Argentine Constitution requires congressional approval for stationing any troops outside of Argentine territory.

56. "Diario de Sesiones de la Honorable Cámara de Diputados," January 18 and 19, 1991, 4034.

57. "Encuesta CEOP: ir o no ir. Intervención de tropas en la ocupación en Haití," *Clarín*, 7 August 1994, 16–17.

58. From the military perspective, this form of participation meant that the Argentine troops would arrive on the island within a multinational force composed of 3,000 men from seventeen countries, after the troops involved in the landing operation had eliminated all vestiges of military resistance on the part of the Haitian military government. See "Intervencíon en Haití. 'La Argentina participará en la primera fase,' Di Tella aclaró que las tropas no irán en combate," *Clarín*, 15 September 1994, sección internacional, 32.

59. "La prioridad de James Cheek es lograr la ley patentes," *La Prensa*, August 4, 1993, Sección Economía Nacional, 4. Translation by Deborah L. Norden.

60. In an interesting study of the presidential veto during the Alfonsín and Menem governments, Ana María Mustapic shows that this use of the veto against initiatives by legislators of his own party reveal the tensions that exist between the president and his legislative support base. See Mustapic, "Tribulaciones del Congreso en la nueva diplomacia argentina—El veto presidencial bajo Alfonsín y Menem," in *Agora* 3 (winter 1995): 61–74.

61. See Ana María Mustapic, "Oficialistas y diputados: Las relaciones Ejecutivo-Legislativo en la Argentina," paper presented at the Seminar on Legislatures in Latin America: Comparative Perspectives, Centro de Investigaciôn y Docencia Econômica, Mexico City, February 6–7, 1998, 6.

62. Following this transfer, the ministry added the words *International Commerce* to its former name, the Ministry of Foreign Affairs and Worship.

63. The Fundación Invertir was created in 1991. Its activities are closely coordinated with the Secretariat of Industry, Commerce, and Mining within the Ministry of Economics; with Public Works and Services; and with the Secretariat of International

Economic Relations of the Ministry of Foreign Relations, International Commerce and Worship, whose leaders form part of the organization's executive committee.

64. For an interesting discussion of the respective roles of the Ministries of Defense and Foreign Relations during the Menem government, see David Pion-Berlin, "Civil-Military Circumvention: How Argentine State Institutions Compensate for a Weakened Chain of Command.

65. For an explanation of other factors that influenced the proposal, see Jorge Castro, *Basis of the Dollarization Strategy and Treaty of Monetary Association*, Presidencia de la Nación, Secretaria de Planeamiento Estratégico (Buenos Aires: Gráfica Sur SRL, 1999).

66. This possibility came to seem increasingly remote after Menem was arrested in June 2001 in conjunction with a scandal involving prohibited arms sales.

67. Margaret G. Hermann, Charles F. Hermann, and Joe D. Hagan, "How Decision Units Shape Foreign Policy Behavior," in *New Directions in the Study of Foreign Policy*, eds. Charles F. Hermann, Charles W. Kegley Jr., and James N. Rosenau (Boston: Allen and Unwin, 1987), 309–36.

68. The official discourse expressly criticized the "useless confrontationism" of the Alfonsín government, although it was recognized that similar attitudes had character-ized all past Argentine governments—including, of course, the Peronist administrations.

69. *Página 12*, December 9, 1990.

70. Military influence diminished even further following the eventual defeat of the army's rebel movement in 1990.

71. Guido Di Tella, "Prologue," in *Política Exterior Argentina 1989–1999: Historía de un éxito*, ed. Andrés Cisneros (Buenos Aires: Nuevo Hacer, 1998), 15.

72. Guido Di Tella, "Palabras pronunciadas en el Seminario Internacional sobre Derecho de la Integración," pamphlet (Buenos Aires, 1991), 13.

CHAPTER 4: DEFINING THE TERMS OF FRIENDSHIP

1. Carlos Escudé and Andrés Fontana, "Argentina's Security Policies: Their Ratio-nale and Regional Context," in *International Security and Democracy: Latin America and the Caribbean in the Post–Cold War Era*, ed. Jorge I. Domínguez (Pittsburgh: University of Pittsburgh Press, 1998), 55.

2. See Carlos H. Acuña, "Politics and Economics in Argentina of the Nineties," in *Democracy, Markets, and Structural Reform in Latin America: Argentina, Bolivia, Brazil, Chile, and Mexico*, ed. William Smith, Carlos H. Acuña, and Eduardo Gamarra (Miami: North-South Center, 1994), 31–73; and Acuña, "Business Interests, Dictator-ship, and Democracy in Argentina," in *Business and Democracy in Latin America*, ed. Ernest Bartell and Leigh Payne (Pittsburgh: University of Pittsburgh Press, 1995), 3–48.

3. Daniel Chudnovsky, Andrés López, and Fernando Porta, *La nueva inversión extranjera directa en la Argentina: Privatizaciones, mercado interno e integración regional*, Centro de Investigaciones para la Transformación (CENIT), Documento de Trabajo No. 15 (Buenos Aires, May 1994), 4.

4. *Washington Post*, "Menem Signs 'Revolutionary' Treaty with U.S. to Protect Investments," November 15, 1991, A17.

5. President George [H. W.] Bush, "Message to the Senate transmitting the Argentina-United States Investment Treaty." Transcript, *Weekly Compilation of Presidential Documents* 29, no. 3 (January 25, 1993), 71.

6. U.S. Department of State, "1998 Country Report on Economic Policy and Trade Practices: Argentina," Submitted to the Senate Committees on Foreign Relations and to the House Committees on Foreign Affairs and on Ways and Means, January 31, 1999.

7. "Tratado entre la República Argentina y los Estados Unidos de América sobre promoción y protección recíproca de inversiones," Article II, No. 1; reproduced in Consejo Argentino para las Relaciones Internacionales (CARI), *La relación entre la Argentina y los Estados Unidos, 1989–1995: Una nueva etapa*, ed. Ambassador Raúl Granillo Ocampo (Buenos Aires: El Cronista Ediciones, 1996), 426.

8. "Tratado entre la República Argentina y los Estados Unidos de América sobre promoción y protección recíproca de inversiones," Article IV, No. 1, in CARI, *La Relación entre la Argentina y los Estados Unidos*, 427.

9. CARI, *La relación entre la Argentina y los Estados Unidos*, 368.

10. Davide G. Erro, *Resolving the Argentine Paradox: Politics and Development, 1966–1992* (Boulder: Lynne Rienner, 1993), 221.

11. "Argentine Official Coming to U.S. for Help on Budget Deficit," *New York Times*, 15 April 1999, C4.

12. U.S. Department of State, Statement by the Press Secretary. "The State Visit of Argentine President Carlos Menem." Released by the White House, Office of the Press Secretary, January 11, 1999. http://www.state.gov/www/regions/wha/990111_statement.html.

13. "Argentina Suspends U.S. Air Pact in Effort to Save Flagship Carrier," *Wall Street Journal*, February 3, 2000, A24.

14. "De la Rúa pedirá en EE.UU. que se postergue 'cielos abiertos.'" *Clarín*, http://old.clarin.com/diario/2000–06–02/e-02601.htm, 2 June 2000; "Qué negocio esconde la pelea por cielos abiertos," *Clarín*, 18 June 2000. http://old.clarin.com/diario/2000–060–18/-02201.htm.

15. "Argentine Pact Looms Large for Argentina," *Wall Street Journal*, June 12, 2000, A24.

16. CEPAL (Comisión Económica para América Latina y el Caribe), "La inversión extranjera en América Latina y el Caribe," Informe 1998 (Santiago de Chile, 1998), 34. The most notorious examples of these holdings are those of Citibank Equity Invest-

ment and of the Exxel Group. The first of these is composed of the Citibank Corporation, the Hicks Group, and the local group, República Holding. The Exxel Group operates with essentially American funds, from CIBC Oppenheimer, General Motors, and others.

17. CARI, *La relación entre la Argentina y los Estados Unidos*, 278.

18. U.S. Department of State, "1998 Country Report on Economic Policy and Trade Practices: Argentina."

19. República Argentina, Ministerio de Relaciones Exteriores, Comercio Internacional y Culto, Dirección América del Norte, "Relación bilateral con los Estados Unidos de América" (Buenos Aires, 2000), 12.

20. "U.S. Lifts Ban on Beef from Argentina," *Wall Street Journal*, June 25, 1997, A14.

21. In August 2000, Argentina beef sales encountered a further obstacle, after a few cases of foot-and-mouth disease were identified in the country's northeast. Argentina took rapid measures to slaughter some 3,000 cattle in the region, and temporarily halted most fresh beef exports. The United States responded by also temporarily banning imports of the beef. See Clifford Krauss, "U.S., Seeing Threat of Disease, Halts Trade in Argentine Beef," *New York Times*, August 12, 2000, A6.

22. CARI, *La relación entre la Argentina y los Estados Unidos*, 296.

23. Ibid.

24. Department of State, "1998 Country Report on Economic Policy and Trade Practices: Argentina."

25. "Fernández Meijide salió a defender a los laboratorios." *Clarín*, 16 February 2000. http://old.clarin.com/diario/2000–02-16/0-01801d.htm.

26. CARI, *La relación entre la Argentina y los Estados Unidos*, 294.

27. U.S. Department of State, "1998 Country Report on Economic Policy and Trade Practices: Argentina"; Section 7, Protection of U.S. Intellectual Property.

28. "Argentina Faces Sanctions by U.S. over Drug Patents." *Wall Street Journal*, January 16 1997, A11.

29. A March 2000 proposal sought to add a clause to the law that would require that foreign companies produce pharmaceuticals within Argentina to be able to benefit from their patents. See "Cruzada de Economía contra retoques a la Ley de Patentes," *Clarín*, March 28, 2000. http://old.clarin.com/diario/2000–03–28/0–01901d.htm

30. "Software Makers Assail Argentine Piracy Ruling." *Wall Street Journal*, February 6, 1998, A17.

31. República de Argentina, Ley 25.036 "Propiedad Intelectual," November 11, 1998.

32. "U.S. Presses Argentina on Patents." *New York Times*, May 3, 1993, D3.

33. Ibid.

34. "Cruzada de Economía contra retoques a la Ley de Patentes," *Clarín*, March 28, 2000. http://old.clarin.com/diario/2000–03–28/0–01901d.htm.

35. "The Buck Doesn't Stop Here: Now Argentina May Adopt It," *New York Times*, February 25, 1999, A14.

36. Shirley Christian, "Debate on 'Dollarization' is Growing in Argentina," *New York Times*, December 28, 1989, D2.

37. Felipe A. M. de la Balze, *Remaking the Argentine Economy* (New York: Council on Foreign Relations Press, 1994), 51.

38. David Wessel, "U.S. Walks Lightly over Dollar Policy from Argentina." *Wall Street Journal*, March 15, 1999, A15.

39. CARI, *La relación entre la Argentina y los Estados Unidos*, 274.

40. U.S. Department of State, "Argentina Country Report on Human Rights Practices for 1998." Released by the Bureau of Democracy, Human Rights, and Labor, February 26, 1999.

41. Patrice McSherry, *Incomplete Transition: Military Power and Democracy in Argentina* (New York: St. Martin's Press, 1997), 256.

42. The United States is, of course, not immune to anti-Semitism, either. On August 10, 1999, a lone gunman entered a Los Angeles Jewish community center and randomly shot five people, including three young children. A member of a neo-Nazi group, he claimed that his act was a "wake-up call" to kill Jews.

43. See Jacobo Timerman, *Prisoner without a Name, Cell without a Number* (New York: Alfred A. Knopf, 1981).

44. McSherry, *Incomplete Transition*, 257.

45. See CARI, *La relación entre la Argentina y los Estados Unidos*, 289.

46. See U.S. Department of State, "Argentina Country Report on Human Rights Practices for 1998."

47. "Trail Heats Up in '94 Argentina Bombing." *Los Angeles Times*, December 6, 1997, A2.

48. "F.B.I. Report Cites Iran in Argentine Bombing," *New York Times*, August 8, 1998, A5.

49. Groups within the military carried out four rebellions between April 1987 and December 1990, largely in protest against the government's efforts to establish control and justice. See Deborah L. Norden, *Military Rebellion in Argentina: Between Coups and Consolidation* (Lincoln: University of Nebraska Press, 1996).

50. Ibid., 103.

51. Ibid., 104.

52. Ibid., 140.

53. Anabella Busso, *Las relaciones Argentina-Estados Unidos en los noventa: El caso Cóndor II* (Rosario: CERIR, 1999).

54. Antonio Palá, "Peacekeeping and its Effects on Civil-Military Relations: The Argentine Experience," in *International Security and Democracy: Latin America and the Caribbean in the Post–Cold War Era*, ed. Jorge I. Domínguez (Pittsburgh: University of Pittsburgh Press, 1998), 144.

55. Rut Diamint, "El Gobierno Norteamericano ante el caso del Condor II: Sistema burocrático y toma de decisiones," in *Papers from the Junior Scholars Training Pro-*

*gram, 1995–96*, Woodrow Wilson International Center for Scholars no. 224 (1997), 11.

56. "Argentina, Acceding to U.S., Ends Missile Program." *New York Times*, May 30, 1991, A9.

57. Escudé and Fontana, "Argentina's Security Policies: Their Rationale and Regional Context," 62.

58. "Memorandum of understanding between the government of the United States of America and the government of the Republic of Argentina on the Transfer and Protection of Strategic Technology." Reproduced in CARI, *La relación entre la Argentina y los Estados Unidos 1989–1995*, 321–22.

59. "Agreement between the United States Department of Energy and the National Atomic Energy Commission of Argentina." Reproduced in CARI, *La relación entre la Argentina y los Estados Unidos 1989–1995*, 315–16.

60. Secretary of State Warren Christopher, "The U.S. and Argentina: Strengthening the Partnership." Transcript, *US Department of State Dispatch 7*, no. 10 (March 4, 1996).

61. *International Narcotics Control Strategy Report*, 1998. Released by the Bureau for International Narcotics and Law Enforcement Affairs, U.S. Department of State, Washington, D.C., February 1999.

62. Office of Applied Studies, Substance Abuse and Mental Health Services Administration, U.S. Department of Health and Human Services, *National Household Survey on Drug Abuse 1998*, Section II, Table 1A, "1998 NHSDA Sample Sizes and U.S. Population Totals, by Age within Gender," and Table 2A, "Any Illicit Drug Use by Gender within Age Group for Total Population in 1998."

63. Secretaría de Programación para la Prevención de la Drogadicción y la Lucha contra el Narcotráfico, República Argentina, "Primer Estudio Nacional sobre Drogas" (June 1999), 1, 4.

64. *International Narcotics Control Strategy Report*.

65. See CARI, *La relación entre la Argentina y los Estados Unidos*, 283. According to the 1998 *International Narcotics Control Strategy Report*, the United States did finance hiring a U.S. expert to organize an anti-drug media campaign in Argentina. However, it is the U.S. government's reluctance to deal with drug use in the United States that is at issue.

66. CARI, *La relación entre la Argentina y los Estados Unidos*, 283.

67. Estado Mayor del Ejército Argentino, "Ejes conceptuales que sirvieron de base a la Ponencia del JEMGE en la XIX Conferencia de Ejércitos Americanos," 1990, 3.

68. CARI, *La relación entre la Argentina y los Estados Unidos*, 270.

69. During 1997, Deborah Norden worked in the Pentagon's Inter-American Affairs office and participated in the BWG with Argentina. She observed that, realistically, the Pentagon does not have enough personnel dealing with Argentina on an ongoing basis to thoroughly staff these committees.

70. CARI, *La relación entre la Argentina y los Estados Unidos*, 269.

71. "Argentine Arms Embargo," press release from Foreign Commonwealth Office, News Department (London, December 17, 1998).

72. "U.S. Approves Sale of Warplanes to Argentina." *New York Times* (February 6, 1994), 8.

73. Department of State, Statement by the Press Secretary. "The State Visit of Argentine President Carlos Menem." Released by the White House, Office of the Press Secretary, January 11, 1999.

74. See White House, Office of the Press Secretary. Press Briefing by Ambassador James Dobbins, Assistant Secretary of State for Inter-American Affairs Jeffrey Davidow, and Mike McCurry, October 16, 1997; see also "U.S. Alliance Brings Prestige to Argentines," *New York Times*, October 20, 1997, A9.

75. Prior Major Non-NATO Allies were Israel, Egypt, Jordan, Japan, South Korea, and Australia.

76. Escudé and Fontana, "Argentina's Security Policies: Their Rationale and Regional Context," 57.

77. Calvin Sims, "Some in Latin America Fear End of U.S. Ban Will Stir Arms Race," *New York Times*, August 3, 1997, 11.

CHAPTER 5: INTERNATIONAL INSTITUTIONS

1. This issue is discussed in chapter 1. See also Carlos Escudé, *Gran Bretaña y la declinación argentina* (Buenos Aires: Editorial de Belgrano, 1983), 26.

2. Argentina and Brazil are the Latin American countries most frequently elected to be represented in the Security Council. In addition to the periods mentioned above, Argentina was a nonpermanent member during the periods 1948–49, 1959–60, 1966–67 and 1971–72.

3. Emilio J. Cárdenas, "La República Argentina en el Nuevo Consejo de Seguridad," *Archivos del Presente* 1, no. 2 (primavera austral 1995): 79.

4. The Conference on Disarmament was established in 1979 by the United Nations General Assembly, replacing prior arenas for disarmament negotiations. Among other important instruments, the conference has produced the Treaty on the Non-Proliferation of Nuclear Weapons, the Convention on Biological Arms, the Treaty on Denuclearization of the Seabeds, and the Convention on the Prohibition of Military or Any Other Hostile Use of Environmental Modification Techniques. Regarding Argentina's role, see Roberto García Moritán and Rafael Grossi, "La Convención de Armas Químicas," in *Contribuciones Argentinas a las Naciones Unidas* (Buenos Aires: Comisión Nacional de la República Argentina para el 50° aniversario de las Naciones Unidas, 1995), 345.

5. This information was obtained from data provided by the Department of Public Information of the United Nations, Section on Peace and Security; online at http://www.un.org/.

6. For further data, see Andrés Fontana, "La seguridad internacional y la Argentina en los años 90," in *Política Exterior Argentina 1989–1999: Historia de un éxito*, ed. Andrés Cisneros (Buenos Aires: Nuevo Hacer, 1998), 336.

7. Argentina, Ministerio de Defensa, *Libro Blanco de la Defensa Nacional* (Buenos Aires: 1999), 7.62.

8. Croatia and Cyprus were the most important cases with regard to the number of troops sent.

9. According to the Argentine Ministry of Foreign Affairs, the primary objectives inspiring this initiative included increasing countries' capacity for the prevention and mitigation of disasters, emergency preparation, and the eradication of poverty in developing countries.

10. At present, the coordination of the White Helmets' activities is carried out by the Office of Coordination of Humanitarian Affairs of the United Nations.

11. Argentina is the country that has contributed most to the budget of the White Helmets. It is followed, in order of importance, by Saudi Arabia, Italy, Japan, Germany, and France.

12. The project, cosponsored by forty-nine countries, was brought to the UN Assembly by the Argentine representative, Ambassador Emilio Cárdenas, on November 23, 1994, and was approved by consensus on December 20, 1994.

13. President William Jefferson Clinton, "Remarks to the 49th Session of the United Nations General Assembly in New York City." Transcript, *Weekly Compilation of Presidential Documents* 30, no. 39 (October 3, 1994), 1862 ff. See also *Cascos Blancos*, vol. 1, no. 1 (September–November 1997): 9.

14. For more details, see Verónica Pittner, *La relación de la Argentina con los Estados Unidos al final de la era Menem: un estudio de casos*, Undergraduate thesis in International Studies, Universidad Torcuato Di Tella, 1999, 7–21.

15. Declaración de Santiago sobre América Latina, *Tratados y Documentos Internacionales*, Recopilación y notas de José I. García Girelli (Buenos Aires: Zavalía, 1992), 356–60.

16. Andrés Fontana, "La Seguridad Hemisférica en los Noventa: Hacia una Comunidad de Estados Democráticos," unpublished paper, Buenos Aires, 3–4; translation by Deborah L. Norden.

17. Following the failure of this proposal and the collapse of negotiations with Panama to establish a center there, the United States established bilateral agreements with some Caribbean and Latin American countries to carry out flights to monitor narcotics trafficking.

18. "Propuestas del Ministro de Defensa Jorge Domínguez: tres puntos argentinos," *Clarín*, October 7, 1996, Sección Política, 2.

19. Drafted under the influence of the traumatic experience from the year of the Proceso military regime, the Internal Security Law explicitly vetoes the possibility that the armed forces carry out internal intelligence functions, in domestic conflicts as

well as in the fight against narcotics trafficking, in coordination with the Defense Law, of which it is a subsidiary. Consequently, the military can only offer logistical support to the police and security forces.

20. "Habló Corach en la Asamblea General de la OEA: Proponen nuevo rol para los militares." *Clarín*, June 9, 1999, on-line at: http://old.clarin.com/diario/99–06–09.

21. The conference, which united thirty-four ministers charged with internal security in the Western Hemisphere, was the continuation of the conference carried out in Lima in April 1996.

22. The Mar del Plata conference gained importance for the United States after terrorist attempts against U.S. embassies in Kenya and Tanzania on August 7, 1998.

23. This committee was created during the Sixteenth Assembly of the OAS, carried out in the city of Guatemala in November 1996. At present, the committee includes all member states in the region. It offers technical support and help in developing juridical, administrative, and operative capabilities to confront the drug problem and, in particular, is an arena for dialogue and cooperation in these matters.

24. The Rio Action Plan was adopted during the Special Inter-American Conference on Narcotics Trafficking carried out in Rio de Janeiro in November 1986. For more details, see Martín Gómez Bustillo, "Una alianza hemisférica contra las drogas, un desafío a la Organización de los Estados Americanos para el siglo XXI," thesis presented to the Instituto del Exterior de la Nación for promotion to the rank of minister of embassy, 22–32.

25. Regarding the bias toward the supply side in North American policies, see Mathea Falco, "America's Drug Problem and the Policy of Denial," *Current History* 97, no. 618 (April 1998), 145–149.

26. The Missile Technology Control Regime was created in April 1987, initiated by the United States and other developed countries (Canada, West Germany, France, Italy, Japan, and the United Kingdom) with the objective of restricting the proliferation of missiles and their technology. It is not actually an international treaty, but rather a voluntary agreement between countries that share a common aim to stop missile proliferation.

27. Julio C. Carasales, "Desarme, no proliferación e interés nacional," *Documento de Trabajo del ISEN* no. 5 (February 1995): 22.

28. Argentina and the United States subscribed to the convention on January 13, 1995. Argentina ratified it on October 2 of that year, while the United States did so on April 25, 1997.

29. "Pese al senado, Clinton dijo que no habrá más ensayos," *La Nación*, October 15, 1999, on-line at: http://www.lanacion.com.ar/99/10/15/?origen=Ediciones Anteriores.

30. These statistics resemble similar voting profiles by the Latin American countries with the greatest weight. For example, Buenos Aires and Brasilia coincided with Washington, D.C. in 1985 between 16.4 percent and 16 percent of the time, respectively. In

1986, Argentina also coincided with the United States 16.4 percent of the time, while Mexico's overlap with the United States was 17.6 percent. In 1987, Argentina and Brazil coincided with the United States 12.4 percent and 13.3 percent, respectively. U.S. Department of State, Bureau of International Organization Affairs, "Voting Practices in the United Nations: A Report to Congress for the Years 1994/1999."

31. Argentina's changing position was not limited to quantitative aspects. Within the realm of the First Committee (Disarmament and International Security), Argentina became integrated into the Barton Group, equivalent to the Western Group in the Conference on Disarmament.

32. U.S. Department of State, Bureau of International Organization Affairs, "Voting Practices in the United Nations: A Report to Congress for the Year 1999," March 2000.

33. Argentina and the United States voted in opposite ways on eleven resolutions referring to the Middle East question. The resolutions range from topics such as the Syrian Golán, to the peace accord regarding the Palestinian question, the Israeli settlements in occupied territories, and Palestinian refugees.

34. Nevertheless, the Argentine position regarding the Cuban question oscillated during 1996. Argentina voted in favor of condemnation in the Human Rights Committee, abstained in the United Nations Economic and Social Council (ECOSOC), and finally, returned to condemnation in the General Assembly. The changed vote in ECOSOC occurred because the Argentine Foreign Affairs Office sought to assure Cuban support in the UN Committee on Decolonization regarding the former's position on the Falklands/Malvinas question. The strong pressure of the U.S. executive on the Menem government pushed Argentina to resume its position condemning Cuba within a short time, as expressed in the General Assembly.

35. The only exception occurred in 1995, when the Chinese motion of "no action" was rejected, even though the subsequent vote on the basic question resulted in China's favor.

36. The "no action" motion resulted in twenty-two votes in favor, seventeen opposed (including the United States), and fourteen abstentions (including Argentina). Commission on Human Rights, *Report on the Period of Sessions (43rd to 54th)*, Economic and Social Council, Official Documents of the United Nations.

37. Instituto Nacional de Estadística y Censos (Argentina), *Indec Informa* (Buenos Aires: INDEC, March 2000), 87.

38. Argentina was a member of the Human Rights Commission during the years 1957–62, 1966–68, 1980–93 and 1997–99, and was reelected for the period 2000–2003. The United States belonged to the committee consistently from 1948 through 2001.

39. In the Human Rights Commission, the result of the vote went against Iran: twenty-three supported the resolution (including the United States), sixteen opposed and fourteen abstained (including Argentina).

40. INDEC, *Indec Informa*, (Buenos Aires: INDEC, March 2000), 87.

41. INDEC, *Indec Informa* (Buenos Aires: INDEC, May 2001), 86.

42. The new rotating permanent members would be chosen by the respective regional group and ratified by the General Assembly for a period of four years or for the term that each regional group were to determine; the new members would also have veto power in accord with established criteria.

43. See, for example, Exposição do Ministro das Relações Exteriores, Embaixador Luiz Felipe Lampreid, perante a Comissão de Relaoes Exteriores da Camara dos Deputados, "O Brasil e a reforma do Cohselho de Segurana," August 28, 1997, Ministerio de Relaes Exteriores, Gabinete do Ministro de Estado: 10–11.

44. Guido Di Tella, "Por qué necesitamos una Corte Penal Internacional," in *Clarín*, March 13, 1998, on-line at: http://old.clarin.com/diario/98–03–13.

45. Discurso del Ministro de Justicia de Argentina, Raúl Granillo Ocampo, at the Conference Plenary, in *Clarín*, June 18, 1998, on-line at: http://old.clarin.com/diario/98–06–18; translation by Deborah L. Norden.

46. Ibid., June 18, 1998. Translation by Deborah L. Norden; original English unavailable. Richardson's words express the concern of the United States that the Court could be used by countries with which it is in conflict to accuse U.S. citizens, particularly soldiers.

47. The International Penal Court, situated in La Haya, will be composed of eighteen judges and will begin to function when sixty states ratify the agreement.

48. This group had significant differences with that of the "noninterventionists," whose most important members were Brazil, Colombia, and especially Mexico, which occupied precisely the opposite position of that of Argentina. See Richard J. Bloomfield, "Making the Western Hemisphere Safe for Democracy? The OAS Defense of Democracy Response," *Washington Quarterly* 17, no. 2 (1994): 162.

49. The collective action mechanism in Resolution 1080 was exercised on three occasions in the 1990s: Haiti (1991), Peru (1992), and Guatemala (1993). It was not applied in the political crises in Venezuela (1992), Paraguay (1996 and 1999), and Ecuador (1997), since these did not produce the grounds envisioned in the resolution.

50. OAS General Assembly, XVI Extraordinary Period of Sessions, December 1992.

51. The United Nations Security Council considered the Haitian situation to be a threat to international peace and security in the region. Nevertheless, a number of countries, such as Brazil, Colombia, and Mexico, did not consider the crisis to threaten the region. According to these countries, allowing the Security Council to extend its jurisdiction into matters such as democracy would eliminate any limits to intervention in internal affairs.

52. The posture adopted by these governments was a key factor in the democratic outcome of the crisis, although not the only one. The government of the United States, the OAS, popular mobilization in defense of democratic institutions, and the firm position of opposition forces in Paraguay played equally central roles.

53. According to Argentina's Minister of Foreign Affairs, Guido Di Tella, "This clause is intended to avoid the repetition of situations like the ones experienced in

Paraguay." "La cumbre del MERCOSUR dio un fuerte respaldo a los reclamos por Malvinas," *La Prensa,* June 26, 1996 seccíon política, 3.

54. Declaración Presidencial sobre Compromiso Democrático en el Mercosur, Potrero de los Funes, Provincia de San Luis, República Argentina; and Protocolo de Ushuaia sobre Compromiso Democrático en el Mercosur, Ushuaia, Provincia de Tierra del Fuego, República Argentina, July 24, 1998, Ministerio de Relaciones Exteriores, Comercio Internacional y Culto, República Argentina.

55. Jorge Campbell, "Un grito de Buenos Aires contra los subsidios agrícolas: el Grupo Cairns debe obtener los compromisos de la Ronda Uraguay," *La Nación,* August 28, 1999, on-line at: http://www.lanacion.com.ar/99/08/28/; translation by Deborah L. Norden.

56. In August 1999, Buenos Aires was the site of the Nineteenth Ministerial Meeting of the Cairns Group, which concluded with a tough declaration—strongly pushed by Argentina—against protectionism and agricultural subsidies. The United States, which participated as an observer and special guest, made the commitment through Secretary of Agriculture Dan Glickman to "partially support" the demands of the group. "Cautela de los EE.UU. en el negocio agrícola," *La Nación,* August 29, 1999, on-line at: http://www.lanacion.com.ar/99/08/29.

57. With respect to this, of the $362 billion in agricultural subsidies by the countries of the OECD in 1998, nearly $100 billion corresponded to the United States.

58. See "La agenda de la ronda del milenio: entrando en la etapa de definiciones," *Panorama del Mercosur/CEI* 3 (July 1999): 155.

59. See "Rotundo fracaso en la OMC," *La Nación,* December 5, 1999, on-line at: http://www.lanacion.com.ar/99/12/05/.

60. See "La agenda de la ronda del milenio: entrando en la etapa de definiciones," 158.

61. Interview with Jorge Campbell, former Secretary of International Economic Relations, Ministry of Foreign Affairs, "Hay que reconstruir los vínuculos políticos," *La Nación,* December 11, 1999, on-line at: http://www.lanacion.com.ar/99/12/11/EO8.htm.

62. In terms of genetically modified products, soy represents half of that harvested, cultivated only in the United States and Argentina, along with Canada. In second place is corn—principally "BT"—which is grown in Argentina, Canada, Spain, the United States, France, and South Africa. Next comes cotton—resistant to insects and tolerant of herbicides—distributed among Argentina, Australia, China, the United States, Mexico, and South Africa. For further details, see "Los productos transgénicos, el comercio agrícola y el impacto sobre el agro argentino," *Panorama del Mercosur/CEI* 4 (November 1999).

63. The Convention on Biological Diversity was signed in Rio de Janeiro in 1992. Argentina ratified it in November 1994, whereas the United States did not even sign it.

64. For more details regarding the dispute on this theme in other settings, see "La agenda de la ronda del milenio: entrando en la etapa de definiciones," 158–59.

65. See Gustavo Svarzman, "La Argentina y el Mercosur ante el proceso de integración hemisférica," *Boletín Informativo Techint* 295 (July/September 1998): 40.

66. Ibid., 41.

67. See Roberto Bouzas, "Las perspectivas del Mercosur: desafíos, escenarios y alternativas para la próxima década," *Documento de Trabajo de FLACSO* (August 1999): 3.

68. Ibid., 4.

69. See Javier Corrales and Richard E. Feinberg, "Regimes of Cooperation in the Western Hemisphere: Power, Interests, and Intellectual Traditions," *International Studies Quarterly* 43 (1999): 16.

70. For more details, see Bouzas, "Las perspectivas del Mercosur," 7.

71. Stuart Eizenstat, Undersecretary for Economic, Business, and Agricultural Affairs, "Our Future Trade Agenda," Remarks before the House of Representatives International Relations Subcommittee, Washington, D.C., September 24, 1997.

72. Instituto de Relaciones Europeo—Latino Americanas, IRELA, "Argentina en los 90: Avances y perspectivas durante el Gobierno de Menem," *Dossier IRELA* 54 (June 1995): 54.

73. The fast-track mechanism would assure that Congress would consider negotiated trade agreements as a package that could not be amended, and would merely need to be approved or rejected. This would reassure foreign governments that agreements reached with the executive branch would not need to be renegotiated in Congress.

74. Scott Ottemann, "The FTAA: Its Dilemma Today and its Prospects in the Future," paper presented at the Andean Development Corporation Conference on Trade and Investment in the Americas, September 1999, 27.

75. See Svarzman, "La Argentina y el Mercosur ante el proceso de integración hemisférica," 45.

76. See Alberto van Klaveren, "Defensa de la democracia en el ámbito iberoamericano," *Revista Diplomacia* (September 1996), 34.

77. "Política Exterior Argentina," Discurso del Señor Ministro de Relaciones Exteriores, Comercio Internacional y Culto, Buenos Aires (May 30, 2000), Ministerio de Relaciones Exteriores, Comercio Internacional y Culto, República Argentina, 3.

78. Adalberto Rodríguez Giavarini, "Hacia la integración latinoamericana," *La Nación*, August 30, 2000, 17.

CHAPTER 6: CONCLUSION

1. Adalberto Rodríguez Giavarini, "Política Exterior Argentina," Discurso del Señor Ministro de Relaciones Exteriores, Comercio Internacional y Culto, Buenos Aires, May 30, 2000: 5; on-line at http://www.cancilleria.gov.ar/ministerio/canciller/disc6.html.

2. For a complete list of the bilateral agreements signed between Argentina and the United States, see *Argentina–Estados Unidos: Acuerdos bilaterales 1853–2000*, Buenos Aires: CARI/CEPE, 2000. The first bilateral treaty, signed in 1853, dealt with the unrestricted navigation of the Paraná and Uruguay rivers.

3. The Helms-Burton Law extended U.S. pressures on Cuba, seeking to restrict even business outside the United States from trading with Cuba.

4. Carlos Escudé, "La política exterior de Menem y su sustento teórico implícito," *América Latina/Internacional* 8, no. 27 (January–March 1991): 396–97. Translation by Deborah L. Norden, emphasis in the original.

5. Roberto Russell and Juan Tokatlian call this form of autonomy "relational." See Russell and Tokatlian, "Globalización y autonomía: una visión desde el Cono Sur," Draft, Universidad Torcuato Di Tella, julio de 2000: 20. Translation by Deborah L. Norden.

6. Celso Lafer, "Brazilian International Identity and Foreign Policy: Past, Present, and Future," *Daedalus* 129, no. 2 (Spring 2000): 229.

7. Carlos Escudé, "La política exterior de Menem y su sustento teórico implícito," *América Latina/Internacional* 8, no. 27 (January–March 1991): 405–6.

8. Di Tella: pasó la etapa de las *relaciones carnales.* 'Ahora podemos criticar a los Estados Unidos,' dijo" *La Nación*, May 24, 1997, on-line at: http://www. lanacion.com.ar/97/05/24/p06.htm; translation by Deborah L. Norden.

9. "Solicitud de ayuda que llegó por carta," *La Nación*, January 30, 2002, 6. A few days before, Duhalde had communicated to President Bush over the telephone his government's total commitment to maintain tight relations with the United States. See Ana Barón, "La Argentina es un amigo querido de los EE.UU," *Clarín*, January 19, 2002, 4.

10. Manuel Mora y Araujo, "Opinión pública y política exterior de la Presidencia Menem," in *Política exterior argentina 1989–1999: Historia de un éxito*, ed. Andrés Cisneros (Buenos Aires: Nuevohacer-GEL, 1998), 348.

11. Significantly, the preference for the United States was particularly high among business people (50 percent), journalists (42 percent), and members of the military (39 percent). "Cómo lo ve la gente. Menem, 10 años Argentinos, a evaluar" *La Nación* (July 4, 1999), on-line at http://www.lanacion.com.ar/suples/enfoques/9927/nota.asp?pag=PO9.htm.

12. "Para el 89% de los argentinos el gasto excesivo causó la crisis," La Nación, January 19, 2002, 10. The poll covered 819 cases nationally and has a confidence level of 95%.

13. Ibid.

14. Education, health, and Argentines' standard of living elicited more critical responses, with scores from 4 to 4.4, while the worst scores were given to areas such as justice (3.0), work (3.3), security and crime (3.0) and, over all, corruption (2.8). Ibid.

15. Ibid.

16. Marc Falcoff, "Estados Unidos, un país previsible," *Archivos del Presente*, 2, no. 4 (southern autumn 1996): 55; translation by Deborah. L. Norden.

17. Data supplied by the U.S. Consulate in Argentina, cited in "Crece la tendencia de

ir a estudiar a EE.Uu," *La Nación*, July 19, 1999, http://www.lanacion.com.ar/99/07/19/g08.htm.

18. The Fulbright Commision is the primary organization granting financial support for studies in the United States, along with the National Fund for the Arts, the Antorchas Foundation, the Yacimientos Petrolíferos Fiscales Foundation, and the Ministry of Education.

19. *El turismo en cifras 1990–1997*, (Buenos Aires: Argentine Secretary of Tourism, 1997), 18.

20. "Eligios de los Estados Unidos," *La Nación*, December 15, 1999; sección política 6, translation by Deborah L. Norden.

21. Despite the difficult economic situation at the time, the De la Rúa government indicated that it would deal with the expense of sending troops by treating this as a high-level political action and as "a contribution to a medium and long-range strategic alliance with the United States." See "La ONU pedirá hoy la intervención," *La Nación*, December 19, 2001, on-line at: http://www.lanacion.com/01/12/19/dp_360472.asp.

22. "De la Rúa: 'Para el 2001 quiero eliminar el déficit" *La Nación*, January 7, 2000, sección política, 1 and 6; translation by Deborah L. Norden.

23. *La Nación*, "Texto completo de mensaje del presidente de la Nación, Fernando de la Rúa, tras jurar ayer ante la Asamblea Legislativa" on-line at: http://www.lanacion.com.ar/99/12/11/PO6.htm. December 11,1999.

24. See Roberto Russell, "Las relaciones Argentina-UE en los años noventa: adelantos y perspectivas," *Documento de Trabajo de IRELA* 42 (1999).

25. Lucio García del Solar, "Nuestro país cedió espacio," *Clarín*, October 13, 1997, on-line at: http://old.clarin.com/diario/97-10-13/i-01912d.htm, translation by Deborah L. Norden.

26. Ana Baron, "Clinton envió felicitaciones por el triunfo electoral de la Alianza, *Clarín*, October 26, 1999, on-line at: http://old.clarin.com/diario/99-10-26/t-0220ld.htm. Original English not available. Translation by Deborah L. Norden.

27. See María O'Donnell, "Una buena noticia para los Estados Unidos," *La Nación*, October 24, 1999, 10.

28. This includes approximately 1,833,000 people, to which should be added another 14.5 percent underemployed, equivalent to 1,973,400 Argentines.

29. Susana Torrado, "Balance de diez años de ajuste," *Clarín*, November 30, 1999, 17; translation by Deborah L. Norden.

30. Alberto Amato, "Dos años para dilapidar un caudal político ganado en tres décadas," Clarín, December 21, 2001, 18.

31. For an excellent description of the events leading to Vice-President Alvarez's resignation, see Joaquín Morales Solá, *El Sueño Eterno: Ascenso y caída de la Alianza*, Buenos Aires: Editorial Planeta/La Nación, 2001.

32. Manuel Pastor and Carol Wise, "From Poster Child to Basket Case," *Foreign Affairs* 80, no. 6 (November/December 2001), 63.

33. "El déficit de 2001 llegó a 16.500 millones de dólares," *La Nación*, Section 2, January 30, 2002, 1.

34. "El nuevo gobierno: asumió hasta diciembre de 2003 y aseguró que no se presentará a la reelección," on-line at: http://www.clarin.com.ar/diario/2002-01-02/p.00215.htm.

35. Natalio R. Botana, "¡Qué se vayan! Y después?, *La Nación*, February 2, 2002, 17.

36. See Mariano Grondona, "Nos ignoran y, además, ignoran," *La Nación*, February 6, 2002, 3.

37. Federico Pinedo, *Argentina en la vorágine* (Buenos Aires: Mundo Forense, 1943), 62–63; translation by Deborah L. Norden.

## DEBORAH L. NORDEN

*Ph.D., Department of Political Science, University of California at Berkeley.*

Dr. Norden is currently assistant professor of political science at Whittier College, Whittier, California. Her publications include *Military Rebellion in Argentina* (University of Nebraska Press, 1996) and various articles on democratization and civil-military relations in Latin America, international peacekeeping, Latin America political parties, and military insurrection in both Argentina and Venezuela.

## ROBERTO RUSSELL

*Ph.D., The Paul Nitze School of Advanced International Studies,*
*The Johns Hopkins University, Washington D.C.*

Dr. Russell coordinates the International Studies Programs of the University Torcuato Di Tella, Buenos Aires, where he teaches Argentine foreign policy. He is also a professor at the Institute of the Foreign Service in Argentina, and has been visiting professor at the University of London (1981), Georgetown University (1988), Universidad de Salamanca España (1999) and the Instituto Universitario Ortega y Gasset, Madrid (2001). Russell has written extensively about international relations theory, the international relations of Latin America, and Argentine foreign policy. His most recent book, coauthored with Mónica Hirst, is *Los cambios en el sistema político internacional y el Mercosur* (Buenos Aires: Fundación OSDE, 2001) .